Genesis According to the Saints

Edited by Daniel M. Clough, M.A.

Loreto Publications
Fitzwilliam, NH 03447
A.D. 2016

Loreto Publications
P. O. Box 603
Fitzwilliam, NH 03447
www.loretopubs.org
603-239-6671

ISBN: 978-1-622-92106-5

Printed and Bound in the USA

Genesis According to the Saints

This book is dedicated to

My Mother

who taught me from my youth

to take and read and

to love the Holy Scriptures.

Our help is in the name of the Lord, Who made heaven and earth.

Psalm 123:8

Table of Contents

Preface

This book was inspired by the *Catena Aurea* of St. Thomas Aquinas where he presented the Gospel commentaries of the Fathers of the Church in a systematic fashion. This work will follow a similar style to what St. Thomas presented, but it will focus exclusively on the first three chapters of the book of Genesis. It will not only draw from the Fathers but from other saints as well. The formatting style for the quotations was also inspired by *The Teaching of the Church Fathers*, by Fr. John Willis. It began first as my notes, and then it became the book that it is now, which can serve as a reference for others in their study of the first book of the Bible.

Many of the modern commentaries on Genesis deal with theories regarding the literary origins of the text, and oftentimes include brief explanations of the text, but these do no more than scratch the surface. I had a desire to go deeper into the mystery of creation, and I found many more interesting things that were said by the Fathers and Doctors of the Church. I compiled this book in order to make available to scholars and to everyone the great treasury of catholic tradition which has been drawn from many different sources.

The commentaries of the saints are drawn from in order to show forth examples of the living tradition in studies on sacred scripture. This living tradition is one of the principles laid down by *Dei Verbum* as being essential to a correct hermeneutic of interpretation. This principle was often repeated in papal teaching, most recently in the Apostolic Exhortation, *Verbum Domini*, of Benedict XVI.

As St. Caesarius of Arles says: "Now if our holy fathers of old with such great zeal and pious labor wrote innumerable volumes for the benefit of all the churches, how will we appear among them if we neglect to distribute to our children what we find has been compiled by them?" (Sermon 1:15)

My hope is that this book will aid in bringing about a renewal in biblical studies which relies more upon our catholic tradition and also brings with it refreshment of spirit. When we enter upon the task of studying the bible, it is easy to treat it as an ordinary literary document on the natural level alone, but it must be treated as a supernatural work. The writings of the saints help us because they, by their holiness of life and their intellectual rigor, remind us that the deeper we go into the study of creation, the more mysterious it can become; hence the need to humble ourselves before such an awesome mystery. May we come to learn more and more, and gain a greater grasp upon the truths revealed by God in the book of Genesis as explained in the writings of the saints. Thus starting from the beginning of God's revelation, may it lead us onward towards our last end, which is union with God in Heaven.

Abbreviations

The following sources are drawn from in this book with the permission of the publishers when needed:

AF: *The Apostolic Fathers*, trans. Alexander Roberts et al. (Edinburgh: T & T Clark, 1868).

ANF: A. Cleveland Coxe, editor, *The Ante-Nicene Fathers* (New York: Charles Scribner's Sons, 1926).

Brev: St. Bonaventure, *Breviloquium, Works of St. Bonaventure – Volume IX*, trans. Dominic Monti, OFM (St. Bonaventure, NY: Franciscan Institute Publications, 2005).

CC: *Corpus Christianorum*, Ser. Lat. LXXII (Turnholti: Brepols, 1959).

CF: Victor Warkulwiz, editor, *St. Lawrence of Brindisi on Creation and the Fall: A Verse by Verse Commentary on Genesis 1-3*, trans. Craig Toth (Mount Jackson, VA: Kolbe Center, 2012).

DS: Heinrich Denzinger and Adolf Schönmetzer, editors, *Enchiridion Symbolorum definitionum et declarationum de rebus fidei et morum* (Rome Herder, 1965).

EH: St. Ephrem the Syrian, *Hymns*, trans. Kathleen McVey (New York: Paulist Press, 1989).

EHP: St. Ephrem the Syrian, *Hymns on Paradise*, trans. Sebastian Brock (Crestwood, NY: St. Vladimir's Seminary Press, 1990).

FCA: St. Augustine, *On Genesis*, trans. Ronald Teske, SJ (Washington, DC: CUA Press, 1991).

FCAm: St. Ambrose, *Hexameron, Paradise, and Cain and Abel*, trans. John Savage (Washington, DC: CUA Press, 2003).

FCB: St. Basil, *Exegetical Homilies*, trans. Sister Agnes Clare Way (Washington, DC: CUA Press, 1963).

FCC: St. John Chrysostom, *Homilies on Genesis*, trans. Robert Hill (Washington, DC: CUA Press, 1986).

FCCs: St. Caesarius of Arles, *Sermons*, Vol. 1, trans. Sister Mary Magdeleine Mueller (New York: Fathers of the Church, Inc., 1956).

FCCy: St. Cyprian, *Treatises*, trans. Roy Deferrari (New York: Fathers of the Church, Inc., 1958).

FCD: St. John of Damascus, *Writings*, trans. Frederic Chase, Jr. (Washington, DC, CUA Press, 1999).

FCE: St. Ephrem the Syrian, *Selected Prose Works*, trans. Edward Matthews, Jr. and Joseph Amar (Washington, DC: CUA Press, 1994).

FCJ: St. Jerome, *Dogmatic and Polemical Works*, trans. John Hritzu (Washington, DC: CUA Press, 1965).

FEF2: William Jurgens, editor, *The Faith of the Early Fathers*, Vol. 2 (Collegeville, MN: The Liturgical Press, 1979). Copyright 1979 by Order of Saint Benedict. Published by Liturgical Press, Collegeville, Minnesota. Reprinted with permission.

FG: Dominic Unger, OFM Cap, *The First Gospel: Genesis 3:15* (St. Bonaventure, NY: The Franciscan Institute, 1954).

GHE: St. Gregory the Great, *Homilies on the Book of the Prophet Ezechiel*, trans. Theodosia Tomkinson (Etna, CA: CTOS, 2008).

IP: St. Irenaeus, *The Demonstration of the Apostolic Preaching*, trans. J. Armitage Robinson (New York: The Macmillan Co., 1920).

LMG: St. Augustine, *The Literal Meaning of Genesis*, trans. John Hammond Taylor (New York: Paulist Press, 1982).

MH: St. Augustine, *On The Manichean Heresy* (Edinburgh: T&T Clark, 1872).

NPNF: Philip Schaff and Henry Wace, editors, *Nicene and Post-Nicene Fathers of the Christian Church,* Second Series (New York: Charles Scribner's Sons, 1904).

OG: Taken from *On Genesis 1-3* by Severian of Gabala and Bede the Venerable, edited by Michael Glerup, and translated by Robert C. Hill and Carmen S. Hardin. Copyright (c) 2010 by the estate of Robert C. Hill, Carmin S. Hardin, Michael Glerup, Thomas C. Oden, Gerald L. Bray and the Institute for Classical Christian Studies (ICCS). Used by permission of InterVarsity Press, P.O. Box 1400, Downers Grove, IL 60515, USA. www.ivpress.com

OTI: St. Athanasius, *On the Incarnation*, trans. John Behr (Yonkers, NY: St. Vladimir's Seminary Press, 2011).

RC: *Roman Conferences of St. Maximilian Kolbe*, trans. Peter Damian Fehlner, FI (New Bedford, MA: Academy of the Immaculate, 2004).

SA: St. Augustine, *Nicene and Post-Nicene Fathers of the Christian Church*, First Series, editor, Philip Schaff (Grand Rapids, MI: Eerdmans Publishing Company, 1979).

SB: St. Bonaventure, *Omnia Opera*, Vol. 7 (Paris: Ludovicus Vivès, 1866).

SCG: St. Thomas Aquinas, *The Summa Contra Gentiles of St. Thomas Aquinas*, trans. The English Dominican Fathers (London: Burns, Oates, & Washbourne, 1923).

SSA: St. Anthony of Padua, *Sermons for Sundays and Festivals*, Vol. 1, trans. Paul Spilsbury (Padova: Edizioni Messaggero Padova, 2007).

ST: Anton Pegis, Editor, *Basic Writing of Saint Thomas Aquinas* (New York: Random House, 1945).

STC: St. Thomas Aquinas, *Summa Theologiae*, Vol. IV (Ottawa: Dominican College, 1941).

TDM: Excerpt from St. Louis de Montfort, *True Devotion to Mary*, trans. Frederick Faber (Rockford, IL: TAN Books, 1985), TAN Books, Charlotte, NC (www.tanbooks.com) used with permission.

WI: *Ante-Nicene Christian Library: The Writings of Irenaeus*, trans. Alexander Roberts and W.H. Rambaut (Edinburgh: T & T Clark, 1868).

WSF: St. Francis of Assisi, *The Writings of Saint Francis of Assisi*, trans. Pascal Robinson (New Delhi, India: Isha Books, 2013).

Quotes from sacred scripture in the footnotes are taken from the Douay-Rheims version of the bible.

Prologue

Moses and the Origins of Genesis

St. John Chrysostom, *Homilies on Genesis*, Homily 2:4: You, see, when God formed human beings in the beginning, He used to speak to them personally, in a way that was possible for human beings to understand Him. This was the way, by example, that He came to Adam, the way He upbraided Cain, the way He conversed with Noah, the way He accepted Abraham's hospitality. And even when all humankind fell into evil ways, the creator of all did not abandon the human race. Instead, when they then proved unworthy of His converse with them, He wanted to renew His love for them; He sent them letters as you do to people far away from you, and this drew all mankind back again to Him. It was God who sent them letters. Moses delivered them. What do the letters say? "In the beginning, God made heaven and earth." FCC, 31

St. Ephrem, *Commentary on Genesis*, Prologue: 2: But, when the sons of Abram went astray in Egypt and deserved to become godless along with the entire world, they too became estranged from those noble commandments that are fixed in nature, and they considered substances, which had come into being out of nothing, to be self-existent beings, and they called created things that had been made out of something 'gods.' FCE, 67-68

St. Ephrem, *Commentary on Genesis*, Prologue: 4: After the mighty works [of God that occurred] in Egypt, both in the sea and in the desert, [Moses] wrote about the substances that were created out of nothing so that [the descendants of Abraham] might know that they were falsely called self-existent beings. And [Moses] wrote about the creatures that were made out of something and were erroneously worshipped as gods. FCE, 68

St. Ephrem, *Commentary on Genesis*, Prologue: 2: Still, God willed to set right once more, through Moses, those things that had become confused in Moses' generation, lest the evil tradition be transmitted throughout the entire world. FCE, 68

St. Theophilus of Antioch, *To Autolycus*, Book 2, Ch. 10: And Moses, who lived many years before Solomon, or, rather, the Word of God by him as by an instrument, says, "In the beginning God created the heavens and the earth." ANF, Vol. 2, 98

St. Justin Martyr, *First Apology*, Ch. 5: For the truth shall be spoken; since of old these evil demons, effecting apparitions of themselves, both defiled women and corrupted boys, and showed such fearful sights to men, that those who did not use their reason in judging of the actions that were done, were struck with terror; and being carried away by fear, and not knowing that these were demons, they called them gods, and gave to each the name which each of the demons chose for himself. ANF, Vol. 1, 164

St. Ambrose, *Hexameron*, Book 1, Ch. 2: He was, of course, Moses, a man learned in all the science of the Egyptians. He was rescued from the river by the daughter of Pharao, who cherished him as if he were her own son and desired that he be trained and instructed in all phases of secular learning with aid furnished from the royal treasury. FCAm, 5-6

St. Ambrose, *Hexameron*, Book 6, Ch. 2: Surely Moses was skilled in all the wisdom of the Egyptians. Yet he welcomed the Spirit of God. As His minister he preferred the way of truth to that vain and self-styled philosophical system. FCAm, 231

St. Methodius, *On Free Will*, Ch. 2: I began to praise the creator, as I saw the earth fast fixed, and living creatures in such variety, and the blossoms with their many hues. But my mind did not rest upon these things alone; but thereupon I began to inquire whence they have their origin—whether from some source eternally co-existent with God, or from Himself alone, none co-existing with Him; for that He has made nothing out of that which has no existence appeared to me the right view to take, unless my reason were altogether untrustworthy. ANF, Vol. 6, 357

St. Ambrose, *Hexameron*, Book 6, Ch. 2: He laid down for us what he considered suited to our hopes, namely, that God made the earth, that the earth produced plant life and all kinds of animal life at the command of almighty God and by the operation of the Lord Jesus. FCAm, 231-32

St. Basil, *On the Hexameron*, Homily 1:1: He who, banished by those to whom he had been a benefactor, gladly left the uproar of the Egyptians and went to Ethiopia and, spending there all his time apart from others, devoted himself for forty entire years to the contemplation of creation... FCB, 4

St. Ambrose, *Hexameron*, Book 1, Ch. 2: There, removed from all other cares, he gave himself wholly to divine contemplation, in order that he might behold the glory of God face to face. FCAm, 6

St. Ephrem, *Commentary on Genesis*, Prologue: 3: On account of these things He enlightened him . . . Moreover, Moses was also anointed with a radiance so that the radiance of his face would manifest the Spirit who spoke with his tongue. FCE, 68

St. Gregory the Great, *Homilies on the Book of the Prophet Ezechiel*, Book 2, Homily 4: In this matter we must also be aware that the knowledge of the spiritual fathers grew with the advances of the ages. For Moses was more learned in the knowledge of Almighty God than Abraham, the Prophets more than Moses, and the Apostles more than the Prophets. GHE, 326

The Literary Character of the Narrative

St. Augustine, *Contra Faustum*, Book XII, 8: The whole narrative of Genesis, in the most minute details, is a prophecy of Christ and of the Church, with reference either to the good Christians or to the bad. MH, 209

St. Augustine, *De Genesi ad litteram*, Book VIII, Ch. 1: The narrative in these books is not written in a literary style proper to allegory, as in the Canticle of Canticles, but from beginning to end in the style proper to history, as in the Books of Kings and the other works of that type. LMG, Vol. 2, 33

St. Augustine, *De Genesi ad litteram*, Book VIII, Ch. 1: But since those historical books contain matters familiar to us from common human experience they are easily and readily taken in a literal sense at the first reading, so that the meaning of the historical events in relation to the future may also be subsequently drawn from them. LMG, Vol. 2, 33

St. Augustine, *De Genesi ad litteram*, Book VIII, Ch. 1: But in Genesis, since there are matters beyond the ken of readers who focus their gaze on the familiar course of nature, they are unwilling to have these matters taken in the literal sense but prefer to understand them in a figurative sense. Accordingly, they assume that history, that is, the literal narrative of events that happened, begins at the point where Adam and Eve, dismissed from Paradise, were joined in sexual union and begot children. LMG, Vol. 2, 33

St. Augustine, *De Genesi ad litteram*, Book VIII, Ch. 1: I say that the creation of natures narrated here is something unfamiliar, because it is the creation of things for the first time. For what is so unique and unparalleled in the constitution of the things of the world as the world itself? Surely we are not to believe that God did not make the world because He does not make worlds today, or that He did not make the sun because He does not make suns today. LMG, Vol. 2, 33

St. Ephrem, *Commentary on Genesis*, Prologue: 5: [Moses] then wrote about the work of the six days that were created by means of a mediator who was of the same nature and equal in skill to the maker. FCE, 69

St. Augustine, *City of God*, Book XI, Ch. 4: Was the prophet present when God made the heavens and the earth? No; but the wisdom of God, by whom all things were made, was there. SA, Vol. 2, 206

St. Thomas Aquinas, *Summa Theologiae*, I, Q 46, Art. 2: Therefore the newness of the world is known only by revelation, and hence it cannot be proved demonstratively. ST, 453

St. Gregory the Great, *Homilies on the Book of the Prophet Ezechiel*, Book 1, Homily 1: Prophecy concerning the past: "In the beginning, God created Heaven and earth"—for man speaks of a time when man was not. GHE, 27

St. John Chrysostom, *Homilies on Genesis*, Homily 2:5: Notice this remarkable author, dearly beloved, and the particular gift he had. I mean, while all the other inspired authors told either what would happen after a long time or what was going to take place immediately, this blessed author, being born many generations after the event, was guided by the deity on high and judged worthy to narrate what had been created by the Lord of all from the very beginning. FCC, 31

St. Justin Martyr, *First Apology*, Ch. 59: And that you may learn that it was from our teachers—we mean the account given through the prophets—that Plato borrowed his statement that God, having altered matter which was shapeless, made the world, hear the very words spoken through Moses, who, as above shown, was the first prophet, and of greater antiquity than the Greek writers; and through whom the Spirit of prophecy, signifying how and from what materials God at first formed the world, spoke thus: "In the beginning God created the heaven and the earth. And the earth was invisible and unfurnished, and darkness was upon the face of the deep; and the Spirit of God moved over the waters. And God said, Let there be light; and it was so." ANF, Vol. 1, 182

Errors Concerning Creation

St. Athanasius, *De Incarnatione Verbi Dei*, Ch. 1:2: The making of the world and the creation of all things have been taken differently by many, and each has propounded as each has wished. OTI, 50

St. Athanasius, *De Incarnatione Verbi Dei*, Ch. 1:2: Some say that all things have come into being spontaneously and as by chance, such as the Epicureans who, according to themselves fantasize that there is no providence over the universe, speaking in the face of clear and apparent facts. For if all things came into being spontaneously without providence, as they claim, all things would necessarily have simply come into being and be identical and without difference. Everything would have been as a single body, sun or moon, and regarding human beings, the whole world would have been hand or eye or foot. But, now, this is not the case: we see here, the sun, there the moon, there the earth; and again regarding human bodies, here a foot, there a hand, and there a head. Such order indicates that they did not come into being spontaneously, but shows that a cause preceded them, from which one can apprehend the God who ordered and created all things. OTI, 50

St. Athanasius, *De Incarnatione Verbi Dei*, Ch. 1:2: Others, amongst whom is Plato, that giant among the Greeks, declare that God made the universe from pre-existent and uncreated matter, as God is not able to make anything unless matter pre-existed, just as a carpenter must already have wood so that it may be used. They do not realize that saying such things is to impute weakness to God: for if He is not Himself the cause of matter, but simply makes things from pre-existent matter, then he is weak, not being able without matter to fashion any of things that exist, just as the weakness of the carpenter is certainly his inability to make any required thing without wood. According to the argument, unless there were matter, God would not have made anything. How would He then still be called 'maker' and 'creator,' if He had his ability to make from something else; I mean from the matter? And if this is so, as they thus have it, according to them, God is only a craftsman and not the creator of being, if he fashions underlying matter but is not Himself the cause of matter. He could in no way be called 'creator,' if He does not create matter, from which created things come into being. OTI, 50-51

St. Irenaeus, *Fragment*, No. 33: Inasmuch as certain men, impelled by what considerations I know not, remove from God the half of His creative power, by asserting that He is merely the cause of quality resident in matter, and by maintaining that matter itself is uncreated. . . ANF, Vol. 1, 573

St. Irenaeus, *Adversus Haereses,* Book II, Ch. 10:4: For, to attribute the substance of created things to the power and will of Him who is God of all, is worthy both of credit and acceptance. It is also agreeable [to reason], and there may be well said regarding such a belief, that "the things which are impossible with men are possible with *God*" [Lk. 18:27]. While men, indeed, cannot make anything out of nothing, but only out of matter already existing, yet God is in this point pre-eminently superior to men, that He Himself called into being the substance of His creation, when previously it had no existence. WI, Vol. 1, 145-6

St. Athanasius, *Four Discourses Against the Arians,* No. 1:29: However, not to leave even a weak argument unnoticed, they must be told, that although God always had the power to make, yet the things originated had not the power of being eternal. For they are out of nothing, and therefore were not before they originated; but things which were not before their origin, how could these coexist with the everlasting God? Wherefore God, looking to what was good for them, then made all when He saw that, when originated, they were able to abide . . . But the Son, not being a work, but proper to the Father's offspring, always is. NPNF, Vol. IV, 323

St. Irenaeus, *Fragment,* No. 33: But further, if matter be uncreated, it has been made altogether according to a certain quality, and this immutable, so that it cannot be receptive of more qualities, nor can this be the thing of which the world is made. But if the world be not made from it, [this theory] entirely excludes God from exercising power on the creation [of the world]. ANF, Vol. 1, 573-74

St. Athanasius, *De Incarnatione Verbi Dei,* Ch. 1:2: Others, again, from the heretics fabricate for themselves another creator of all things besides the Father of our Lord Jesus Christ, being greatly blinded even in what they say. For the Lord said to the Jews, "Have you not read that he who made them from the beginning made them male and female, and said, 'For this reason a man shall leave his father and mother and will cleave to his wife, and the two will be one flesh.'" Then, referring to the creator, he says. "What God has put together, let not man put asunder" (Mt. 19:4–6). How then do they introduce a creation alien to the Father? OTI, 51

St. Ambrose, *Hexameron,* Book 3, Ch. 7: Do you recognize the fact that you are the work of Christ? With His own hands He formed you, as we read, yet you, Manichean, you assume for yourself another author. FCAm, 91

St. Thomas Aquinas, *Summa Theologiae*, I, Q 65, Art 1 ad 2: Corporeal creatures according to their nature are good, though this good is not universal, but partial and limited.[1] ST, 610

St. Athanasius, *De Incarnatione Verbi Dei*, Ch. 1:3: But the inspired teaching and faith according to Christ casts out their vain talk as godlessness. For it knows that neither spontaneously, as it is not without providence, nor from pre-existent matter, as God is not weak, but from nothing and having absolutely no existence God brought the universe into being through the Word. OTI, 51

St. Augustine, *Contra Faustum*, Book XXII, 4: [how Faustus misinterprets Genesis] These books, moreover contain shocking calumnies against God Himself. We are told that He existed from eternity in darkness, and admired the light when He saw it; that He was so ignorant of the future, that He gave Adam a command, not foreseeing that it would be broken; that His perception was so limited that He could not see Adam when, from the knowledge of his nakedness, he hid himself in a corner of Paradise; that envy made Him afraid lest His creature man should taste of the tree of life, and live forever. MH, 402

St. Basil, *On the Hexameron*, Homily 1:2: The wise men of the Greeks wrote many works about nature, but not one account among them remained unaltered and firmly established, for the later account always overthrew the preceding one. FCB, 5

St. Basil, *On the Hexameron*, Homily 1:2: For this reason, some had recourse to material origins, referring the beginning of the universe to the elements of the world. FCB, 5

---

[1] 1Tim. 4:4-5: "For every creature of God is good, and nothing to be rejected that is received with thanksgiving: For it is sanctified by the word of God and prayer."

St. Basil, *On the Hexameron*, Homily 1:2: And others imagined that the nature of visible things consisted of atoms and indivisible particles, of molecules and interstices; indeed, that, as the indivisible particles now united with each other and now separated, there were produced generations and deteriorations; and that the stronger union of the atoms of the more durable bodies was the cause of their permanence. FCB, 5

St. Basil, *On the Hexameron*, Homily 1:2: Truly, it is a spider's web that these writers weave, who suggest such weak and unsubstantial beginnings of the heavens and earth and sea. It is because they did not know how to say: "In the beginning God created the heavens and the earth." FCB, 5

St. Basil, *On the Hexameron*, Homily 1:2: They were deceived by the godlessness present within them into thinking that the universe was without guide and without rule, as if borne around by chance.[2] FCB, 5-6

St. Basil, *On the Hexameron*, Homily 1:2: In order that we might not suffer this error, he who directed the creation of the world immediately, in the very first words, enlightened our mind with the name of God, saying: "In the beginning God created." FCB, 6

St. Basil, *On the Hexameron*, Homily 9:2: Consider the word of God moving through all creation, having begun at that time, active up to the present, and efficacious until the end, even to the consummation of the world . . . It begets a horse as the successor of a horse, a lion of a lion, and an eagle of an eagle; and it continues to preserve each of the animals by uninterrupted successions until the consummation of the universe. FCB, 136-37

St. Augustine, *City of God*, Book XII, Ch. 16: I own that I do not know what ages passed before the human race was created, yet I doubt that no created thing is co-eternal with the creator. SA, Vol. 2, 236

---

2 Wis. 14:3, Jn. 5:17, Heb. 1:3

St. Hippolytus, *Against the Heresy of Noetus*, Ch. 10: God, subsisting alone, and having nothing contemporaneous with Himself, determined to create the world . . . Beside Him there was nothing; but He, while existing alone, yet existed in plurality. ANF, Vol 5, 227

St. Thomas Aquinas, *Summa Contra Gentiles*, Book II, Ch. 31: Now it is not necessary that God will the creature always to have been; since neither is it necessary that God will a thing to be at all . . . Therefore it is not necessary that creatures should have been always. SCG, 63

St. Ambrose, *Hexameron*, Book 1, Ch. 5: Certainly not without reason do we read that the world was made, for many of the Gentiles who maintain that the world is co-eternal with God, as if it were a shadow of divine power, affirm also that it subsists of itself. FCAm, 17

St. Ambrose, *Hexameron*, Book 1, Ch. 5: Although they admit that the cause of it is God, they assert that the cause does not proceed from His own will and rule. Rather, they make it to be analogous to the shadow in respect to the body. For the shadow stays close to the body and a flash follows the light more by natural association than by exercise of free will. FCAm, 17

St. Basil, *On the Hexameron*, Homily 1:2: He placed first 'the beginning,' that no one might believe that it was without a beginning. Then he added the word, 'created,' that it might be shown that what was made required a very small part of the power of the creator. FCB, 6

St. Thomas Aquinas, *Summa Theologiae*, I, Q 46, Art 1: On the contrary, It is said (Jn. 17:5), "Glorify Me, O Father, with Thyself with the glory which I had before the world was"; and (Prov. 8:22), "The Lord possessed Me in the beginning of His ways, before He made anything from the beginning."[3] ST, 449

---

[3] 1Cor. 2:7

St. Gregory Nazianzen, *Orations,* No. 40:45: Believe that all that is in the world, both all that is seen and that is unseen, was made out of nothing by God, and is governed by the providence of its creator, and will receive a change to a better state. NPNF, Vol. VII, 377

St. Theophilus of Antioch, *To Autolycus*, Book 2, Ch. 4: But the power of God is manifested in this, that out of things that are not He makes whatever He pleases; just as the bestowal of life and motion is the prerogative of no other than God alone. ANF, Vol. 2, 95

St. Thomas Aquinas, *Summa Theologiae,* I, Q 46, Art 1 ad 10: Therefore from the eternal action of God an eternal effect did not follow; but such an effect as God willed, an effect, to wit, which has being after not being. ST, 451-52

St. Ambrose, *Hexameron,* Book 1, Ch. 1: On the other hand, Plato ventures to assert that the world did not always exist, but that it will always exist. A great many writers, however, give us evidence from their works that they believe that the world did not always exist and that it will exist forever. FCAm, 4

St. Basil, *On the Hexameron,* Homily 1:3: It is absolutely necessary that things begun in time be also brought to an end in time. If they have a beginning in time, have no doubt about the end. FCB, 7

St. Basil, *On the Hexameron,* Homily 2:2: If matter itself is uncreated, it is, in the first place, of equal rank with God, worthy of the same honors. FCB, 23

St. Thomas Aquinas, *Summa Theologiae,* I, Q 46, Art 2: But that God is the creator of the world in such a way that the world began to be is an article of faith. ST, 453

St. Thomas Aquinas, *Summa Theologiae,* I, Q 46, Art 2 ad 1: For some said that the substance of the world was not from God, which is an intolerable error; and therefore it is refuted by proofs that are cogent. Some, however, said that the world was eternal, although made by God. For they hold that the world has a beginning, not of time, but of creation, so that in a certain hardly intelligible way it was always made. ST, 453-54

St. Augustine, *City of God*, Book XI, Ch. 4: But why did God choose then to create the heavens and earth which up to that time He had not made? If they who put this question wish to make out that the world is eternal and without beginning, and that consequently it has not been made by God, they are strangely deceived and rave in the incurable madness of impiety. For, though the voices of the prophets were silent, the world itself, by its well-ordered changes and movements and by the fair appearance of all visible things, bears a testimony of its own, both that it has been created and also that it could not have been created save by God, whose greatness and beauty are unutterable and invisible. SA, Vol. 2, 207

St. Ambrose, *Hexameron*, Book 1, Ch. 1: They maintain that God, acting not as a creator of matter but as a craftsman who reproduced a model, that is, an idea, made the world out of matter. FCAm, 3

St. Irenaeus, *Adversus Haereses*, Book I, Ch. 22:1: The rule of truth which we hold is, that there is one God Almighty, who made all things by His Word, and fashioned and formed, out of that which had no existence, all things which exist. WI, Vol. 1, 84-85

St. Irenaeus, *Adversus Haereses*, Book IV, Ch. 38:3: His power and goodness [appear] in this, that of His own will He called into being and fashioned things having no previous existence. WI, Vol. 2, 43

St. Methodius, *On Free Will*: For man will exist even without the art of building unless the man be previously in being. Whence we must say that it is in the nature of things for arts to be produced in men out of what has no existence. If, then, we have shown that this is so in the case of men, why was it improper to say that God is able to make not only qualities, but also substances, out of that which has no existence? For as it appears possible for something to be produced out of what exists not, it is evident that this is the case with substances. ANF, Vol. 6, 360

St. Athanasius, *Defense of the Nicene Definition*, Ch. 11: For God creates, in that He calls what is not into being, needing nothing thereunto; but men work some existing material, first praying, and so gaining the wit to make, from God who has framed all things by His proper Word.[4] NPNF, Vol. IV, 157

St. Athanasius, *Defense of the Nicene Definition*, Ch. 11: As then men create not as God creates, as their being is not such as God's being, so men's generation is in one way, and the Son is from the Father in another. NPNF, Vol. IV, 157

St. Ambrose, *Hexameron*, Book 2, Ch. 1: God, therefore, created the heavens and the earth and those things which He as Author ordained to exist, not just as a designer of their form but as a creator of their nature. FCAm, 46

St. Ambrose, *Hexameron*, Book 1, Ch. 4: We can find it easy to understand, then, that the creator of Angels, Dominations, and Powers is He who in a moment of His power made this great beauty of the world out of nothing, which did not itself have existence and gave substance to things or causes that did not themselves exist. FCAm, 16

St. Ambrose, *Hexameron*, Book 1, Ch. 3: For God is Melchisedech, that is, "He is king of peace and justice, having neither the beginning of days nor end of life" [Heb. 7:2–3]. No wonder, therefore that God, who is without end, gave a beginning to all things, so that what was not began to exist. FCAm, 9

---

[4] 2Mac. 7:21-28

St. Ambrose, *Hexameron*, Book 1, Ch. 3: Do not then believe that it was without beginning because the world is said to be, as it were, a sphere in which there would appear to be no beginning. FCAm, 10

St. Basil, *On the Hexameron*, Homily 1:3: Do not, then, imagine, O man, that the things which you see are without a beginning, and do not think, because the bodies moving in the heavens travel around in a circle and because the beginning of the circle is not easily discerned by our ordinary means of perception, that the nature of bodies moving in a circle is without a beginning. FCB, 6

St. Ambrose, *Hexameron*, Book 1, Ch. 3: To perceive by one's senses the beginning of a circle is considered to be impossible. You cannot discover the beginning of a sphere or from what point the round disk of the moon begins or where it ends its monthly wanings. FCAm, 10

St. Basil, *On the Hexameron*, Homily 1:3: But, even if it does escape our observation, assuredly, He who drew it with a center and a certain radius truly began from some point. FCB, 7

Why God Created[5]

St. John Damascene, *De Fide Orthodoxa*, Book 2, Ch. 2: Now, because the good and transcendentally good God was not content to contemplate Himself, but by a superabundance of goodness saw fit that there should be some things to benefit by and participate in His goodness, He brings all things from nothing into being and creates them, both visible and invisible and man, who is made up of both.[6] FCD, 205

---

[5] Cf. First Vatican Council: Dei Filius, Ch. 1:3. DS, 3002: *"Hic solus verus Deus bonitate sua et 'omnipotenti virtute' non ad augmendum suam beatitudinem nec ad acquirendam, sed ad manifestandam perfectionem suam per bona, quae creaturis impertitur, liberrimo consilio 'simul ab initio temporis utramque de nihilo condidit creaturam, spiritualem et corporalem ...' "*

[6] Prov. 16:4

St. Augustine, *De Genesi ad litteram*, Book IV, Ch. 15: Hence, where Holy Scripture says that God rested from all the works He had made, He is not represented as taking delight in any works in such a way as to imply that He needed to make it, or that He would have lacked something if He had not made it, or that He was happier after He had made it. For whatever comes from God is dependent upon Him that it owes its existence to Him, but He does not owe His happiness to any creature He has made. LMG, Vol. 1, 120-21

St. Augustine, *De Genesi ad litteram*, Book IV, Ch. 15: He placed Himself in His love above the works He had made, for He did not sanctify the day on which He began to make them, nor that on which He finished them, lest there appear to be an increase of His joy because of the undertaking or completion of these works. But He did sanctify that day on which He rested from them in Himself. LMG, Vol. 1, 121

St. Theophilus of Antioch, *To Autolycus*, Book 2: And first, [the prophets] taught us with one consent that God made all things out of nothing; for nothing was coeval with God; but He being His own place, and wanting nothing, and existing before all ages, willed to make man by whom He might be known; for him, therefore, He prepared the world. For he that is created is also needy; but He that is uncreated stands in need of nothing. ANF, Vol. 2, 97-98

St. Bonaventure, *Breviloquium*, Part II, Ch. 4:5: All corporeal beings were made to serve humankind, so that through these things humanity might ascend to loving and praising the creator of the universe whose providence disposes all. Brev, 71

St. Thomas Aquinas, *Summa Theologiae*, I, Q 47, Art 1: And because His goodness could not be adequately represented by one creature alone, He produced many and diverse creatures, so that what was wanting to one in the representation of the divine goodness might be supplied by another. ST, 459

St. Augustine, *City of God*, Book XI, Ch. 24: And by the words, "God saw that it was good", it is sufficiently intimated that God made what was made not from any necessity, nor for the sake of supplying any want, but solely from His own goodness, *i.e.*, because it was good. SA, Vol. 2, 219

St. Gregory Nazianzen, *Orations*, No. 38:9: But since this movement of self-contemplation alone could not satisfy Goodness, but Good must be poured out and go forth beyond Itself to multiply the objects of Its beneficence, for this was essential to the highest Goodness, He first conceived the Heavenly and Angelic Powers. NPNF, Vol. VII, 347

St. Hippolytus, *Against the Heresy of Noetus*, Ch. 10: When He willed, and as He willed, He manifested His word in the times determined by Him, and by Him He made all things. When He wills, He does; and when He thinks, He executes; and when He speaks, He manifests; when He fashions, He contrives in wisdom. For all things that are made He forms by reason and wisdom—creating them in reason and arranging them in wisdom. He made them, then, as He pleased, for He was God. ANF, Vol 5, 227

St. Irenaeus, *Adversus Haereses*, Book II, Ch. 1:1: But of His own free will, He created all things, since He is the only God, the only Lord, the only creator, the only Father, alone containing all things, and Himself commanding all things into existence. WI, Vol. 1, 117

St. Thomas Aquinas, *Summa Contra Gentiles*, Book II, Ch. 31: Now God does not act out of necessity in producing creatures, as we have proved above. Wherefore it is not absolutely necessary for the creature to be, as regards necessity dependent on the efficient cause. Likewise neither is it necessary as regards the necessity that depends on the final cause. For things directed to an end do not derive necessity from the end, except in so far as without them the end either cannot be—as preservation of life without food—or cannot be so well—as a journey without a horse. SCG, 63

St. Ambrose, *Hexameron*, Book 1, Ch. 5: Rather, He created it as a good man makes what would be of use, as a philosopher propounding his best thoughts, as one all-powerful foreseeing what is to be the most magnificent. FCAm, 17

St. Thomas Aquinas, *Summa Contra Gentiles*, Book II, Ch. 35: Because the object of the divine will is not only the existence of the effect, but also the time of its existence. Wherefore the thing will, namely that a creature should exist at such and such a time, is not delayed; because the creature began to exist at the time appointed by God from all eternity. SCG, 74-75

St. Athanasius, *Four Discourses against the Arians*, No. 1:29: And that creatures should not be in existence, does not disparage the maker; for He has the power of framing them, when He wills . . . Wherefore his works were framed, when He would, through His Word. NPNF, Vol. IV, 323

Chapter One
The Six Days of Creation

The Creation of All Things by God[7]

Genesis 1:1: *In the beginning. . .*

St. John Damascene, *De Fide Orthodoxa*, Book 2, Ch. 1: Before the framing of the world, when there was no sun to separate day from night, there was no measureable age, but only an age co-extensive with eternal things after the fashion of some sort of temporal period and interval. In this sense, there is one age in respect to which God is said to be of the ages, and, indeed, before the ages, for He made the very ages—since He alone is God without beginning and Himself creator both of the ages and of the things that are. FCD, 204

St. Thomas Aquinas, *Summa Theologiae*, I, Q 46, Art 3: The words of Genesis, "In the beginning God created heaven and earth," are inter-

---

[7] Some of the headings are based on the 1909 decree of the Pontifical Biblical Commission, Cf. DS, 3514: "*...rerum univerarum creatio a Deo facta in initio temporis; pecularis creatio hominis; formatio primae mulieris ex primo homine; generis humani unitas; originalis protoparentum felicitas in statu iustitiae, integritas et immortalitatis; praeceptum a Deo homini datum ad eius obedientiam probandam; divini praecepti, diabolo sub serepentis specie suasore, transgressio; protoparentum deiectio ab illo primaevo innocentiae statu; nec non Reparatoris futuri promissio.*"

preted in a threefold sense in order to exclude three errors. For some said that the world always was, and that time had no beginning and to exclude this the words "In the beginning" are interpreted to mean "the beginning of time." ST, 456

St. Thomas Aquinas, *Summa Contra Gentiles*, Book II, Ch. 35: But God brought into being both the creature and time together. SCG, 75

St. Augustine, *City of God*, Book X, Ch. 31: Plato, however, in writing concerning the world and the gods in it, whom the Supreme made, most expressly states that they had a beginning and yet would have no end but, by the sovereign will of the creator, would endure eternally. SA, Vol. 2, 201

St. Ambrose, *Hexameron*, Book 1, Ch. 4: Therefore, He who uttered these words, "In the beginning God created heaven and earth," teaches us that there is a beginning. The term 'beginning' has reference either to time or to number or to foundation.[8] FCAm, 11

St. Thomas Aquinas, *Summa Theologiae*, I, Q 46, Art 3: And some said that there are two principles of creation, one of good things and the other of evil things, against which "In the beginning is expounded —in the Son." ST, 456

St. Anthony of Padua, *Sermon on Septuagesima,* 3: These words refer to that which contains and that which is contained. God the Father created, and he re-creates, "in the Beginning" (that is, in the Son). He created in six days, resting on the seventh; he creates anew in six articles of faith, promising eternal rest on the seventh.[9] SSA, 10

---

[8] Ecclus. 51:11: "I remembered thy mercy, O Lord, and thy works, which are from the beginning of the world."

[9] Ps. 103:24: "Thou hast made all things in wisdom." Prov. 8:30: "I was with him forming all things; and was delighted every day, playing before him at all times." Col. 1:16: "For in him were all things created in heaven and on earth,

St. Ambrose, *Hexameron*, Book 1, Ch. 2: So in the Gospel, in answer to those who were inquiring of Him "Who art thou?" He replied: "I am the beginning, I who speak with you." All this was that you might know that He gave to all created things their beginnings and that He is the creator of the world—not one who imitates matter under the guidance of some Idea, from which He formed His work, not in accordance with His will, but in compliance with a self-proposed model. FCAm, 5

St. Jerome, *Hebraicae Quaestiones in Libro Geneseos*, p. 3: Whence also in the psalter He says of Himself "in the head of the book it is written of me", that is, in the beginning of Genesis [Ps. 39:8].[10] CC, 3

St. Ambrose, *Hexameron*, Book 1, Ch. 4: A beginning in a mystical sense is denoted by the statement: "I am the first and the last, the beginning and the end." The words of the Gospel are significant in this connection, especially wherein the Lord, when asked who He was, replied: "I am the beginning, I who spoke with you." In truth, He who is the beginning of all things by virtue of His divinity is also the end, because there is no one after Him. According to the Gospel, the beginning of the ways of God is in His work, so that the race of men might learn by Him to follow the ways of the Lord and to perform the works of God.[11] FCAm, 14-15

---

visible and invisible, whether thrones, or dominations, or principalities, or powers. All things were created by him and in him." Jn. 1:1-3: "In the beginning was the Word, and the Word was with God, and the Word was God. The same was in the beginning with God. All things were made by him: and without him was made nothing that was made."

10 My translation: *Unde et in psalterio de se ipso ait in capitulo libri scriptum est de me, id est in principio Geneseos.*

11 Apoc. 1:8: "I am the Alpha and Omega, the beginning and the end, saith the Lord God."

St. Ambrose, *Hexameron*, Book 1, Ch. 4: Therefore, in the beginning, that is, in Christ, God created heaven and earth, because "All things were made through him and without him was made nothing that was made" [Jn. 1:3]. Again: "In him all things hold together and he is the firstborn of every creature" [Col. 1:15]. Moreover, He was before every creature because He is holy. FCAm, 15

St. Thomas Aquinas, *Summa Theologiae*, I, Q 46, Art 3: But others have said that corporeal things were created by God through the medium of spiritual creatures; and to exclude this the words of *Genesis* are interpreted thus: "In the beginning" *i.e., before* all things "God created heaven and earth". ST, 456

St. Ambrose, *Hexameron*, Book 1, Ch. 2: Fittingly, too, Moses says: "In the beginning He created," in order that, where He had made clear the effect of the operation already completed, before giving an indication of its having been begun, He thus might express the incomprehensible speed of the work. FCAm, 5

St. Ambrose, *Hexameron*, Book 1, Ch. 4: Finally, others have interpreted the Greek phrase ἐν κεφαλαίῳ as if *in capite*, by which is meant that in a brief moment the sum of the operation was completed. FCAm, 15

St. Ambrose, *Hexameron*, Book 1, Ch. 2: Under the inspiration of the Holy Spirit, Moses, a holy man, foresaw that these errors would appear among men and perhaps had already appeared. FCAm, 5

St. Ambrose, *Hexameron*, Book 1, Ch. 2: He linked together the beginnings of things, the creator of the world, and the creation of matter in order that you might understand that God existed before the beginning of the world or that He was Himself the beginning of all things. FCAm, 5

Genesis 1:1: *God created heaven and earth.*

St. Lawrence of Brindisi, *Explanatio in Genesim*, Ch. 1: Therefore, since Moses, inspired by the Holy Ghost, wrote *bara Elohim*, literally, 'the gods he-created' (a plural subject with a singular verb), without doubt we understand the sense of these words: he means plurality of divine Persons in the word *Elohim* and the unity of essence in the singular verb 'he-created'. That is to say, three divine Persons are not three gods, but the one God. CF, 13

St. Thomas Aquinas, *Summa Theologiae*, I, Q 65, Art 3: Now it is impossible that anything should have been created, save by God alone. ST, 614

St. Augustine, *City of God,* Book, XI, Ch. 4: Of all visible things, the world is the greatest; of all invisible, the greatest is God. SA, Vol. 2, 206

St. Thomas Aquinas, *Summa Theologiae*, I, Q 65, Art 4: Accordingly, the corporeal forms that bodies had when first produced came immediately from God, Whose bidding alone matter obeys, as its own proper cause. ST, 616

St. Ephrem, *Commentary on Genesis*, Part 1:2: Therefore, it is evident that heaven and earth came to be from nothing because neither water nor wind had yet been created, nor had fire, light or darkness been given their natures, for they were younger than heaven and earth. FCE, 75

St. Ambrose, *Hexameron*, Book 1, Ch. 5: And the world was therefore created and that which was not began to exist. FCAm, 17

St. Ephrem, *Commentary on Genesis*, Part 1:14–15: Heaven, earth, fire, wind, and water were created from nothing as Scripture bears witness . . . Although it is not written that fire, water, and wind were created, neither is it said that they were made. Therefore, they came to be from nothing just as heaven and earth came to be from nothing... [fire] had no existence in and of itself but existed in something else and it was created together with that thing in which it came to be. FCE, 85

St. Thomas Aquinas, *Summa Theologiae*, I, Q 46, Art 3: For four things are stated to be created together—*viz.*, the empyrean heavens, corporeal matter, by which is meant the earth, time, and the angelic nature. ST, 456

Time

St. Thomas Aquinas, *Summa Theologiae*, I, Q 66, Art 4 ad 4: Among the first created things are to be reckoned those which have a general relationship to things. And, therefore, among these time must be included, as having the nature of a common measure. ST, 628

St. Ambrose, *Hexameron*, Book 1, Ch. 6: Time proceeds from this world, not before the world. And the day is a division of time, not its beginning. FCAm, 19

St. Thomas Aquinas, *Summa Theologiae*, I, Q 66, Art 4: Augustine says: "Both spiritual and corporeal creatures were created at the beginning of time." ST, 627

St. Bonaventure, *Breviloquium*, Part II, Ch. 6:3: The First Principle, by the very fact of being first, produced all things from nothing, not only those things that are "close to nothing," but also those that are close to it. Brev, 77

St. Bonaventure, *Breviloquium*, Part II, Ch. 6:3: It was therefore proper that it produce not only a substance that is far removed from it (which is the corporeal nature) but also one that is kindred to it. Brev, 77

St. Ephrem, *Commentary on Genesis*, Part 1:1: So let no one think that there is anything allegorical in the work of the six days . . . there was no other thing signified by the names 'heaven' and 'earth.' The rest of the works and things made that followed were not meaningless significations either, for the substances of their natures correspond to what their names signify. FCE, 74

St. Augustine, *De Genesi ad litteram*, Book I, Ch. 1: But perhaps we should take 'heaven' to mean spiritual beings in a state of perfection and beatitude from the first moment of their creation and take 'earth' to mean bodily matter in a state that is not yet complete and perfect. LMG, Vol. 1, 20

St. Thomas Aquinas, *Summa Theologiae*, I, Q 66, Art 4: It is commonly said that the first things created were these four: the angelic nature, the empyrean heaven, formless corporeal matter, and time. ST, 627

Heaven of the Blessed

St. Thomas Aquinas, *Summa Theologiae*, I, Q 66, Art 3: Strabo says that in the passage, "In the beginning God created heaven and earth, heaven denotes not the visible firmament, but the empyrean or fiery heaven." ST, 624-25

St. Thomas Aquinas, *Summa Theologiae*, I, Q 66, Art 3: The empyrean heaven rests only on the authority of Strabo and Bede, and also of Basil; all of whom agree in one respect, namely, in holding it to be the place of the blessed.[12] ST, 625

St. Bede, *In principium Genesis*, Book I: One should remember that the higher heaven had not been created without form

[12] Mt. 25:34: "The kingdom prepared for you from the foundation of the world."

and void, nor is it granted that any place in it or any abyss has remained in the darkness because the Lord God illuminates it, and his lamp is the Lamb. OG, 115

St. Augustine, *City of God*, Book XI, Ch. 1: We have learned that there is a city of God, and its Founder has inspired us with a love which makes us covet its citizenship.[13] SA, Vol. 2, 205

St. Thomas Aquinas, *Summa Theologiae*, I, Q 66, Art 3: Now the spiritual glory began with the beginning of the world, in the blessedness of the angels, equality with whom is promised to the saints. It was fitting, then, that even from the beginning, there should be made some beginning of bodily glory in something corporeal, free at the very outset from the servitude of corruption and change, and wholly luminous, even as the whole bodily creation, after the Resurrection, is expected to be. So, then, that heaven is called the empyrean, *i.e.* fiery, not from its heat, but from its brightness. ST, 625

St. Ambrose, *Hexameron*, Book 1, Ch. 6: He stretched it out as you would skin over tents, the dwelling places of the saints, or as a scroll, that the names of many be inscribed therein who merited the grace of Christ by their faith and devotion. To all such it is said: "Rejoice in this that your names are written in heaven" [Lk. 10:20].[14] FCAm, 20

St. Thomas Aquinas, *Summa Theologiae*, I, Q 66, Art 4 ad 5: Place is said to be in the empyrean heaven considered as the boundary of the universe. And since place has reference to things permanent, it was created at once in its totality. ST, 628

---

[13] Heb. 11:16: "for he hath prepared for them a city."

[14] Isa. 40:22: "It is he that sitteth upon the globe of the earth, and the inhabitants thereof are as locusts: he that stretcheth out the heavens as nothing, and spreadeth them out as a tent to dwell in."

St. Lawrence of Brindisi, *Explanatio in Genesim*, Ch. 1: The Holy Roman Church professes that, from the beginning, God at once created corporeal creatures (those belonging to the world) and spiritual creatures (the angels). CF, 17

St. Lawrence of Brindisi, *Explanatio in Genesim*, Ch. 1: Even the original Hebrew text of Genesis seems to be in agreement with this belief, where for *heaven* it reads *hashamayim*, a noun in the dual number, as if there were two kinds of heavens, to wit, a spiritual heaven and a corporeal heaven. CF, 17

St. Thomas Aquinas, *Summa Theologiae*, I, Q 74, Art 1 ad 1: According to Augustine, the work of creation belongs to the production of formless matter, and of the formless spiritual nature, both of which are outside of time, as he himself says. Thus, then, the creation of either is set down before there was any day. ST, 674

Genesis 1:2: *And the earth was void and empty, and darkness was upon the face of the deep.*

St. Ambrose, *Hexameron*, Book 1, Ch. 6: On the nature and position of the earth there should be no need to enter into discussion at this point with respect to what is to come. It is sufficient for our information to state what the text of the Holy Scriptures establishes, namely, that, "he hangeth the earth upon nothing" [Job 26:7]. FCAm, 20

St. Ambrose, *Hexameron*, Book 1, Ch. 6: When we read: "I have established the pillars thereof," [Ps. 74:4] we cannot believe that the world was supported actually by columns, but rather by that power props up the substance of the earth and sustains it. FCAm, 21

St. Ephrem, *Commentary on Genesis*, Part 1:3: I am not saying that the void and desolation were something. Rather [I am saying] that the earth, which does exist, was known [to exist] in something which does not exist, for the earth existed alone without any other thing. FCE, 76

Formless Matter

St. Augustine, *De Genesi ad litteram*, Book I, Ch. 15: But we must not suppose that unformed matter is prior in time to things that are formed; both the thing made and the matter from which it was made were created together. LMG, Vol. 1, 36

St. Thomas Aquinas, *Summa Theologiae*, I, Q 66, Art 3: But the question of the darkness is explained, according to St. Augustine, by supposing that the informity, signified by darkness, preceded form not by duration, but by origin. ST, 625

St. Lawrence of Brindisi, *Explanatio in Genesim*, Ch. 1: St. Gregory Nazianzus (in his *Sermon on the Holy Ghost*), Lactantius (in Book 2 of his *On the Origin of Error*), St. Augustine (in Book 12 of his *Confessions*), the Venerable Bede, and Hugh of St. Victor, too, think that prime matter ought to be understood by the name *earth*; from prime matter, everything contained under the heavens, even to the center of the earth, was then made. CF, 19

St. Augustine, *Confessions*, Book XII, Ch. 12: But this Thou didst not leave formless, since before all days, in the beginning Thou createdst heaven and earth—these two things of which I spoke. But the earth was invisible and without form, and darkness was upon the deep. By which words its shapelessness is conveyed unto us—that by degrees those minds may be drawn on which cannot wholly conceive the privation of all form without coming to nothing—whence another heaven might be created, and another earth visible and well-formed, and water beautifully ordered, and whatever besides is, in the formation of the world, recorded to have been, not without days created. SA, Vol. 1, 179

St. Augustine, *De Genesi ad litteram*, Book I, Ch. 1: These words seem to indicate the formless state of bodily substance. Or does the second statement imply the formless state of both substances, so that bodily substance is referred to in the words, "The earth was invisible and formless", but the spiritual substance in the words, "Darkness was over the abyss"? LMG, Vol. 1, 20

St. Augustine, *De Genesi ad litteram*, Book I, Ch. 1: In this interpretation we should understand 'dark abyss' as a metaphor meaning that life which is formless unless it is turned towards its creator. Only in this way can it be formed and cease being an abyss, and be illumined and cease being dark. LMG, Vol. 1, 20

St. Augustine, *De Genesi ad litteram*, Book I, Ch. 1: And then what is the meaning of the statement, "Darkness was over the abyss"? Was there no light? If there was any light at all, there would be a great abundance of it, for that is the way it is in the case of a spiritual creature that turns to God, the changeless and incorporeal Light. LMG, Vol. 1, 20

St. Thomas Aquinas, *Summa Theologiae*, I, Q 66, Art 1: Basil, Ambrose, and Chrysostom, hold that the informity of matter preceded in time its formation. ST, 619

St. Basil, *On the Hexameron*, Homily 2:3: "God created the heaven and the earth," not each one by halves, but the entire heavens and the whole earth, including the substance itself with the form. He is not the inventor of the shapes, but the creator of the very nature of all that exists. FCB, 24-25

St. John Chrysostom, *Homilies on Genesis*, Homily 2:12: He shows it to you first formless and imperfect so that you would not attribute the earth's gifts to it but to the one who brought it into existence from nothing. FCC, 36

St. Ambrose, *Hexameron*, Book 1, Ch. 7: And perhaps they may say: Why did not God, in accordance with the word, "He spoke and they were made," [Ps. 148:5] grant to the elements at the same time as they arose their appropriate adornments, as if He, at the moment of creation, were unable to cause the heavens immediately to gleam with studded stars and the earth to be clothed with flowers and fruit? That could very well have happened. FCAm, 28-29

St. Ambrose, *Hexameron*, Book 1, Ch. 7: Add to this the fact that God willed it that we be imitators of Himself, so that we first make something and afterwards beautify it. FCAm, 29

St. Lawrence of Brindisi, *Explanatio in Genesim*, Ch. 1: Nonetheless, we do not say that this matter had been created entirely without any form but, according to the opinion of St. Augustine, we say it was formless to the extent that it does not have a definite, specific form (from which it might be drawn out to a determined being) and was utterly lacking every definite outward shape. Rather it was clothed with a kind of form, disordered and imperfect, which had the weakest and most imperfect act, with which it could be the common subject to all forms, and in that form there existed the desire to be perfected through the forms in contact with it. CF, 21

St. Thomas Aquinas, *Summa Theologiae*, I, Q 66, Art 1 ad 1: The *earth* is taken differently in this passage by Augustine, and by other writers. Augustine holds that by the words *earth* and *water*, in this passage, primarily matter itself is signified. For it was impossible for Moses to make the idea of such matter intelligible to an ignorant people, except under the similitude of well-known things. Hence he uses a variety of figures in speaking of it, calling it not water only, nor earth only, lest they should think it to be in very truth water or earth. ST, 620

St. Lawrence of Brindisi, *Explanatio in Genesim*, Ch. 1: St Augustine thinks that 'abyss' means the same prime matter from which, since it was created from nothing, all things were created. He says that it is called "heaven and earth" in so far as these things were made of it. It is called "the indivisible and shapeless earth" because among the element of the world, the earth seems less formed than the others . . . It is called 'water' above which the Spirit of God moved, just as the will of an artisan operates above the handiwork that he will make . . . Finally, the 'abyss' is said to be dark because of its disorder. It was without shape, and by no outward appearance could it be discerned or touched.[15] CF, 23

St. Thomas Aquinas, *Summa Theologiae,* I, Q 66, Art 1 ad 1: In this respect, then, the earth is said to be "void and empty", or "invisible and shapeless", because matter is known by means of form. Hence, considered in itself, it is called 'invisible' or 'void', and its potentiality is filled by form; and that is why Plato says that matter is 'place'. ST, 620

St. Augustine, *De Genesi ad litteram,* Book I, Ch. 9: But by the expression, "earth without shape or form", and by the dark abyss, is meant the imperfect material substance from which temporal things would be made, of which the first light would be. LMG, Vol. 1, 27

The Formless Earth

St. Thomas Aquinas, *Summa Theologiae,* I, Q 66, Art 1 ad 1: But other holy writers understand by 'earth' the element *earth,* and we have said how, in this sense, the earth was, according to them, without form. ST, 620

St. Thomas Aquinas, *Summa Theologiae,* I, Q 66, Art 1: And the earth lacked beauty in two ways: first, that beauty which it acquired when its watery veil was withdrawn, and so we read that "the earth was void", or 'invisible', inasmuch as the water covered and concealed it from

15 Wis. 11:18: "For thy almighty hand, which made the world of matter without form."

view; secondly, that which it derives from being adorned by herbs and plants, for which reason it is called 'empty', or, according to another reading, 'shapeless'—that is, unadorned. ST, 619-20

St. Ambrose, *Hexameron*, Book 1, Ch. 7: And justly is the earth called invisible, because it was without order, not having as yet received from its creator its appropriate form and beauty. FCAm, 28

St. Ambrose, *Hexameron*, Book 1, Ch. 7: Yet Scripture points out that things were first created and afterwards put in order, lest it be supposed that they were not actually created and that they had no beginning, just as if the nature of things had been, as it were, generated from the beginning and did not appear to be something afterwards. FCAm, 29

St. Ambrose, *Hexameron*, Book 1, Ch. 7: For that reason, God created first and afterwards beautified, in order that we may believe that He who made and He who adorned were one and the same person. FCAm, 29

St. John Damascene, *De Fide Orthodoxa*, Book 2, Ch. 10: Some say that the earth is spherical in form; others, that it is conical. FCD, 229

St. Basil, *On the Hexameron*, Homily 9:1: Moses gave no discussion concerning the shape of the earth and did not say that its circumference contains one hundred and eighty thousand stades. FCB, 136

St. Ambrose, *Hexameron*, Book 6, Ch. 2: What concern has the circumference of the earth for me? Geometers estimate it to be one-hundred-eighty stadia. I gladly admit that I do not know that of which I am ignorant or, rather, that I am aware knowledge of this sort would not be of profit for me. Better than knowledge about the extent of the earth is knowledge about the concrete things in it. FCAm, 231

St. Bonaventure, *Breviloquium*, Part II, Ch. 5:1: But there is order in the way Scripture gives us sufficient teaching about all these things. This is the case, even if it does not explicitly describe the different spheres of the heavens and of the elements; even if it says little or nothing about the motions and powers of the superior bodies, or of the combinations of the elements and their compounds; and even if it says nothing explicitly about the creation of the higher spirits, especially when it describes how the universe came into being. Brev, 72

St. Ephrem, *Commentary on Genesis*, Part 1:5: Because everything that was created was created in those six days, whether it was written down that it was created or not. The clouds must also have been created on the first day, just as fire was created along with wind, although Moses did not write that the clouds were created along with the abyss, just as he did not record the creation of fire along with that of the wind when he wrote about the creation of the wind.[16] FCE, 77-78

Darkness

St. Thomas Aquinas, *Summa Theologiae*, I, Q 66, Art 1: As far as may be gathered from the text of *Genesis*, a threefold beauty was wanting in corporeal creatures, for which reason they were said to be without form. For the beauty of light was wanting to all that transparent body, which we call the heavens, whence it is said that *darkness was upon the face of the deep.* ST, 619

St. Thomas Aquinas, *Summa Theologiae*, I, Q 66, Art 1: Thus after the mention of two created natures, the heaven and the earth, the informity of the heaven is indicated by the words, *darkness was upon the face of the deep*, since the air is included under heaven; and the informity of the earth, by the words, *the earth was void and empty.* ST, 620

[16] Prov. 3:20: "By his wisdom the depths have broken out, and the clouds grow thick with dew."

St. Ambrose, *Hexameron*, Book 1, Ch. 7: Or they might hold that the earth was invisible for the reason that when covered by water it could not be seen by mortal eyes, just as much as that which lies in deep water escapes the notice of our sharpest eyes. FCAm, 28

St. Basil, *On the Hexameron*, Homily 2:1: In accordance with this interpretation, we believe that 'invisible' means that the earth was concealed by the water. Then, of course, since light had not yet been made, it is not to be wondered at that the earth, lying in darkness, because the air above it was not illumined, was for this reason also called by the scripture 'invisible.'FCB, 22

St. Ambrose, *Hexameron*, Book 1, Ch. 7: Invisible, also, was the earth, because the light which illumined the world did not as yet exist, nor did the sun. FCAm, 28

St. Ambrose, *Hexameron*, Book 1, Ch. 8: There was darkness because the brilliance of light was absent; there was darkness because the air itself was dark. Water itself beneath a cloud is dark because "dark are the waters in the clouds of air" [Ps. 17:12]. There was, therefore, darkness over the abyss of waters. FCAm, 31

St. Ephrem, *Commentary on Genesis*, Part 1:5: Just as clouds covered Egypt for three days and three nights, clouds were spread over all of creation on the first night and on the first day. FCE, 78

St. John Damascene, *De Fide Orthodoxa*, Book 2, Ch. 8: This is what scripture meant when it said that "darkness was upon the face of the deep," intending to show that the air does not have light from itself, but that the substance of light is something else. FCD, 222-23

St. Lawrence of Brindisi, *Explanatio in Genesim*, Ch. 1: St. Augustine and Bede think that 'darkness' is simply the lack of light because light had not yet been made.[17] CF, 22

---

[17] Jer. 4:23: "I behold the earth, and lo it was void, and nothing: and the

St. Ambrose, *Hexameron*, Book 1, Ch. 8: And the earth was invisible, because water flowed over it and covered it. Darkness was diffused over it, because there was not yet the light of day, or the rays of the light which can reveal even what lies hid beneath the waters. FCAm, 34

St. Ambrose, *Hexameron*, Book 1, Ch. 8: This darkness was over the abyss of waters. For the Gospel teaches us that the abyss is a mass of deep waters where, in fact, the demons entreated the Saviour "not to command them to depart into the abyss." [Lk. 8:31-32] FCAm, 37

St. John Damascene, *De Fide Orthodoxa*, Book 2, Ch. 9: for the deep is nothing else than a great quantity of water. In the beginning, then, water covered the whole earth. FCD, 224

St. Augustine, *Contra Faustum*, Book XXII, 11: The deep is the unfathomable abyss of waters. MH, 406

St. Ephrem, *Commentary on Genesis*, Part 1:16: Some teachings posit that this [darkness] is an adversary of creatures and they make that thing which has no substance of its own a self-existent being. FCE, 86-87

Genesis 1:2: *and the spirit of God moved over the waters.*

St. Ephrem, *Commentary on Genesis*, Part 1:7: It is indeed said that *it was hovering*, but what came forth from the waters on the first day

---

heavens, and there was no light in them." Ps. 138:12: "But darkness shall not be dark to thee, and night shall be light all the day: the darkness thereof, and the light thereof are alike to thee." Ecclus. 23:28: "And he knoweth not that the eyes of the Lord are far brighter than the sun, beholding round about all the ways of men, and the bottom of the deep, and looking into the hearts of men, into the most hidden parts."

when [the wind] was hovering over the waters? If on the day that it was written that *it was hovering over the waters* nothing came out of the waters, and then on the fifth day when the waters brought forth reptiles and birds, it was not written that the wind *was hovering*, how then can anyone say that this wind took part in the activity of creation? For, although scripture said *it was hovering*, it did not say that anything came out of the waters on the day that it was hovering... Moses wished to make known to us the creation [of the wind]. FCE, 80

St. Ambrose, *Hexameron*, Book 1, Ch. 8: But if, as some would have it, we are to interpret 'spirit' as 'air,' let these people answer the question: How did the Scripture speak of the 'Spirit of God,' when it would have been sufficient to mention simply 'spirit'? FCAm, 33

St. Thomas Aquinas, *Summa Theologiae*, I, Q 74, Art 3 ad 4: But according to the holy writers, the Spirit of the Lord signifies the Holy Ghost, Who is said to *move over the water*—that is to say, over what Augustine holds to mean formless matter, lest it should be supposed that God loved of necessity the works He was to produce, as though He stood in need of them. ST, 679

St. Thomas Aquinas, *Summa Theologiae*, I, Q 66, Art 1 ad 3: Because by the word *Spirit of God* scripture usually means the Holy Ghost, Who is said to *move over the waters*, not, indeed, in bodily shape, but as the craftsman's will may be said to move over the material to which he intends to give a form. ST, 621

St. Thomas Aquinas, *Summa Theologiae*, I, Q 74, Art 3 ad 3: *The Spirit of God*, it is said, *moved over the waters*—that is to say, over the formless matter, signified by water, even as the love of the artist moves over the materials of his art, that out of them he may form his work. ST, 679

St. Thomas Aquinas, *Summa Theologiae*, I, Q 74, Art 3 ad 4: It is the opinion, however, of Basil that the Spirit moved over the element of water, *fostering and quickening its nature and impressing vital power, as the hen broods over her chickens.* For water has especially a life-giving power, since many animals are generated in water, and the seed of all animals is liquid. Also the life of the soul is given by the water of baptism. ST, 680

St. Basil, *On the Hexameron*, Homily 2:6: How, then, was It stirring above the waters? I will tell you an explanation, not my own, but that of a Syrian who was as far removed from worldly wisdom as he was near the knowledge of the truth. Now, he claimed that the language of the Syrians was more expressive and because of its resemblance to the Hebrew language approached somewhat more closer to the sense of the scripture; therefore the meaning of the statement was as follows. FCB, 31

St. Basil, *On the Hexameron*, Homily 2:6: As regards the verb 'was stirring above,' they interpret in preference to that, he says, 'warmed with fostering care,' and he endued the nature of the waters with life through his comparison with a bird brooding upon eggs and imparting some vital power to them as they are being warmed. Some such meaning, they say, was implied by this word, as if the Spirit were warming with fostering care, that is, was preparing the nature of water for the generation of living beings.[18] FCB, 31

St. Ambrose, *Hexameron*, Book 1, Ch. 9: Rightly, therefore, was the Spirit of God sent forth where the divine operation was to begin.[19] FCAm, 38

---

[18] Deut. 32:11: "As the eagle enticing her young to fly, and hovering over them, he spreads out his wings, and hath taken him and carried him on his shoulders."

[19] Ps. 103:30: "Thou shalt send forth thy spirit, and they shall be created: and thou shalt renew the face of the earth."

St. Jerome, *Hebraicae Quaestiones in Libro Geneseos*, pg. 3: From which we understand it to be said not of the spirit of the world, as some have thought, but of the Holy Spirit, who is also Himself said to be from the beginning the vivifier of all things. But if vivifier consequently also the preserver. Now the preserver is also God for he says "you shall send forth your spirit and they shall be created".[20] CC, 3

St. Lawrence of Brindisi, *Explanatio in Genesim*, Ch. 1: In conclusion, first we may notice how the entire Trinity together brought about the establishment of the world. By the word 'God', we understand the Father, who is the beginning of all things, the source and origin of divinity and deity. In the word 'beginning', we understand the Son Himself, who says of himself "I am the beginning who also speak to you". In the words 'Spirit of God', we understand the third Person of the Trinity, namely the Holy Ghost when it is written: "By the word of the Lord the heavens were made and by the breath of his mouth all their host" [Ps. 32:6].[21] CF, 25

Genesis 1:3: *And God said: Be light made. And light was made.*

St. Augustine, *De Genesi ad litteram*, Book I, Ch. 9: In other words, was this movement produced in that spiritual creation which is the heaven of the visible heaven above us? Or shall we say that this was an utterance not only without any sound but also without any temporal

---

[20] My translation: *Ex quo intelligimus non de spiritu mundi dici, ut non nulli arbitrantur, sed de spiritu sancto, qui et ispe vivificator omnium a principio dicitur. Si autem vivificator, consequenter et conditor. Quod si conditor, et deus: emittes enim ait spiritum tuum et creabuntur.*

[21] Jn. 1:32: "And John gave testimony, saying: I saw the Spirit coming down, as a dove from heaven, and he remained upon him." Mt. 3:16: "And Jesus being baptized, forthwith came out of the water: and lo, the heavens were opened to him: and he saw the spirit of God descending as a dove, and coming upon him."

motion of the spiritual creature in whose mind it was placed and impressed, as it were, by the eternal Word of the Father, and that according to it the dark and imperfect corporeal world below was moved and directed towards its form and thus became light? LMG, Vol. 1, 28

St. Augustine, *De Genesi ad litteram*, Book II, Ch. 8: Hence, created light is first in the Word of God according to the form by which it is created, that is to say, in Wisdom coeternal with the Father. And then it exists in created light itself according to the nature in which it is created. In God it is not made but begotten; in the creature it is made because from unformed being it is formed. "And so God said, 'Let there be light,' and light was made", so what was there in the Word might now be here in this work. LMG, Vol. 1, 57

St. Thomas Aquinas, *Summa Theologiae*, I, Q 74, Art 3 ad 5: According to Augustine these three phrases denote the threefold being of creatures. First, their being in the Word, denoted by the command "Let . . . be made"; secondly, their being in the angelic mind, signified by the words, "It was . . . done"; thirdly, their being in their proper nature, by the words, "He made". ST, 680

St. Basil, *On the Hexameron*, Homily 2:7: When we speak of a voice and a word and a command with reference to God, we mean the divine word, not a sound sent out through phonetic organs, nor air struck by the tongue, but we believe that the bent of His will is presented in the form of a command, because it is easily comprehended by those who are being instructed. FCB, 32

St. John Chrysostom, *Homilies on Genesis*, Homily 5:9: He simply spoke, and the work followed. You see, this is God's way: created things are governed by His will.[22] FCC, 70

---

[22] Ps. 148:5: "Praise the name of the Lord. For he spoke, and they were made: he commanded, and they were created."

St. John Damascene, *De Fide Orthodoxa*, Book 2, Ch. 2: By thinking He creates, and with the Word fulfilling and the Spirit perfecting, the object of His thought subsists. FCD, 205

St. Basil, *On the Hexameron*, Homily 3:2: By these means scripture leads us on to the idea of the Only-begotten in a certain orderly way. And surely, for an incorporeal nature there was no need for vocal speech, since the thoughts themselves could be communicated to His Co-worker. So, what need was there of speech for those who are able by the thought itself to share their plans with others? FCB, 39

St. Ambrose, *Hexameron*, Book 1, Ch. 9: The fabricator of nature uttered the word 'light' and also created it. The Word of God is His will; the work of God is nature. FCAm, 38

St. Ambrose, *Hexameron*, Book 1, Ch. 9: God did not speak as one would utter a sound through the vocal organs or as a movement of the tongue might produce an exhortation from heaven or as a sound might strike this air of ours. His purpose was to reveal the knowledge of His will by the effects of His work. FCAm, 39

St. Lawrence of Brindisi, *Explanatio in Genesim*, Ch. 1: In the Hebrew language, 'to say' something denotes an internal idea of the mind and will. CF, 37

St. Augustine, *De Genesi ad litteram*, Book I, Ch. 9: Here is a matter that is difficult to understand. God's decree is not pronounced in time, and it is heard, but not in time, by a creature that transcends all time in the contemplation of truth. But when this creature transmits to being of a lower rank the forms (*rationes*) which are, so to speak, intelligible utterances impressed upon its intellect by the unchangeable Wisdom of God, then there can be movements in the temporal order in being subject to time that are to be formed and governed. LMG, Vol. 1, 28-29

St. Lawrence of Brindisi, *Explanatio in Genesim*, Ch. 1: St. Augustine nevertheless explains this verse in a manner that applies to the nature of the Word. CF, 37

St Augustine, *De Genesi ad litteram*, Book I, Ch. 2: When it is said of the Word, "All things have been made through Him", it becomes quite clear that light was made through Him when God said, "Let there be light", and so this utterance of God is eternal. For the Word of God, true God in the bosom of God and the only Son of God, is coeternal with the Father; and yet through this utterance of God in the eternal Word, creation had been brought about in time. LMG, Vol. 1, 22

Light

St. Thomas Aquinas, *Summa Theologiae*, I, Q 67, Art 1: In its primary meaning, it was intended to signify that which produces clarity in the sense of sight; afterwards it was extended to that which produced clarity in any sort of knowledge. ST, 630

St. Ephrem, *Commentary on Genesis*, Part 1:8: At the end of the twelve hours of that night, the light was created between the clouds and the waters and it chased away the shadow of the clouds that overshadowed the waters making them dark. For Nisan was the first month; in it the number of the hours of day and night were equal. FCE, 80

St. Ambrose, *Hexameron*, Book 1, Ch. 4: Therefore, He created heaven and earth at the time when the months began, from which time it is fitting that the world took its rise. Then there was the mild temperature of spring, a season suitable for all things. FCAm, 12

St. Ambrose, *Hexameron*, Book 1, Ch. 4: Consequently, the year, too, has the stamp of a world coming to birth, as splendor of the springtime shines forth all the more clearly because of the winter's ice and darkness now past. FCAm, 12

St. Ambrose, *Hexameron*, Book 1, Ch. 4: Wherefore, in order to show that the creation of the world took place in the spring, scripture says, "This month shall be to you the beginning of months, it is for you the first in the months of the year," [Ex. 12:2] calling the first month springtime. It was fitting that the beginning of the year be the beginning of generation and that generation itself be fostered by the gentler breezes. FCAm, 13

St. Lawrence of Brindisi, *Explanatio in Genesim*, Ch. 1: Therefore, from the common agreement of all theologians, light in verse three is created, not as a certain quality distinct *per se* from a thing full of light, but in a thing full of light and as it were a cloud full of light not created from nothing but made from matter already pre-existent, so that it would be light and would have the power of giving off light. CF, 28

St. Basil, *On the Hexameron*, Homily 2:5: Therefore, we answer that this darkness did not subsist in substance but is a condition incident to the air because of the deprivation of light. FCB, 29

St. Bede, *In principium Genesis*, Book I: Moses only briefly commented on this upper realm, because he decided to speak about this world, in which humankind was made, for the instruction of the human race, believing it was sufficient if he included the general condition and adornment of the spiritual and invisible creation with the single term of heaven, which he said had been made in the beginning, believing it was necessary to describe the corporeal, visible, and perishable creation in order more profoundly. Remaining silent about those things that are deeper and more profound that people search out by inquiry. OG, 116-117

St. Basil, *The Holy Spirit*, 16, 38: The manner of the creation of the heavenly powers is passed over in silence, for the historian of the creation of the world has disclosed to us only the creation of things that can be perceived by the senses. FEF2, 17

St. Ephrem, *Commentary on Genesis,* 1:3: He did not record for us the day on which the spiritual beings were created. FCE, 76

St. John Chrysostom, *Homilies on Genesis,* Homily 2:7: See the great extent of the considerateness in this statement; there is no mention of unseen powers, nor does he say, "In the beginning, God made the angels, or the archangels". FCC, 32-33

St. Augustine, *City of God,* Book XI, Ch. 9: The angels therefore existed before the stars; and the stars were made on the fourth day. SA, Vol. 2, 210

St. Augustine, *Contra Faustum,* Book XXII, 10: So, when the darkness was over the deep, He who was light, said "Let there be light." From what light this light came is clear; for the words are, "God said." What light is that that was made, is not so clear. MH, 405-6

St. Augustine, *Contra Faustum,* Book XXII, 10: For there has been a friendly discussion among students of the sacred scriptures, whether God the made light in the minds of the angels, or, in other words, these rational spirits themselves, or some material light which exists in the higher regions of the universe beyond our ken. For the fourth day He made the visible luminaries of heaven. And it is also a question whether these bodies were made at the same time as their light, or were somehow kindled from the light made already. MH, 406

Spiritual Light

St. Anthony of Padua, *Sermon on Septuagesima,* 13: The light of which God said *Be light made.* This is the light of contrition of heart, enlightening the soul, the light which shows the knowledge of God, the awareness of our own weakness and the distinction between good and evil in man. SSA, 20

St. Anthony of Padua, *Sermon on Septuagesima,* 14: As the dawn is the beginning of day and the end of night, so contrition is the end of sin and the beginning of repentance. And so the Apostle says: "You were heretofore darkness, but now light in the Lord"; [Eph. 5.8] and again: "The night is passed and day is at hand" [Rom. 13:12].[23] SSA, 21

St. Augustine, *De Genesi ad litteram,* Book IV, Ch. 28: Christ Himself is not called Light in the same way as He is called a stone: He is literally the Light but metaphorically a stone.[24] LMG, Vol. 1, 136

St. Ambrose, *Hexameron,* Book 1, Ch. 9: In fact, God himself was in the light, because He "dwells in light inaccessible," and He "was the true light that enlightens every man who comes into the world."[25] FCAm, 38

St. Augustine, *Contra Faustum,* Book XXII, 11: Nor does it follow that God, before He made light, abode in darkness, because it is said that darkness was over the deep, and then that the Spirit of God moved over the waters. MH, 406

St. Anthony of Padua, *Sermon on Septuagesima,* 4: This light is the Wisdom of God the Father, enlightening every man coming into this

---

[23] Jn. 8:12: "Again therefore, Jesus spoke to them, saying: I am the light of the world: he that followeth me, walketh not in darkness, but shall have the light of life."

[24] 1Jn. 1:5: "God is light and in him there is no darkness."

[25] Ecclus. 24:6: "I made that in the heavens there should rise light that never faileth, and as a cloud I covered all the earth."

Jn. 1:4-10: "In him was life, and the life was the light of men. And the light shineth in darkness, and the darkness did not comprehend it. There was a man sent from God, whose name was John. This man came for a witness, to give testimony of the light, that all men might believe through him. He was not the light, but was to give testimony of the light. That was the true light, which enlighteneth every man that cometh into this world. He was in the world, and the world was made by him, and the world knew him not."

world [cf. Jn. 1:9], and dwelling in inaccessible light [cf. 1Tim. 6:16]; concerning which the Apostle writes to the Hebrews: "Who is the brightness and image of his substance"; [Heb 1:3] and of which the Prophet says: "In thy light we shall see light"; [Ps. 35:10] and in the Book of Wisdom: "Wisdom is the brightness of the eternal light" [Wis. 7:26].[26] SSA, 11

St. Basil, *On the Hexameron*, Homily 2:5: For neither the ranks of angels nor all the heavenly armies, nor, in short, any other of the rational natures, whether named or unnamed, or of all the ministering spirits, lived in darkness; but in light and in all spiritual gladness enjoyed a condition proper to them. FCB, 29

St. Thomas Aquinas, *Summa Theologiae*, I, Q 69, Art 1: The formation of the spiritual nature is recorded in the first place, where it is said that light was made on the first day. For as the spiritual nature is higher than the corporeal, so the higher bodies are nobler than the lower. ST, 648

St. Augustine, *De Genesi ad litteram*, Book II, Ch. 8: It is no wonder that when the holy angels were formed by the first creation of light, God first showed them that He was going to create the works to follow. And indeed they would not have known the mind of God except in so far as He Himself had revealed it to them. LMG, Vol. 1, 57-58

St. Augustine, *Contra Faustum*, Book XXII, 8: From their not distinguishing between the Light which is God, and the light which God made, they imagine that God must have been in darkness before he made light.[27] MH, 404

---

[26] Apoc. 21:23: "And the city hath no need of the sun, nor of the moon, to shine in it. For the glory of God hath enlightened it: and the Lamb is the lamp thereof."

[27] 2Cor. 4:6: "For God, who commanded the light to shine out of darkness, hath shined in our hearts, to give the light of the knowledge of the glory of God, in the face of Christ Jesus."

St. Thomas Aquinas, *Summa Theologiae*, I, Q 67, Art 4: Augustine seems to say that Moses could not have fittingly passed over the production of the spiritual creature, and therefore when we read, "In the beginning God created heaven and earth", a spiritual nature as yet formless is to be understood by the word 'heaven', and the formless matter of the corporeal creature by the word 'earth'. And the spiritual nature was formed first, as being of higher dignity than the corporeal. The forming, therefore, of this spiritual nature is signified by the production of light. For a spiritual nature receives its formation by the illumination whereby it is led to adhere to the Word of God. ST, 633-34

St. Augustine, *De Genesi ad litteram*, Book II, Ch. 8: The angels, therefore, were instructed by God when a knowledge of the creation to follow was implanted in them and when they later acquired a knowledge of the created works in themselves. LMG, Vol. 1, 58

St. John Damascene, *De Fide Orthodoxa*, Book 2, Ch. 3: The angels are secondary spiritual lights, who receive their brightness from that first Light which is without beginning. FCD, 206

St. Augustine, *De Genesi ad litteram,* Book IV, Ch. 28: But it is not true that material light is literally 'light,' and light referred to in Genesis is metaphorical 'light.' For where light is more excellent and unfailing, there day also exists in a truer sense. LMG, Vol. 1, 135

St. Augustine, *De Genesi ad litteram,* Book IV, Ch. 28: Why, then, should that day not have a truer evening and a truer morning? For if in the days with which we are familiar the light wanes as day declines, and we call this evening, and if it rises again at daybreak, and we call this morning, why should we not say that there is also evening when the angels after contemplating the creator gaze down upon a creature, and that there is also morning when they rise from a knowledge of a creature to the praise of the creator? LMG, Vol. 1, 135-36

St. Augustine, *De Genesi ad litteram*, Book I, Ch. 9: But if the light spoken of first of all in the words, "Let there be light, and light was made", must also be supposed to have a primacy in creation, it is nothing other than intellectual life, which must be in a formless and chaotic state unless it is turned to its creator to be illumined. But when it is turned and illumined, the decree, "Let there be light," spoken by the Word of God has been fulfilled. LMG, Vol. 1, 29

St. Augustine, *City of God*, Book XXII, Ch. 1: For it is He who in the beginning created the world full of all visible and intelligible beings, among which He created nothing better than those spirits whom He endowed with intelligence and made capable of contemplating and enjoying Him... It is He Who gave to this intellectual nature free-will of such a kind, that if he wished to forsake God, *i.e.*, his blessedness, misery should forthwith result. SA, Vol. 2, 479

St. Lawrence of Brindisi, *Explanatio in Genesim,* Ch. 1: I agree with St. Augustine that this light brought about day and night by its own movement. Since that light-filled substance, which we understand in this verse by the word 'light', was of a celestial nature, it certainly obtained that movement by which the *primum mobile,* made in the beginning, began to move itself from east to west by its own nature, for that movement brought about day and night as well as evening, morning, and noontide. Therefore, by such a movement, that light brought about the day by its presence and the night by its absence, while the atmosphere was deprived of its own light. CF, 30

St. Thomas Aquinas, *Summa Theologiae,* I, Q 67, Art 4 ad 4: And so we must not understand the production of light to signify the formation of spiritual creatures, not, indeed, with the perfection of glory, in which they were not created, but with the perfection of grace, which they possessed from their creation. ST, 636

Mention of the Angels

St. Thomas Aquinas, *Summa Theologiae*, I, Q 61, Art 1 ad 1: Augustine says that the angels were not passed over in that account of the first creation of things, but are designated by the name of 'heavens', or of 'light'. And they were either passed over, or else designated by the names of corporeal things, because Moses was addressing an uncultured people, as yet incapable of understanding an incorporeal nature. ST, 566

St. Augustine, *City of God*, Book XI, Ch. 9: Where Scripture speaks of the world's creation, it is not plainly said whether or when the angels were created; but if mention of them is made, it is implicitly under the name of 'heaven', when it is said, "In the beginning God created the heavens and the earth," or perhaps rather under the name of 'light'. SA, Vol. 2, 209

St. Thomas Aquinas, *Summa Theologiae*, I, Q 61, Art 1 ad 1: And if it had been divulged that there were creatures existing beyond corporeal nature, it would have proved to them an occasion of idolatry, to which they were inclined, and from which Moses especially wished to remove them. ST, 566

St. Bonaventure, *Breviloquium*, Part II, Ch. 5:9: Yet, because complete silence concerning the creation of the loftiest creatures would have been inconsistent with the sublimity of Scripture, the sacred writings described their creation insofar as a sublime, and saving knowledge requires, but in such a way that, taking a spiritual interpretation, the literal account of the whole creation refers symbolically to the celestial and ecclesiastical hierarchies. Brev, 76

St. Thomas Aquinas, *Summa Theologiae*, I, Q 61, Art 3 ad 1: The Greek Fathers . . . hold that the creation of the angels took place previously to that of the corporeal world. ST, 568

St. John Damascene, *De Fide Orthodoxa*, Book 2, Ch. 3: Now, some say that the angels were made before all creation, as Gregory the Theologian says: "First He conceived the angelic and heavenly powers, and His conception was an accomplished work." FCD, 208

St. John Damascene, *De Fide Orthodoxa*, Book 2, Ch. 3: For my part, I agree with the Theologian, because it was fitting for the spiritual substance to be created first and then the sensible and then finally man himself from both. FCD, 208

St. Thomas Aquinas, *Summa Theologiae*, I, Q 67, Art 4: Other writers think that the production of the spiritual creatures were purposely omitted by Moses, and give various reasons. Basil says that Moses begins his narrative from the beginning of time which belongs to sensible things; but that the spiritual or angelic creation is passed over, as having been created beforehand. ST, 634

St. Basil, *On the Hexameron*, Homily, 1:5: In fact, there did exist something, as it seems, even before this world, which our mind can attain by contemplation, but which has been left uninvestigated because it is not adapted to those who are beginners and as yet infants in understanding. This was a certain condition older than the birth of the world and proper to the supramundane powers, one beyond time, everlasting, without beginning or end. In it the creator and producer of all things perfected the works of His art, a spiritual light befitting the blessedness of those who love the Lord, rational and invisible natures, and the whole orderly arrangement of spiritual creatures which surpass our understanding and of which it is impossible even to discover names. These fill completely the essence of the invisible world, as Paul teaches us when he says: "For in him were created all things," whether visible or invisible, "whether Thrones, or Dominations, or Principalities, or Powers," [Col. 1:16] or Forces, or hosts of Angels, or sovereign Archangels. When at length it was necessary for this world also to be added to what already existed, primarily as a place of training and a school for the souls of men, then was created a fit dwelling place for all things in general which are subject to birth and destruction. FCB, 8-9

St. John Chrysostom, *Homilies on Genesis*, Homily 2:7: It was not idly or without purpose that he took this line in his teaching. I mean, since he was talking to Jews, people quite wrapped up in the world about them and incapable of forming any spiritual notion, he led them along for the time being from visible realities to the creator of all things, so that from created things they might come to learn the architect of all and adore their maker, not stopping short at creatures. FCC, 3

St. Thomas Aquinas, *Summa Theologiae,* I, Q 67, Art. 4: Chrysostom gives as a reason for the omission that Moses was addressing an ignorant people, to whom material things alone appealed, and whom he was endeavoring to draw away from the worship of idols. It would have been to them a pretext of idolatry if he had spoken to them of natures spiritual in substance and nobler than all corporeal creatures; for they would have paid them divine worship, since they were prone to worship as gods even the sun, moon and stars, which was forbidden them (Deut. 4:19). ST, 634

St. John Chrysostom, *Homilies on Genesis,* Homily 2:7: You see, despite the creation of the world, they had not avoided the error of making gods out of creatures, offering worship to the vilest of brutes; so what madness would they have not have fallen into if such considerateness had not been shown them. FCC, 33

St. Ambrose, *Hexameron,* Book 1, Ch. 5: The Angels, Dominations, and Powers, although they began to exist at some time, were already in existence when the world was created. FCAm, 18

St. John Damascene, *De Fide Orthodoxa,* Book 2, Ch. 3: They watch over the parts of the earth and are set over nations and places in accordance with their disposition by their creator. FCD, 207

St. Lawrence of Brindisi, *Explanatio in Genesim,* Ch. 1: Where for 'heaven' it reads *hashamayim,* a noun dual in number as if there were two kind of heavens, to wit, a spiritual heaven and a corporeal heaven. CF, 17

St. Lawrence of Brindisi, *Explanatio in Genesim*, Ch. 1: The happy spirits of that most eminent heaven and the brightest and most splendid stars of all the most excellent empyrean heaven are set there, praising God together in the morning, and this occurred in the beginning of their creation.[28] CF, 17

St. John Damascene, *De Fide Orthodoxa*, Book 2, Ch. 3: But there are others who say that they were made after the creation of the first heaven. However, they all agree that it was before the formation of man. FCD, 208

St. Thomas Aquinas, *Summa Theologiae*, I, Q 61, Art 4: As was observed, one universe is made up of corporeal and spiritual creatures. Consequently spiritual creatures were so created as to bear some relationship to the corporeal creature, and to rule over every corporeal creature. Hence it is fitting for the angels to be created in the highest corporeal place, as presiding over all corporeal nature; whether it be called the empyrean heaven, or whatever else it be called. ST, 569

St. Thomas Aquinas, *Summa Theologiae*, I, Q 61, Art 4 ad 1: The angels were not created in a corporeal place as if depending upon a body either as to their being or as to their production; because God could have created them before all corporeal creation, as many holy Doctors hold. They were made in a corporeal place, on the contrary, in order to show their relationship to corporeal nature, and that they are by their power in touch with bodies. ST, 569

---

[28] Job 38:4, 7: "Where wast thou when I laid the foundations of the earth? . . . When the morning stars praised me together, and all the sons of God made a joyful melody?"

Genesis 1:4: *And God saw the light that it was good . . .*

St. Augustine, *Contra Faustum*, Book XXII, 12: God's seeing His works that they were good, means that the creator approved of His own works as pleasing to Himself. For God cannot be forced to do anything against His will, so that He should not be pleased with His own work; nor can He do anything by mistake so that He should regret having done it. MH, 407

St. Ambrose, *Hexameron*, Book 1, Ch. 9: He did not see that of which He had no knowledge, nor did He approve what He before had neither known nor seen. FCAm, 40

St. Ambrose, *Hexameron*, Book 2, Ch. 5: "And God saw that it was good." The Son does what the Father desires. No degeneration of nature is found in Him whose work does not degenerate from the will of the Father. He saw, it is certain, but not with corporeal eyes. FCAm, 63

St. Ambrose, *Hexameron*, Book 2, Ch. 5: He spoke as if speaking to one who knew all the wishes of His Father. He saw as if He knew all that His Son had accomplished, acting with Him in community of operation. FCAm, 63

St. Ambrose, *Hexameron*, Book 2, Ch. 5: He did not, of course, recognize that of which He was ignorant. FCAm, 63

St. Augustine, *Contra Faustum*, Book XXII, 13: Faustus speaks of God as astonished, which is not said in Scripture; nor does it follow that one must be astonished when he sees anything to be good. There are many good things which we see without being astonished, as if they were better than we expected; we merely approve of them as being what they ought to be. MH, 407

St. Ambrose, *Hexameron*, Book 2, Ch. 5: The Son, too, beholds the work of the Father and the Father that of the Son, as the Lord Himself has declared: "The Son can do nothing of Himself but only what He sees the Father doing." [Jn. 5:19]. He sees, therefore, the Father doing and sees and hears Him in like manner through the hidden power of His invisible nature. FCAm, 64

St. Augustine, *De Genesi ad litteram*, Book II, Ch. 8: Moreover, by the words, "And God saw that it was good," we should understand that the divine Goodness was pleased in the work of creation; and thus the work which God was pleased to make would continue in its existence as a creature, as indicated by the words, "the Spirit of God was stirring above the water." LMG, Vol. 1, 58

The Fall of the Angels

Genesis 1:4: *and he divided the light from the darkness.*

St. Bede, *In principium Genesis*, Book I: Wisely he remained silent about the fall of the lying angel and his allies, since this pertained to those invisible and spiritual creatures. OG, 117

St. Augustine, *City of God*, Book XI, Ch. 19: To me it does not seem incongruous with the working of God, if we understand that the angels were created when the first light was made and that a separation was made between the holy and the unclean angels, when, as is said, "God divided the light from the darkness; and God called the light Day, and the darkness He called Night." For He alone could make this discrimination, who was able also before they fell, to foreknow that they would fall, and that being deprived of the light of truth they would abide in the darkness of pride. SA, Vol. 2, 215

St. Augustine, *City of God*, Book XII, Ch. 6: Thus the true cause of the blessedness of the good angels is found to be this, that they cleave to Him who supremely is. And if we ask the cause of the misery of the bad, it occurs to us, and not unreasonably, that they are miserable because they have forsaken Him who supremely is, and have turned to themselves who have no such essence. . . For when the will abandons what is above itself, and turns to what is lower, it becomes evil, not because that is evil to which it turns, but because the turning itself is wicked. SA, Vol. 2, 229

St. Bonaventure, *Breviloquium*, Part II, Ch. 8:1: So those who turned to God were instantly confirmed in their choice through grace and glory; fully enlightened in their intellect through the knowledge of dawn and dusk; perfectly fortified in their powers of command and execution; and fully ordered in their activities, whether of contemplation or service. Brev, 81

St. Bonaventure, *Breviloquium*, Part II, Ch. 8:2: they not only have a knowledge of dusk, but also of morning, and even a knowledge of full sunlight, through the fullness and absolute purity of that light in comparison to which every created thing may properly be called darkness. Brev, 82

St. Thomas Aquinas, *Summa Theologiae*, I, Q 63, Art 1 ad 3: It is natural for the angel to turn to God by the movement of love, according as God is the source of his natural being. But for him to turn to God as the object of supernatural beatitude comes of infused love, from which he could be turned away by sinning. ST, 586

St. Augustine, *City of God*, Book XI, Ch. 19: But between the light, which is the holy company of angels spiritually radiant with the illumination of the truth, and that opposing darkness, which is the noisome foulness of the spiritual condition of those angels who turned away from the light of righteousness, only He Himself could divide, from whom their wickedness (not of nature, but of will), while yet it was future, could not be hidden or uncertain. SA, 215

St. Ambrose, *Hexameron*, Book 1, Ch. 8: I am not of the opinion that by darkness are to be understood the powers of evil, in that their wickedness was brought about by God. The reason is, of course, that evil is not a substance, but an accident and that is a deviation from the goodness of nature. FCAm, 31-32

St. John Damascene. *De Fide Orthodoxa*, Book 2, Ch. 4: For evil is no more than the privation of good, just as darkness is the absence of light. And good is spiritual light, while in the same way evil is spiritual darkness.[29] FCD, 209

St. John Damascene, *De Fide Orthodoxa*, Book 2, Ch. 4: Now, light was made by the creator and it was good, for "God saw all things which he had made, and they were very good," but darkness came by free will. And together with him a numberless horde of the angels that he had marshaled were torn away, and followed after him and fell. Hence, although they were of the same nature as the angels, they became bad by freely turning from good to evil.[30] FCD, 209

---

[29] Job 4:18: "and in his angels he found wickedness."

[30] Isa. 14:12-15: "How art thou fallen from heaven, O Lucifer, who didst rise in the morning? How art thou fallen to the earth, that didst wound the nations? And thou saidst in thy heart; I will ascend into heaven, I will exalt my throne above the stars of God, I will sit in the mountain of the covenant, in the sides of the north. I will ascend above the height of the clouds, I will be like the most High. But yet thou shalt be brought down to hell, into the depth of the pit."

Apoc. 12:3-4, 7-9: "And there was seen another sign in heaven. And behold a great red dragon, having seven heads and ten horns and on his heads seven diadems. And his take drew the third part of the stars of heaven and cast them to earth. And the dragon stood before the woman who was ready to be delivered: that, when she should be delivered he might devour her son . . . And there was a great battle in heaven: Michael, and his angels fought with the dragon, and the dragon fought, and his angels. And they prevailed not: neither was their place found any more in heaven. And that great dragon was cast out, that old serpent, who is called the devil and Satan, who seduceth the whole world. And he was cast down unto the earth: and his angels were thrown down with him."

St. Thomas Aquinas, *Summa Theologiae*, I, Q 63, Art 2: The first sin of the angel can be none other than pride . . . after pride, there followed the evil of envy in the sinning angel, whereby he grieved over man's good, and also over the divine excellence, according as against the devil's will God makes use of man for the divine glory. ST, 587-88

St. Irenaeus, *Adversus Haereses*, Book IV, Ch. 40:3: Hence we learn that this was the apostate angel and the enemy, because he was envious of God's workmanship, and took in hand to render this [workmanship] at enmity with God. WI, Vol. 2, 50

St. Bonaventure, *Breviloquium*, Part II, Ch. 7:4: His wicked will and action, turned away from God, were turned instead to hatred and envy of humankind; his keen mind, blinded from true light, turned to deceiving humankind by divinations and deceptions; his readiness to serve, averted from true service, turned to seducing humans through temptations; his power, lessened and constrained, turned in as much as God permitted, to performing stupendous feats by bringing about rapid changes in the material creation. Brev, 81

St. Augustine, *City of God*, Book XIV, Ch. 3: For the devil, too, wished to live according to himself when he did not abide in the truth; so that when he lied, this was not of God, but of himself, who is not only a liar, but the father of lies, he being the first who lied, and originator of lying as of sin. SA, Vol. 2, 264

St. Bonaventure, *Breviloquium*, Part II, Ch. 7:1: The first among the angels, Lucifer, laying presumptuous claim to a private good, craved his own excellence and desired to be elevated further than the rest.[31] Brev, 79

---

[31] Ezec. 28:16-17: "By the multitude of thy merchandise, thy inner parts were filled with iniquity, and thou sinned: and I cast thee out from the mountain of God, and destroyed thee, O covering cherub, out of the midst of the

St. Cyprian, *The Good of Patience,* Ch. 19: The devil bore with impatience the fact that man was made to the image of God, and for this reason was the first to perish and cause to perish.[32] FCCy, 281

St. Lawrence of Brindisi, *Explanatio in Genesim,* Ch. 3: He foreshadowed to them His Son Jesus Christ in the shape and figure of a man. Then at length he ordered and promulgated the law that they should adore Him as God.[33] CF, 147

St. Lawrence Brindisi, *Explanatio in Genesim,* Ch. 3: Lucifer, however, marveling at the revelation, began to think very hard thoughts that God's design was not just enough and indeed was unworthy and unfair. To be sure, he thought that this dignity should instead be granted to an angel, whose nature in the whole extent of its own kind is actually much more sublime than man, and especially much more according to the view of the foremost species of angels, which is the most excellent of all. At that moment, looking at himself and contemplating his beauty, appearance and comeliness as well as his lofty gifts, his virtue, and the excellence of his powers, by which he excelled all the others just as does the Sun amid the stars, he began to desire explicitly that God be united to his nature, which he perceived to be the most excellent of all the angels. CF, 148

St. Thomas Aquinas, *Summa Theologiae,* I, Q 63, Art 7: Hence Gregory says that he who sinned was the very highest of all. This seems to be the more probable view, because the angels' sin did not come from any proneness, but from free choice alone. ST, 596

St. Thomas Aquinas, *Summa Theologiae,* I, Q 63, Art 3: In another

---

stones of fire. And thy heart was lifted up with thy beauty: thou hast lost thy wisdom in thy beauty, I have cast thee to the ground."

32 Wis. 2:24: "But by the envy of the devil, death came into the world."

33 Heb. 1:6: "... when he bringeth in the first begotten into the world, he saith: And let all the angels of God adore him."

way, one may desire to be like God in some respect which is not natural to one, *e.g.*, if one were to desire to create heaven and earth, which is proper to God; in which desire there would be sin. It was in this way that the devil desired to be as God . . . But he desired resemblance with God in this, that he desired as the last end of his beatitude something which he could not attain by virtue of his own nature, turning his appetite away from the supernatural beatitude which is attained by God's grace. Or, if he desired as his last end that likeness to God which is bestowed by grace, he sought it by the power of his own nature, and not from divine assistance according to God's ordering. ST, 589-90

St. Lawrence Brindisi, *Explanatio in Genesim*, Ch. 3: That most wicked rival began to desire pressingly for himself the likeness of God and joint seating on the throne at the right hand of God as well as the exaltation of his seat above all the stars of heaven, which from His eternity, God had determined to bestow upon Christ.[34] CF, 148

St. Thomas Aquinas, *Summa Theologiae*, I, Q 63, Art 5: It was impossible for the angel to sin in the first instant by an inordinate act of free choice. For although a thing can begin to act in the first instant of its being, nevertheless, that operation which begins with the being comes from its productive cause.[35] ST, 593

St. Thomas Aquinas, *Summa Theologiae*, I, Q 63, Art 5 ad 1: As

[34] 1Jn. 3:8: "the devil sinneth from the beginning."

[35] Ezec. 28:13-15: "Thou was in the pleasures of the paradise of God: every precious stone was thy covering: the sardius, the topaz, and the jasper, the chrysolite, and the onyx, and the beryl, the sapphire, and the carbuncle, and the emerald: gold the work of thy beauty: and thy pipes were prepared in the day that thou was created. Thou a cherub stretched out, and protecting, and I set thee in the holy mountain of God, thou hast walked in the midst of the stones of fire. Thou wast perfect in thy ways from the day of thy creation, until iniquity was found in thee." Ps. 118:127: "Therefore have I loved thy commandments above gold and the topaz. Therefore was I directed to all thy commandments: I have hated all wicked ways."

Augustine says when it is stated that "the devil sins from the beginning" (1Jn. 3:8), "he is not to be thought of as sinning from the beginning wherein he was created, but from the beginning of sin". That is to say, because he never went back from his sin. ST, 593

St. Augustine, *City of God*, Book XI, Ch. 15: And from this passage, "The devil sinneth from the beginning," it is not to be supposed that he sinned from the beginning of his created existence, but from the beginning of his sin, when by his pride he had once commenced to sin. SA, 213

St. Thomas Aquinas, *Summa Theologiae*, I, Q 63, Art 5 ad 4: Therefore, as all were created in grace, all merited in their first instant. But some of the angels at once placed an impediment to their beatitude, thereby destroying their preceding merit; and consequently they were deprived of the beatitude which they had merited. ST, 594

St. Thomas Aquinas, *Summa Theologiae*, I, Q 63, Art 6: It is said of the devil (Jn. 8:44): "He stood not in the truth"; and, as Augustine says, "we must understand this in the sense, that he was in the truth, but did not remain in it."[36] ST, 594

St. Augustine, *City of God*, Book XI, Ch. 13: The Lord did not say, "The devil was naturally a stranger to the truth," but "The devil abode not in the truth", by which He meant us to understand that he had fallen from the truth, in which, if he had abode, he would have become a partaker of it, and have remained in blessedness along with the holy angels. SA, Vol. 2, 213

St. Thomas Aquinas, *Summa Theologiae*, I, Q 63, Art 6 ad 4: So the first instant in the angels is understood to respond to the operation of the angelic mind, whereby it introspects itself by its evening knowl-

---

[36] Jn. 8:44: "He was a murderer from the beginning: and he stood not in the truth, because the truth was not in him."

edge because on the first day evening is mentioned, but not morning. This operation was good in them all. From such operation some of them were converted to the praise of the Word by their morning knowledge while others, absorbed in themselves, became night, "swelling up with pride", as Augustine says. ST, 595

St. Augustine, *De Genesi ad litteram*, Book IV, Ch. 24: For if the angels turned to themselves or took delight more in themselves than in Him in union with Whom they are happy, they would fall swollen with pride. This is what happened with the devil. LMG, Vol. 1, 132

St. Lawrence of Brindisi, *Explanatio in Genesim*, Ch. 3: Lucifer . . . obtained the first and brightest place over all, and in whom all the gifts of God shown forth more completely and more brightly . . .. Whence in another passage of the Book of Ezekiel, the same prophet, showing his excellence over others, said to Pharaoh, the king of Egypt: "The cedars in the garden of God were not its equal, nor could the fir trees match its bough, neither were the plane trees like its branches; no tree in the garden of God matched its beauty. I made it beautiful, with much foliage, the envy of all Eden's trees in the garden of God" [Ezec. 31:8]. CF, 145-46

St. Thomas Aquinas, *Summa Theologiae*, I, Q 63, Art 7: Gregory says that the chief angel who sinned, "being set over all the hosts of angels", surpassed them all in brightness, "and was by comparison the most illustrious among them". ST, 596

St. John Damascene, *De Fide Orthodoxa*, Book 2, Ch. 4: One of these angelic powers was chief of the terrestrial order and had been entrusted by God with the custody of the earth. Although he was not evil by nature, but good, and although he had been made for good and had in himself not the slightest trace of evil from the creator, he did not keep the brightness and dignity which the creator had bestowed upon him. FCD, 209

St. Bonaventure, *Breviloquium*, Part II, Ch. 7:3: Having free will, Lucifer was able to turn toward the supreme good or to turn toward a private good. But aroused by the sight of his own beauty and eminence, he fell in love with himself and his private good, and so laid presumptuous claim to the eminence he had and sought to gain a further excellence he did not possess. Brev, 80

St. John Damascene *De Fide Orthodoxa*, Book 2, Ch. 4: By his free choice he turned from what was according to nature to what was against it. Having become stirred up against the God who created him and having willed to rebel against Him, he was the first to abandon good and become evil. FCD, 209

St. Bonaventure, *Breviloquium*, Part II, Ch. 7:3: Thus, in his presumption, he set himself up as his own principle by glorying in himself; in his ambition, he established himself as his own supreme good by seeking his end in himself. Since, however, he was neither the supreme Principle nor the supreme Good, he was bound to fall from his inordinate desire, and for the same reason all those of like mind. Brev, 80

St. Thomas Aquinas, *Summa Theologiae*, I, Q 63, Art 7 ad 1: 'Cherubim' is interpreted as "fullness of knowledge", while 'Seraphim' means "those who were on fire, or who set on fire". Consequently Cherubim is derived from knowledge, which is compatible with mortal sin; but Seraphim is derived from the heat of charity, which is incompatible with mortal sin. Therefore the first angel who sinned is called, not a Seraph, but a Cherub.[37] ST, 597

---

[37] Ezec. 28:16-17: "By the multitude of thy merchandise, thy inner parts were filled with iniquity, and thou hast sinned: and I cast thee out from the mountain of God, and destroyed thee, O covering cherub, out of the midst of the stones of fire. And thy heart was lifted up with thy beauty: thou hast lost thy wisdom in thy beauty, I have cast thee to the ground: I have set thee before the face of kings, that they might behold thee."

St. Thomas Aquinas, *Summa Theologiae*, I, Q 63, Art 8 ad 1: Although the demons all sinned in the one instant, yet the sin of one could be the cause of the rest sinning. For the angel needs no delay of time for choice, exhortation, or consent, as man, who requires deliberation in order to choose and consent, and vocal speech in order to exhort; both of which are the work of time. ST, 598

St. Thomas Aquinas, *Summa Theologiae*, I, Q 63, Art 9: More angels stood firm than sinned. For sin is contrary to the natural inclination, while that which is against the natural order happens to the smaller number; for nature procures its effects either always or more often than not.[38] ST, 599

St. Thomas Aquinas, *Summa Theologiae*, I, Q 64 Art 1 ad 3: The creature is darkness in comparison with the excellence of the divine light; and therefore the creature's knowledge in its own nature is called 'evening' knowledge. For the evening is akin to darkness, yet it possesses some light: but when the light fails utterly, then it is night. So then the knowledge of things in their own nature, when referred to the praise of the creator, as it is in the good angels, has something of the divine light, and can be called evening knowledge; but if it be not referred to God, as is the case with the demons, it is not called evening, but *nocturnal* knowledge. Accordingly we read in Genesis (1:5) that the darkness, which God separated from the light, "He called night". ST, 602

St. Augustine, *De Genesi ad litteram*, Book IV, Ch. 22: Hence, if the light originally created is not material but spiritual, then this light [namely, the company of the angels] was made after the darkness in the sense that it turned from its unformed state to its creator and was thus formed. Consequently, after evening, morning is made, when

---

[38] 2Kings 6:16-17: "Fear not: for there are more with us than with them. And Eliseus prayed, and said: Lord, open his eyes, that he may see. And the Lord opened the eyes of the servant, and he saw: and behold, the mountain was full of horses, and chariots of fire round about Eliseus."

after its knowledge of its own nature as something distinct from God, this light directs its praise to the Light that is God, in the contemplation of which it is formed. And because the other creatures below it are not made without its knowledge, the one and same day is repeated each time so that by this repetition as many days may recur as there are kinds of creatures, determined by the perfection of the number six. LMG, Vol. 1, 130

St. Augustine, *De Genesi ad litteram*, Book IV, Ch. 22: Evening of the first day, therefore, is the knowledge spiritual beings have of themselves, inasmuch as they know that they are not God. The morning following the evening concludes the first day, the morning, that is, which begins the second day, is the conversion of spiritual beings, by which they direct to the praise of their creator the gift of their creation, and receive from the Word of God a knowledge of the creature next made, namely, the firmament. LMG, Vol. 1, 130

Material Light

St. Bonaventure, *Breviloquium*, Part II, Ch. 5:10: Thus, the foregoing reveals the sufficiency and truth of the scriptures in the diverse opinions of the saints, that is, of Augustine and others. If we understand them correctly, they do not contradict one another, but are true. Brev, 76

St. Augustine, *Contra Faustum*, Book XXII, 10: But whoever reads the sacred writings in the pious spirit which is required to understand them, must be convinced that whatever the light was which was made when, at the time that darkness was over the deep, God said, "Let there be light," and it was created light, and the creating Light was the maker of it. MH, 406

St. John Damascene, *De Fide Orthodoxa*, Book 2, Ch. 7: "In the beginning," then, which is to say, on the first day, God made the light to adorn and enhance all visible creation. For, remove the light and everything will be in darkness and be indistinguishable and incapable of displaying its inherent comeliness. FCD, 215

St. Thomas Aquinas, *Summa Theologiae*, I, Q 74, Art 1 ad 4: The nature of light, as existing in a subject, was made on the first day; and the making of the luminaries on the fourth day does not mean that their substance was produced anew, but that they then received a form that they had not before, as said above. ST, 674

St. Lawrence of Brindisi, *Explanatio in Genesim*, Ch. 1: The light (*i.e.* solar light) had been created unformed on the first day, since light had not yet been accommodated to and deposited in the solar body—placed, as it were, in a very convenient vehicle. CF, 29

St. Thomas Aquinas, *Summa Theologiae*, I, Q 68, Art 1: For as Dionysius says, the light of the sun was without form during the first three days, and afterwards, on the fourth day, received its form. ST, 638

St. Ephrem, *Commentary on Genesis*, Part 1:9: It is said that from this light, now diffused, and from fire, which were both created on the first day, the sun, which was in the firmament, was fashioned, while the moon and the stars came to be from the same first light. FCE, 81-82

St. Augustine, *Contra Faustum*, Book XXII, 21: God was not taken by surprise by the unexpected appearance of light, but that light owes its existence to Him as its creator, as it owes its continued existence to His approval. MH, 415

The Seven Days

Genesis 1:5: *And he called the light Day, and the darkness Night; and there was evening and morning one day.*

Genesis 2:4: *These are the generations of the heaven and the earth, when they were created, in the day that the Lord God made heaven and the earth.*

St. Thomas Aquinas, *Summa Theologiae*, I, Q 74, Art 2: On this question Augustine differs from other expositors. His opinion is that all the days that are called seven are one day represented in a sevenfold aspect. ST, 675

St. Augustine, *De Genesi ad litteram*, Book IV, Ch. 33: But if the angelic mind can grasp simultaneously all that the sacred text sets down separately in an ordered arrangement according to causal connection, were not all these things also made simultaneously, the firmament itself, the waters gathered together and the bare land that appeared, the plants and the trees that sprang forth, the light and the stars that were established, the living creatures in the water and on the earth? Or were they rather created at different times on appointed days? LMG, Vol. 1, 141

St. Augustine, *De Genesi ad litteram*, Book IV, Ch. 33: Creation, therefore, did not take place slowly in order that a slow development might be implanted in those things that are slow by nature; nor were the ages established at the plodding pace at which they now pass. Time brings about the development of these creatures according to the laws of their numbers, but there were no passages of time when they received these laws at creation. LMG, Vol. 1, 141-42

St. Augustine, *De Genesi ad litteram*, Book V, Ch. 3: Hence, you must understand that this day was seven times repeated, to make up the seven days. And when you hear that all things were made after day was made, you may possibly understand this sixfold or sevenfold repetition which took place without lapse of time. If you cannot understand it, you should leave the matter for the consideration of those who can. LMG, Vol. 1, 150

St. Augustine, *De Genesi ad litteram*, Book IV, Ch. 26: All creation, then, was finished by the sixfold recurrence of this day whose evening and morning we may interpret as explained above. And there was the morning that terminated the sixth day, at which time there was the beginning of the seventh, which would have no evening, since God's rest is not a creature. LMG, Vol. 1, 133

St. Augustine, *De Genesi ad litteram*, Book IV, Ch. 26: Hence, we can no longer take 'day' to mean the form of the work created and 'evening' its completion and 'morning' the beginning of another work. Otherwise we might be forced to say, against the evidence of scripture, that beyond the works of the six days a creature was made on the seventh day, or that the seventh day itself was not a creature. LMG, Vol. 1, 133-34

St. Augustine, *De Genesi ad litteram*, Book V, Ch. 3: Holy Scripture, indeed, speaks in such a way as to mock proud readers with its heights, terrify the attentive with its depths, feed great souls with its truth, and nourish little ones with sweetness. LMG, Vol. 1, 150

St. Bonaventure, *Breviloquium*, Part II, Ch. 2:5: Now if, from another point of view, it is said that all things were made at once, this is simply considering the work of the seven says from the perspective of the angels. Brev, 66

St. Bonaventure, *Breviloquium*, Part II, Ch. 5:10: Again [in a spiritual sense], the 'seven days' stand for the seven states of the Church through the succession of the seven ages. The same series of seven days also signify the seven illuminations through which the angels rise from the creature to God. Brev, 76

St. Augustine, *De Genesi ad litteram*, Book IV, Ch. 33: It follows, therefore, that He, who created all things together, simultaneously created these six days, or seven, or rather one day six or seven times repeated. Why, then, was there any need for six distinct days to be set forth in the narrative one after the other? The reason is that those who cannot understand the meaning of the text, "He created all things together" [Eccles. 18:1], cannot arrive at the meaning of scripture unless the narrative proceeds slowly step by step. LMG, Vol. 1, 142

St. Thomas Aquinas, *Summa Theologiae*, I, Q 74, Art 2: For Augustine understands by the word 'day' the knowledge in the mind of the angels, and hence, according to him, the first day denotes their knowledge of the first of the divine works, the second day their knowledge of the second work, and similarly with the rest. ST, 676

St. Augustine, *De Genesi ad litteram*, Book V, Ch. 23: But in the beginning He created all things together and completed the whole in six days, when six times He brought the 'day' which He made before the things which He made, not in a succession of periods of time but in a plan made known according to causes. LMG, Vol. 1, 175-76

St. Thomas Aquinas, *Summa Theologiae*, I, Q 74, Art 2: So the distinction of days denotes the natural order of the things known, and not a succession in the knowledge acquired, or in the things produced. ST, 676

St. Augustine, *De Genesi ad litteram*, Book IV, Ch. 26: But that day, which God has made, recurs in connection with His works not by a material passage of time but by spiritual knowledge, when the blessed company of angels contemplate the beginning in the Word of God the divine decree to create. LMG, Vol. 1, 134

St. Augustine, *De Genesi ad litteram*, Book IV, Ch. 26: Thus, in all the days of creation there is one day, and it is not to be taken in the sense of our day, which we reckon by the course of the sun; but it must have another meaning, applicable to the three days mentioned before the creation of the heavenly bodies. LMG, Vol. 1, 134

St. Augustine, *De Genesi ad litteram*, Book V, Ch. 2: One might easily think that this day was a day made up of a material light by whose circuit the hours of day and night are brought to us. But when we recall the order in which creatures were made, we find that "all the grass of the field" was created on the third day, before the sun was made (for it was made on the fourth day), and it is by the presence of the sun that the day with which we are familiar is constituted. LMG, Vol. 1, 148

St. Augustine, *De Genesi ad litteram*, Book V, Ch. 2: When, therefore, we hear, "When day was made, God made heaven and earth, and all the grass of the field," we are admonished to think that day which may perhaps be a corporeal thing consisting in some sort of light unknown to us, or a spiritual thing made up of the united company of angels. But at least we know that it is different from the ordinary day with which we are familiar. LMG, Vol. 1, 148

St. Thomas Aquinas, *Summa Theologiae*, I, Q 74, Art 2: In the opinion of the others, however, the days signify a succession both in time, and in the things produced. ST, 676

St. Thomas Aquinas, *Summa Theologiae*, I, Q 74, Art 2: While others consider there were seven distinct days, and not only one. ST, 675-76

St. Thomas Aquinas, *Summa Theologiae*, I, Q 74, Art 3 ad 7: The words *one day* are used when day is first established to denote that one day is made up of twenty-four hours. Hence, by mentioning 'one', the measure of a natural day is fixed. Another reason may be to signify that a day is completed by the return of the sun to the point from which it commenced its course. And yet another, because at the completion of a week of seven days, the first day returns, which is 'one' with the eighth day. The three reasons above are those given by Basil. ST, 681

St. Basil, *On the Hexameron*, Homily 2:8: Now, henceforth, after the creation of the sun, it is day when the air is illuminated by the sun shining on the hemisphere above the earth, and night is the darkness of the earth when the sun is hidden. Yet, it was not at that time according to solar motion, but it was when that first created light was diffused and again drawn in according to the measure ordained by God, that day came and night succeeded. FCB, 33

St. Basil, *On the Hexameron*, Homily 2:8: It is as if one would say that the measure of twenty-four hours is the length of one day, or that the return of the heavens from one point to the same point once more occurs in one day; so that, as often as through the revolution of the sun evening and morning traverse the world, the circle is completed, not in a longer period of time, but in the space of one day. FCB, 34

St. Basil, *On the Hexameron*, Homily 2:8: Or, is the reason handed down in the nature of time, set as measures and limits for it the intervals of the days, and the measuring out for a week, He orders the week, in counting the change in time, always to return again in a circle to itself? Again, He orders that one day by recurring seven times complete a week; and this, beginning from itself and ending on itself, is the form of a circle. FCB, 34

St. Thomas Aquinas, *Summa Theologiae*, I, Q 69, Art 1 ad 5: Thus we find it said at first that "He called the light Day", for the reason that later on a period of twenty-four hours is also called day, where it is said that "there was evening and morning, one day". ST, 650

St. Thomas Aquinas, *Summa Theologiae*, I, Q 66, Art 4 ad 2: so time was in a manner formless before it was fully formed and distinguished into day and night. ST, 627

St. Lawrence of Brindisi, *Explanatio in Genesim*, Ch. 1: *Yom* in Hebrew sometimes means the 'time' in which the solar light is upon the earth, as noted above: "He called the light Day". Moreover, it is as often joined with *laylah*, night, as it is called 'day' and 'night', as below. Sometimes, indeed, it encompasses a day and a night together, which is said to be a natural day contained in the space of twenty-four hours, wherein the sun travels its circle in relation to the motion of the *primum mobile*. According to this definition, a day must be understood when we read "And it happened evening and morning day one". CF, 32

St. Basil, *On the Hexameron*, Homily 2:8: In fact, it is also characteristic of eternity to turn back upon itself and never to be brought to an end. Therefore, He called the beginning of time not a 'first day,' but 'one day,' in order that from the name it might have kinship with eternity. For, the day which shows a character of uniqueness and nonparticipation with the rest is properly and naturally called 'one.' FCB, 34-35

St. Ambrose, *Hexameron*, Book 1, Ch. 10: In notable fashion has scripture spoken of a 'day,' not the 'first day.' Because a second, then a third day, and finally the remaining days were to follow, a 'first day' could have been mentioned, following in this way the natural order. But scripture established a law that twenty-four hours, including both day and night, should be given the name of day only, as if one were to say the length of one day is twenty-four hours in extent. FCAm, 42

St. Lawrence of Brindisi, *Explanatio in Genesim*, Ch. 1: Nevertheless, it seems to be that one must admit that the phrase 'one day' is in line with the Hebrew idiom; for among the Jews one is not infrequently used as an ordinal number. Therefore, very often in the language 'one' is used for 'first.' Such a manner of speaking is found frequently in the Gospels, the idiom of which is almost entirely Hebraic. CF, 36

St. Bonaventure, *Breviloquium*, Part II, Ch. 2:5: Now God could have done all these things simultaneously, but preferred to accomplish them over a succession of times. First of all, this would serve as a clear and distinct manifestation of God's power, wisdom, and goodness. Secondly, there was a fitting correspondence between these operations and having various 'days' or times. Finally, the primal production of the world ought to contain the seeds of all things that would later be accomplished, as a prefiguration of future ages. Brev, 65

St. Bonaventure, *Breviloquium*, Part II, Ch. 2:5: At any rate, the first manner of speaking is more in keeping with the Scripture and with the authority of the saints, both those before and after St. Augustine. Brev, 66

St. Ambrose, *Hexameron*, Book 4, Ch. 3: Night is a shadow of the earth. FCAm, 134

St. Lawrence of Brindisi, *Explanatio in Genesim*, Ch. 1: "God named the light Day and the darkness Night" because He said this in the Word co-eternal with Himself, *i.e.* by the internal and eternal designs of unchangeable Wisdom, not by the bodily sound of a voice. CF, 42

St. Thomas Aquinas, *Summa Theologiae*, I, Q 69, Art 1 ad 5: So, by the expression "He called" we are to understand throughout that "the nature or property He bestowed corresponded to the name He gave". ST, 650

St. Ambrose, *Hexameron*, Book 2, Ch. 1: Hence such a day should be distinguished from the others as 'one day,' and should not be compared with other days as 'the first day,' for on it the foundations of all things were laid and there began to come into existence the causes of all things on which the substance of this world and of the entire visible creation is based. FCAm, 46

St. Thomas Aquinas, *Summa Theologiae*, I, Q 66, Art 4 ad 2: Just as in the opinion of some holy writers matter was in some measure formless before it received its form, so time was in a manner formless before it was formed and distinguished into day and night. ST, 627

St. Anthony of Padua, *Sermon on Septuagesima*, 11: We have described briefly and in passing these seven days and seven articles. We now approach the task of expounding morally the six virtues of the faithful soul. We shall make them concordant with the six hours referred to in the Gospel reading; and with the meaning of the penny and of the Sabbath. SSA, 1

St. Anthony of Padua, *Sermon on Septuagesima*, 3: On the first day God said: "Be light made. And light was made". [Gen. 1:3] The first article of faith is the Nativity. On the second day God said: "Let there be a firmament made amidst the waters, and let it divide the waters from the waters". [Gen. 1:6] The second article of faith is Baptism. On the third day God said: "Let the earth bring forth the green herb, and such as may seed, and the fruit-tree yielding fruit after its kind". [Gen. 1:11] The third article is the Passion. On the fourth day God said: "Let there be two great lights in the firmament". [cf. Gen. 1:14] The fourth article is the Resurrection. On the fifth day God made the birds of the air [cf. Gen. 1:20]. The fifth article is the Ascension. On the sixth day God said: "Let us make man to our image and likeness . . . And he breathed into his face the breath of life, and man became a living soul". [Gen. 1:26; 2:7] The sixth article is the sending of the Holy Spirit. On the seventh day God rested from all the work which he had done [cf. Gen. 2:2]. The seventh article is the coming to judgment, in which we shall rest from all our works and labors. SSA, 10-11

St. Anthony of Padua, *Sermon on Septuagesima*, 13: Note that there are six virtues of the soul, namely: contrition of heart, confession by the mouth, satisfaction in works, love of God and neighbor, the exercise of the active and contemplative life, and the completion of final perseverance. SSA, 18

The Day of the Lord

St. Basil, *On the Hexameron*, Homily 2:8: For, Scripture knows as a day without evening, without succession, and without end, that day which the psalmist called the eighth, because it lies outside this week of time. Therefore, whether you say 'day' or 'age' you will express the same idea. If, then, that condition should be called day, it is one and not many, or, if it should be named age, it would be unique and not manifold. In order, therefore, to lead our thoughts to a future life, he called that day 'one,' which is an image of eternity, the beginning of days, the contemporary of light, the holy Lord's day, the day honored by the Resurrection of the Lord. "There was, then evening and morning, one day," he said.[39] FCB, 35

St. Basil, *On the Hexameron,* Homily 2:8: But darkness, certainly, for those who are deserving of darkness.[40] FCB, 35

St. Augustine, *De Genesi ad litteram,* Book V, Ch. 5: Finally, made aware of the repose of its creator, who rested from all His works in rest that had no evening, the day thereby deserved to be blessed and sanctified.[41] LMG, Vol. 1, 155

St. Bonaventure, *Breviloquium,* Part II, Ch. 2:5: That is why, to six days of work was added a seventh day of rest: a day to which no dusk is ascribed [in scripture]—not that this day was not followed by night, but because it was to prefigure the repose of souls that shall have no end.[42] Brev, 65-66

St. Ambrose, *Hexameron,* Book 1, Ch. 10: Moreover, scripture teaches us that the everlasting day of eternal reward is to be one in which there is no interchange or intermission of day and night. FCAm, 43

St. John Damascene, *De Fide Orthodoxa,* Book 2, Ch. 1: For, after the resurrection, time will not be numbered by days and nights at all; rather, there will be one day without evening, with the Sun of Justice shining brightly upon the just and a deep and endless night reserved for sinners. FCD, 204

---

39 Joel 2:11: "for the day of the Lord is great and very terrible: and who can stand it?"

40 Amos 5:18 : "the day of the Lord is darkness, and not light."

41 Ps. 117:24: "This is the day which the Lord hath made: let us be glad and rejoice therein."

42 Apoc. 22:5: "And night shall be no more. And they shall not need the light of the lamp, nor the light of the sun, because the Lord God shall enlighten them. And they shall reign for ever and ever."

The Firmament

Genesis 1:6: *And God said: Let there be a firmament made amidst the waters.*

St. Thomas Aquinas, *Summa Theologiae*, I, Q 68, Art 1: If, however, we take these days to denote an order of nature, as Augustine holds, and not a succession in time, there is then nothing to prevent our saying, while holding any one of the opinions given above, that the substantial formation of the firmament belongs to the second day. ST, 638-39

St. Thomas Aquinas, *Summa Theologiae*, I, Q 74, Art 2: First, because Augustine takes the earth and water, as first created, to signify matter totally without form; but the making of the firmament, the gathering of the waters, and the appearing of the dry land, to denote the impression of forms upon corporeal matter. ST, 676

St. Thomas Aquinas, *Summa Theologiae*, I, Q 68, Art 1 ad 1: According to another theory, touched upon by Augustine the heaven made on the first day was the starry heaven, and the firmament made on the second day was that region of the air where the clouds are collected, which is also called heaven, but equivocally. ST, 639

St. Thomas Aquinas, *Summa Theologiae*, I, Q 68, Art 2: If, however, we understand that part of the air in which the clouds are collected, then the waters above the firmament must be the vapors resolved from the waters which are raised above a part of the atmosphere, and from which the rain falls.[43] But to say, as do some writers alluded to by Augustine, that waters resolved into vapor must be lifted above the starry heaven, is a mere absurdity. ST, 641

---

[43] Job 37:16: "Knowest thou the great paths of the clouds, and the perfect knowledges?"

St. Lawrence of Brindisi, *Explanatio in Genesim*, Ch. 1: The Hebrew word is *raqia*, means an extension or a certain spreading out, derived from the verb *raqa*, which means to stretch out and to spread out by hammering out, just as it reads in Exodus.[44] CF, 43

St. Ambrose, *Hexameron*, Book 2, Ch. 4: It seems to me that the word 'heaven' is a generic term, because scripture testifies to the existence of very many heavens. The word 'firmament' is more specific, since here we read: "And he called the firmament, heaven." FCAm, 60

St. Ambrose, *Hexameron*, Book 2, Ch. 4: Therefore, the firmament is called because of its firmness or because it has been made firm by divine power, just as Scripture teaches us, saying: "Praise ye him in the firmament of his power" [Ps. 150:1]. FCAm, 62

St. Augustine, *De Genesi ad litteram*, Book IV, Ch. 22: The firmament, therefore, was first made in the knowledge of spiritual creatures, as indicated by the words, "And so it was done", and afterwards in the actual firmament produced in nature itself, as revealed in the words that follow next, "And so it was done, And God made the firmament." LMG, Vol. 1, 130

Genesis 1:6-7: *and let it divide the waters from the waters. And God made a firmament, and divided the waters that were under the firmament, from those that were above the firmament, and it was so.*

St. Basil, *On the Hexameron*, Homily 3:2: These words seem to involve something more because the utterance did not stop with a bare

[44] Isa. 42:5: "Thus saith the Lord God that created the heavens, and stretched them out: that established the earth, and the things that spring out of it: that giveth breath to the people upon it, and spirit to them that tread thereon." Job 26:8: "He bindeth up the waters in his clouds, so that they break not out and fall down together." Ecclus. 43:1, 16: "The firmament on high is his beauty, the beauty of heaven with its glorious show. By his greatness he hath fixed the clouds, and the hailstones are broken."

command but in addition it specified the reason which required the firmament. It says, 'to divide the waters.'[45] FCB, 38

St. Basil, *On the Hexameron*, Homily 3:4: But, let not this be forgotten, that, after God gave the command, "Let there be a firmament," Scripture did not say simply, "and the firmament was made," but, "And God made the firmament"; and again, "God divided." Hear, ye deaf, and look up, ye blind. And who is deaf, except he who does not hear the Spirit when He calls so loudly? And who is blind? He who does not discern such clear arguments concerning the Only-begotten. "Let there be a firmament." This is the utterance of the first and principal Cause. "God made the firmament." This is the testimony of the efficient and creative Power. [46] FCB, 43-44

St. Thomas Aquinas, *Summa Theologiae*, I, Q 68, Art 2: We must hold, then, these waters to be material, but their exact nature will be differently defined according as opinions on the firmament differ. ST, 640

St. Thomas Aquinas, *Summa Theologiae*, I, Q 68, Art 3 ad 3: Because the air and other similar bodies are invisible, Moses includes all such bodies under the name of water, and thus it is evident that waters are found on each side of the firmament, whatever be the sense in which the word is used. ST, 644

St. Thomas Aquinas, *Summa Theologiae*, I, Q 68, Art 2: For if by 'firmament' we understand the starry heaven, and if we understand it as being of the nature of the four elements, for the same reason it may be believed that the waters above the heaven are of the same nature as the elemental waters. ST, 640-41

---

[45] Ps. 32:7: "Gathering together the waters of the sea, as in a vessel; laying up the depths in storehouses."

[46] Ps. 32:6, 9: "By the word of the Lord the heavens were established; and all the power of them by the spirit of his mouth . . . For he spoke and they were made: he commanded and they were created."

St. Thomas Aquinas, *Summa Theologiae*, I, Q 68, Art 2: Again, if the firmament is held to be of a nature other than the elements, it may be said to divide the waters, if we understand by waters not the element but formless matter. Augustine, in fact, says that whatever divides bodies from bodies can be said to divide waters from waters. ST, 641

St. Augustine, *De Genesi contra Manichaeos*, Book I, Ch. 11: Since we said that matter was called water, I believe that the firmament of heaven separated the corporeal matter of visible things from the incorporeal matter of invisible things. For though heaven is a very beautiful body, every invisible creature surpasses even the beauty of heaven, and perhaps for that reason the invisible waters are said to be above the heaven. For few understand that they surpass the heaven, not by the places they occupy, but by the dignity of their nature, although we should not rashly affirm anything about this, for it is obscure and remote from the senses of men. Whatever the case may be, before we understand it, we should believe. FCA, 64-65

St. Thomas Aquinas, *Summa Theologiae*, I, Q 69, Art 1: Hence, the formation of the higher bodies is indicated in the second place, by the words, "Let there be made a firmament"; by which is to be understood the impression of celestial forms on formless matter, that preceded with priority, not of time, but of origin only. ST, 648

St. Thomas Aquinas, *Summa Theologiae*, I, Q 68, Art 2 ad 3: According to the third opinion given, the waters above the firmament have been raised in the form of vapors, and serve to give rain to the earth. ST, 642

St. Augustine, *De Genesi ad litteram*, Book II, Ch. 8: But when we hear "And so it was done", we should realize that in the created intellects of the angels there has been produced a knowledge of the essence (in the Word of God) of a creature to be made. Thus, the created work was in a sense first made in the angelic nature, which by a mysterious operation first saw in the Word of God Himself that the creature was to be made. Finally, then, when we hear the repetition of the words, "God made", we should recognize that the created work itself is now produced in its own order of being. LMG, Vol. 1, 58

St. Anthony of Padua, *Sermon on Septuagesima*, 5: The firmament in the midst of the waters is Baptism, separating the upper waters from the lower waters; that is to say, separating the faithful from the unfaithful, who are rightly called "lower waters" because they seek the things that are below and daily fall short by their defects. "The waters above", however, stand for the faithful who, according to the Apostle, should "seek the things that are above, where Christ is seated at the right hand of God". [Col 3.1] SSA, 12-13

St. Anthony of Padua, *Sermon on Septuagesima*, 17: The firmament is confession, which firmly binds a man so that he does not slip into dissipation. The Lord reproves the sinful soul which lacks this firmament, through Jeremiah: "How long wilt thou be dissolute in deliciousness, O wandering daughter?" [Jer. 31:22] and through Isaiah: "Pass thy land as a river, O daughter of the sea; for thou hast a girdle no more". [Is. 23:10] The wretched soul is called "daughter of the sea", sucking the pleasure of the world as from the devil's breast: sweet-tasting but giving rise to eternal bitterness. So James says: "When concupiscence hath conceived, it bringeth forth sin; but sin when it is completed begetteth death". [Jas. 1:15] SSA, 23

St. Anthony of Padua, *Sermon on Septuagesima*, 17: Alternatively, the mind of the just man possesses "waters above", that is to say, reason, which is the superior power of the soul, and which always urges man to good. The "waters below", on the other hand, namely sensuality, always tend to drag him down. So the firmament of confession divides the upper waters from the lower, so that whoever confesses goes out of Sodom and up into the hills, not looking back like Lot's wife who was turned into a statue or pillar of salt [cf. Gen. 19:17, 26]. SSA, 24

Genesis 1:8: *And God called the firmament, Heaven.*

St. Ambrose, *Hexameron*, Book 6, Ch. 2: When we read of 'heaven,' we should understand this to mean what it says. When we read of 'earth,' we should understand the fruit bearing earth. FCAm, 231

St. Ambrose, *Hexameron*, Book 2, Ch. 2: The question also arises whether there are two heavens or more. FCAm, 49

St. Thomas Aquinas, *Summa Theologiae*, I, Q 69, Art 1 ad 5: In like manner, it is said that "the firmament", that is, the air, "He called heaven", for that which was first created was also called *heaven*. ST, 650

St. Thomas Aquinas, *Summa Theologiae*, I, Q 68, Art 1 ad 1: According to Chrysostom, Moses prefaces his record by speaking of the works of God collectively, in the words, "In the beginning God created heaven and earth", and then proceeds to explain them part by part. In somewhat the same way, one might say: "This house was constructed by that builder", and then add: "First he laid the foundations, then built the walls, and thirdly put on the roof." ST, 639

St. John Chrysostom, *Homilies on Genesis*, Homily 2:11: Notice how the divine nature shines out of the very manner of creation, how He executes His creation in a way contrary to human procedures, first stretching out the heavens and then laying out the earth beneath, first the roof and then the foundation. Who has ever seen the like? Who has ever heard of it? No matter what human beings produce, this could never have happened—whereas, when God decides, everything yields to His will and becomes possible. FCC, 35

St. Thomas Aquinas, *Summa Theologiae*, I, Q 68, Art 1 ad 1: In accepting this explanation we are, therefore, not bound to hold that a different heaven is spoken of in the words, "In the beginning God created heaven and earth," and when we read that the firmament was made on the second day. ST, 639

St. Thomas Aquinas, *Summa Theologiae*, I, Q 68, Art 1 ad 1: We may also say that the heaven recorded as created in the beginning is not that same as that made on the second day; and there are several senses in which this may be understood. ST, 639

St. Thomas Aquinas, *Summa Theologiae*, I, Q 68, Art 1 ad 1: Augustine says that the heaven recorded as made on the first day is the formless spiritual nature, and that the heaven on the second day is the corporeal heaven. ST, 639

St. Augustine, *De Genesi ad litteram*, Book I, Ch. 9: Thus, we must suppose that before the beginning of days, He wrought the work referred to in the words, "In the beginning God created heaven and earth". And then by the expression 'heaven' we must understand a spiritual created work already formed and perfected, which is, as it were, the heaven of this heaven which is the loftiest of the material world. On the second day, God made the firmament, which He called heaven again. LMG, Vol. 1, 27

St. Thomas Aquinas, *Summa Theologiae*, I, Q 68, Art 1 ad 1: According to Bede and Strabo, the heaven made on first day is the empyrean, and the firmament made on the second day, the starry heaven. ST, 639

St. Bede, *In principium Genesis*, Book I: Described in these verses is the creation of our heaven in which the stars are fixed. It is established that the firmament is in the midst of the waters, for we understand that waters were placed beneath the firmament and in the air and on land. OG, 119

St. Thomas Aquinas, *Summa Theologiae*, I, Q 68, Art 1 ad 1: According to Damascene, that of the first day was "spherical in form and without stars". . . while by the firmament made on the second day he understands the starry heaven. ST, 639

St. John Damascene, *De Fide Orthodoxa*, Book 2, Ch. 6: Now, since scripture speaks of 'heaven,' the "heaven of heaven," and the "heavens of heavens," and says that the blessed Paul was caught up to the "third heaven," [2Cor. 12:2] we say that in the creation of the universe we consider as heavens that which the pagan philosophers, making the teachings of Moses their own, call a starless sphere.[47] FCD, 211

St. John Damascene, *De Fide Orthodoxa*, Book 2, Ch. 6: It is also customary in the Hebrew tongue to speak of heaven in the plural as "heavens." So, when scripture meant to say "heaven of heaven," it said "heavens of heavens," which would mean precisely "heaven of heaven"—that which is over the firmament and the waters which are above the heavens, whether over the air and the firmament or over the seven spheres of the firmament, or over the firmament expressed in the plural as 'heavens' according to the Hebraic usage. FCD, 213

St. John Damascene, *De Fide Orthodoxa*, Book 2, Ch. 6: And again, God called heaven the 'firmament,' which He ordered to be made in the midst of the water and so arranged that it was separated from the midst of the water above the firmament and from the midst of that which is below the firmament. Instructed by sacred scripture, the divine Basil says that its substance was subtle—like smoke, as it were.[48] FCD, 211

St. Thomas Aquinas, *Summa Theologiae*, I, Q 68, Art 4: On this point there seems to be a diversity of opinion between Basil and Chrysostom. The latter says that there is only one heaven and that the words "heavens of heavens" are merely the translation of the Hebrew idiom according to which the word is always used in the plural, just as in Latin there are many nouns that are wanting in the singular. ST, 644

---

[47] Ps. 148:4: "Praise him ye heavens of heavens."

[48] Isa. 51:6: "for the heavens shall vanish like smoke."

St. John Chrysostom, *Homilies on Genesis*, Homily 4:10: Now, those with a precise knowledge of that language tell us that among the Hebrews the word 'heaven' is used in the plural, and those who know the language of the Syrians confirm this. In that language—that is, the language they use—no one would say 'heaven', but 'the heavens'. FCC, 57

St. Thomas Aquinas, *Summa Theologiae*, I, Q 68, Art 4: On the other hand, Basil, whom Damascene follows, says that there are many heavens. ST, 644

St. John Damascene, *De Fide Orthodoxa*, Book 2, Ch. 6: So there is a heaven of heaven, which is the first heaven and is above the firmament. But now, because God also called the firmament 'heaven,' there are two heavens. FCD, 213

St. Basil, *On the Hexameron*, Homily 3:3: Secondly, we must examine whether this firmament, which was also called the heavens, is different from the heavens created in the beginning, and whether, in short, there are two heavens. FCB, 39

St. Basil, *On the Hexameron*, Homily 3:3: We, however, are so far from doubting the second heavens that we seek for the third, of the sight of which the blessed Paul was considered worthy. The psalm, too, speaking of the heavens of heavens, [Ps. 148:4] gives us an idea of even more. FCB, 40

St. Basil, *On the Hexameron*, Homily 3:3: Now, some of those before us have said that this is not the generation of a second heaven but a more detailed account of the first, because on the former occasion the creation of the heavens and the earth was presented to us in brief, but here the scripture teaches us in greater detail the manner in which each was made. FCB, 41

St. Basil, *On the Hexameron*, Homily 3:3: We, however, say that, since both from second name and a function peculiar to the second heaven was recorded, this is a different one from that created in the beginning, one of a more solid nature and furnishing a special service for the universe. FCB, 41-42

St. Thomas Aquinas, *Summa Theologiae*, I, Q 68, Art 4: The difference, however, is more verbal than real. For Chrysostom means by the one heaven the whole body that is above the earth and the water, for which reason the birds that fly in the air are called "birds of heaven" (Ps. 8:9). But since in this body there are many distinct parts, Basil said that there are more heavens than one. ST, 644-45

St. John Damascene, *De Fide Orthodoxa*, Book 2, Ch. 6: However, it is customary for sacred Scripture to call the air heaven, too, because of its being seen above, as it says: "O all ye fowls of the heaven, bless the Lord," [Dan. 3:80] meaning the air, although the air is not heaven but a medium of passage for the fowls. FCD, 213

St. Thomas Aquinas, *Summa Theologiae*, I, Q 68, Art 4: there are metaphorical uses of the word heaven, as when this is applied to the Blessed Trinity, Who is the Light and the Most High Spirit. It is explained by some, as thus applied, in the words, "I will ascend into heaven" (Isa. 16:13), whereby the devil is represented as seeking to make himself equal with God. ST, 645

St. Thomas Aquinas, *Summa Theologiae*, I, Q 68, Art 4: Sometimes also spiritual blessings, the recompense of the saints, are signified by the word heaven and, in fact, they are so signified, according to Augustine, in the words, "Your reward is very great in heaven" (Mt. 5:12). ST, 645

St. Ephrem, *Commentary on Genesis*, Part 1:20: Although God said that the light which came to be on the first day "was very good", He did not say this about the firmament which came to be on the second day, because the firmament had not yet been finished, neither in its structure nor in its adornment. FCE, 89

St. Lawrence of Brindisi, *Explanatio in Genesim*, Ch. 1: I am more convinced that Moses refrained from saying "That it was good" because the firmament was still imperfect since it was missing the ornament of the stars that constitute its chief beauty. However, it achieved this perfection on the fourth day, and accordingly in that narrative Moses writes "And God saw that it was good." CF, 53-54

Genesis 1:9: *God also said: Let the waters that are under the heaven, be gathered together into one place: and let the dry land appear. And it was so done.*

St. John Damascene, *De Fide Orthodoxa*, Book 2, Ch. 9: Now, the fact that scripture speaks of one gathering does not mean that they were gathered together into one place, for notice that after this it says: "And the gathering together of the water he called seas." Actually, the account meant that the waters were segregated by themselves apart from the earth. And so the waters were brought together into their gathering places and the dry land appeared. FCD, 224-25

St. Ambrose, *Hexameron*, Book 3, Ch. 1: This is not the only example of the obedience of water available to us, for elsewhere we find it written: "The waters saw thee, O God, the waters saw thee and they were afraid" [Ps. 76:17]. What is said here of the waters does not seem to be without a semblance of truth, since elsewhere the Prophet also speaks in the same manner: "The sea saw and fled: Jordan was turned back" [Ps. 113:3]. Who does not know how in actual fact the sea fled at the crossing of the Hebrews? When the waters were divided, the people crossed over, believing because of the dust under their feet that the sea had fled, and that the waters had vanished. Therefore, the Egyptian believed what he saw and entered in, but the waters which had fled returned on him. The waters, then, know how to congregate, how to fear, and how to flee, when commanded to do so by God. Let us imitate those waters and let us recognize one congregation of the Lord, one Church. FCAm, 67-68

St. Thomas Aquinas, *Summa Theologiae*, I, Q 69, Art 1: In the third place, the impression of elemental forms on formless matter is recorded, also with a priority of origin only. Therefore the words, "Let the waters be gathered together, and the dry land appear", mean that corporeal matter was impressed with the substantial form of water, so as to have such movement and with the substantial form of earth, so as to have such an appearance. ST, 648

St. Thomas Aquinas, *Summa Theologiae*, I, Q 69, Art 1: For according to Augustine, in all his commentaries on Genesis, there is no order of duration, but only of origin and nature. He says that the spiritual and corporeal natures were first created formless (the latter are first indicated by the words 'earth' and 'water') in the sense that this formlessness preceded formation, not in time, but only in origin. Nor did one formation precede another in duration, but merely in the order of nature. ST, 647-48

St. Augustine, *De Genesi ad litteram*, Book I, Ch. 15: God the creator did not first make unformed matter and later, as if after further reflection, form it according to the series of works He produced. He created formed matter. It is true that the material out of which something is made, though not prior in time, is in a sense by its origin prior to the object produced. Accordingly, the sacred writer was able to separate in the time of his narrative what God did not separate in time in His creative act. LMG, Vol. 1, 36

St. Thomas Aquinas, *Summa Theologiae*, I, Q 69, Art 1: According, however, to other holy writers, an order of duration in the works is to be understood, by which is meant that the formlessness of matter preceded its formation, and one from another, in the order of time. ST, 648

St. Thomas Aquinas, *Summa Theologiae*, I, Q 69, Art 1: Nevertheless, they do not hold that the formlessness of matter implies the total absence of form, for heaven, earth, and water already existed, since these three are named as already clearly perceptible to the senses; rather they understand by formlessness the want of due distinction and of perfect beauty, and in respect to these three scripture mentions three kinds of formlessness. ST, 648

St. Thomas Aquinas, *Summa Theologiae*, I, Q 69, Art 1: Heaven, the highest of them, was without form so long as 'darkness' filled it, because it was the source of light. The formlessness of water, which holds the middle place, is called the 'deep', because, as Augustine says, this word signifies the mass of waters without order. Thirdly, the formless state of the earth is touched upon when the earth is said to be 'void' or 'invisible', because it was covered by the waters. ST, 648

St. Thomas Aquinas, *Summa Theologiae*, I, Q 69, Art 1 ad 2: We need not suppose that the earth was first covered by the waters, and that these were afterwards gathered together, but that they were produced in this very gathering together. ST, 649

St. John Damascene, *De Fide Orthodoxa*, Book 2, Ch. 9: Thus it was that the waters were brought together into their gathering places, and this is the cause of the mountains being made. FCD, 226

St. John Damascene, *De Fide Orthodoxa*, Book 2, Ch. 10: But at God's command the receptacles for the waters were made. Then the mountains came into being and by the divine command the earth assumed its natural beauty and was adorned with every sort of verdure and plant. FCD, 228

St. Augustine, *De Genesi contra Manichaeos*, Book I, Ch. 12: This gathering into one place is the formation of these waters that we see and touch. For every form is reduced to a rule of unity. What else should we understand is meant by the words "Let the dry land appear" than that this matter receives the visible form which this earth that we see and touch now has? Hence the previous expression "the earth was invisible and without form" signified the confusion and obscurity of matter, and the expression "the water over which the Spirit of God was borne" signified that same matter. But now this water and earth are formed from that matter which is called by their names before it had received the forms that we now see. FCA, 65-66

St. Basil, *On the Hexameron*, Homily 3:5: Therefore, the immense mass of water was poured around the earth, not in proportion to it, but exceeding it many times over, since the mighty craftsman from the beginning was looking toward the future and arranging the first things according to the consequent need. FCB, 44

St. Basil, *On the Hexameron*, Homily 4:5: At the same time, lest we attribute to the sun the cause of the drying of the earth, the creator contrived the drying of the earth before the generation of the sun. FCB, 61

St. Thomas Aquinas, *Summa Theologiae*, I, Q 69, Art 1 ad 3: Or, "one place" is to be understood not simply, but contrasted with the place of dry land, so that the sense would be, "Let the waters be gathered together in one place", that is, apart from dry land. ST, 649

St. Ambrose, *Hexameron*, Book 3, Ch. 3: Still, there are some lakes and standing waters which are not connected with other waters, such as Lake Como, Lake Garda, the Alban Lake—and many others. How then can one speak of one mass of water? But, just as God made two luminaries, the sun and the moon—although there still exist, to be sure, the lights of the stars—in like manner, we speak also of one mass of water, although there are very many such. The reason is that what has not been taken in consideration in any enumeration is not reckoned in the sum total. FCAm, 79

Genesis 1:10: *And God called the dry land, Earth; and the gathering together of the waters, he called Seas. And God saw that it was good.*

St. Thomas Aquinas, *Summa Theologiae*, I, Q 69, Art 1 ad 5: And here, again, it is said that "the dry land", that is, the part from which the waters had withdrawn, "He called Earth", as distinct from the sea; although the name 'earth' is equivocally applied to that which was covered with waters or not. ST, 650

St. Ambrose, *Hexameron*, Book 3, Ch. 4: The word 'dry' is the expression of a natural characteristic; the word 'earth' is a simple name of a thing which has in itself that same characteristic. FCAm, 80

St. Basil, *On the Hexameron*, Homily 4:3: It was necessary for them to flow that they might reach their own place; then, being in the places appointed, to remain by themselves and not to advance further. For this reason, according to the saying of Ecclesiastes, "All the rivers run into the sea, yet the sea doth not overflow" [Eccles. 1:7]. It is through the divine command that waters flow, and it is due to that first legislation, "Let the waters be gathered into one place," that the sea is enclosed within boundaries. FCB, 58

St. Lawrence of Brindisi, *Explanatio in Genesim*, Ch. 1: "Let the waters below the heavens", *i.e.* let bodily matter be reduced to form so that this water be what we observe. CF, 55

St. Lawrence of Brindisi, *Explanatio in Genesim*, Ch. 1: According to Hebrew idiom, all assembled waters, whether salt water or sweet, are called seas, so the term is not just applied to the ocean. Accordingly, we frequently read in the Gospels about the sea of Galilee or of Tiberias, even though it is a kind of large body of water that Luke called the lake of Genesareth. CF, 59

St. Jerome, *Hebraicae Quaestiones in Libro Geneseos*, 3: It may be noted that all the gathering of waters, whether salty or sweet, are called seas according to the Hebrew idiom.[49] CC, 3

St. Louis de Montfort, *True Devotion to Mary*, Ch.1, Art. 2:23: God the Father made an assemblage of all the water and He named it the sea (*mare*). He made an assemblage of all His graces and He called it Mary (*Maria*). This great God has a most right treasury in which He laid up all that He has of beauty and splendor, of rarity and preciousness, including even His own Son: and this immense treasury is none other than Mary, whom the saints have named the Treasure of the Lord, out of whose plenitude all men are made rich. TDM, 14-15

The Plants

Genesis 1:11-12: *And he said: Let the earth bring forth the green herb, and such as may seed, and the fruit tree yielding fruit after its kind, which may have seed in itself upon the earth. And it was so done. And the earth brought forth the green herb, and such as yieldeth seed according to its kind, and the tree that beareth fruit having seed each one according to its kind. And God saw that it was good.*

Genesis 2:5: *And every plant of the field before it spring up in the earth, and every herb of the ground before it grew: for the Lord God had not rained upon the earth; and there was not a man to till the earth.*

St. Ambrose, *Hexameron*, Book 3, Ch. 6: Before the light of the sun shall appear, let the green herb be born, let its light be prior to that of the sun. Let the earth germinate before it receives the fostering care of the sun, lest there be an occasion for human error to grow. Let everyone be informed that the sun is not the author of vegetation. FCAm, 87

---

49 My translation: *Notandum quod omnis congregatio aquarum, siue salsae sint siue dulces, iuxta idioma hebraicae maria nuncupentur.*

St. Thomas Aquinas, *Summa Theologiae*, I, Q 102, Art 1 ad 5: According to Augustine, the plants were not produced actually on the third day, but in their seminal principles; whereas after the work of the six days, the plants, both of paradise and others, were actually produced. ST, 946

St. Thomas Aquinas, *Summa Theologiae*, I, Q 69, Art 2: Therefore, the production of plants in their causes, within the earth, took place before they sprang up from the earth's surface. And this is confirmed by reason, as follows. In these first days, God created all things in their origin or causes, and from this work He subsequently rested. Yet afterwards, by governing His creatures, in the work of propagation, "He worketh until now". Now the production of plants from out of the earth is a work or propagation, and therefore they were produced in act on the third day, but in their causes only. ST, 651

St. Thomas Aquinas, *Summa Theologiae*, I, Q 69, Art 2: However, in a accordance with other writers, it may be said that the first constitution of species belongs to the work of the six days, but the reproduction among them of like from like, to the government of the universe. And scripture indicates this in the words, "before it sprung up in the earth" and "before it grew", that is before like was produced from like; just as now happens in the order of nature through seeds. ST, 651-52

St. Thomas Aquinas, *Summa Theologiae*, I, Q 69, Art 2: Therefore Scripture says pointedly (Gen. 1:11): "Let the earth bring forth the green herb, and such as may seed", as indicating the production of perfection of perfect species, from which the seed of others should arise. ST, 652

St. Augustine, *De Genesi ad litteram*, Book V, Ch. 4: From these words it appears rather that the seeds sprang from the crops and the trees, and that the crops and trees themselves came forth not from seeds but from the earth. This is what the word of God itself declares. For it does not say, "Let the seeds in the earth bring forth the grain and the fruit-bearing tree"; but it says, "Let the earth bring forth the grain scattering its seed". It thus reveals that the seed is from the crops, not the crops from the seed. LMG, Vol. 1, 152

St. Thomas Aquinas *Summa Theologiae*, I, Q 69, Art 2: For other commentators, in accordance with the surface meaning of the text, consider that the plants were produced in act in their various species on this third day. ST, 651

St. Thomas Aquinas, *Summa Theologiae*, I, Q 102, Art 1 ad 5: According to other holy writers, we ought to say that all the plants were actually produced on the third day, including the trees of paradise; and what is said of the trees of paradise being planted after the world of the six days is to be understood, they say, by way of recapitulation. Whence our text reads: "The Lord God had planted a paradise of pleasure from the beginning" (Gen. 2:8). ST, 946

St. Ambrose, *Hexameron*, Book 3, Ch. 6: Let us pay heed to the words of truth! Their content is the salvation of those who hear! For that first declaration of God is a law of nature which requires that every creature be born. This law has continued in force for all ages, with the intent to prescribe how a continuous succession of plants may experience in time to come modes of generation and fructification. FCAm, 86

St. Ambrose, *Hexameron*, Book 3, Ch. 6: How serviceable, how effective, is the speech: "Let the earth bring forth the green herb," that is so say, let the earth bring forth of itself, let it not seek the aid of another, let it not be needful of any other ministrations. FCAm, 86-87

St. Ambrose, *Hexameron*, Book 3, Ch. 8: And forthwith the earth in labor brought forth new plants; girding herself with the garments of verdure, she luxuriated in fecundity, and decked it in diverse seedlings, she claimed them as her own fitting adornments. We marvel at the speed of that productivity. FCAm, 92

St. Bede, *In principium Genesis*, Book I: It is evident from these words that the adornment of the world was completed in the springtime, for that is the season when living plants typically appear on the earth and trees are laden with fruit. OG, 121

St. Bede, *In principium Genesis*, Book I: Likewise, it must be noted that the first shoots of the trees and plants did not come from seed, but they sprang forth from the earth; for the earth, which appeared dry in accordance with the command of the creator, suddenly was beautified with plants and arrayed with flowering groves, and fruits of every type continuously came forth from the seeds they bear. OG, 121

St. Lawrence of Brindisi, *Explanatio in Genesim*, Ch. 1: God wished to show how He could produce perfectly and in an instant, without middle causes, all the effects of middle causes. CF, 62

St. Thomas Aquinas, *Summa Theologiae*, I, Q 66, Art 1 ad 2: But God produces being in act out of nothing, and can, therefore, produce a perfect thing in an instant, according to the greatness of His power. ST, 620

St. Ephrem, *Commentary on Genesis*, Part 1:22: Although the grasses were only a moment old at their creation, they appeared as if they were months old. Likewise, the trees, although only a day old when they sprouted forth, were nevertheless like [trees] years old as they were fully grown and fruits were already budding on their branches. FCE, 90

St. Bede, *In principium Genesis*, Book 1: It was fitting that in the beginning whatever the form of each thing, it came forth according to the command of God as mature; in the same manner it must be believed that man, for when all things on earth had been created, was fashioned in mature form, that is, as a youthful man. OG, 121

St. Basil, *On the Hexameron*, Homily 5:6: all came into existence in a moment of time, although they were not previously upon the earth, each one with its own peculiar nature, separated from other varieties by most evident differences, and each one known by its own character. FCE, 74

St. Lawrence of Brindisi, *Explanatio in Genesim*, Ch. 2: God made every plant and herb by His omnipotence *before they existed, i.e.* outside the natural causes that were suitable for every plant and herb to come into existence, and they were brought forth into being before their natural causes from which they naturally had to be produced. CF, 105-6

St. Augustine, *De Genesi ad litteram*, Book IV, Ch. 33: Otherwise, if we think that, when they were first created by the Word of God, there were the processes of nature with the normal duration of days that we know, those creatures that shoot forth roots and clothe the earth would need not one day but many days to germinate beneath the ground, and then a certain number of days, according to their natures, to come forth from the ground; and the creation of vegetation, which scripture places on one day, namely the third, would have been a gradual process. LMG, Vol. 1, 142

St. Lawrence of Brindisi, *Explanatio in Genesim*, Ch. 2: But at that time when these things were brought forth, there had been no rain nor man to cultivate the earth. CF, 106

St. Lawrence of Brindisi, *Explanatio in Genesim*, Ch. 1: Along with Basil, I think we must not fittingly understand by this verse of Genesis that this law of bringing forth and bearing fruit for the earth was ordained by this command of God, and, along with Augustine, I think that the earth received the power to bring forth, and, along with Chrysostom, I think that the earth produced vegetation and fruits by the order of God without any middle effect of second causes. CF, 63

St. Augustine, *De Genesi ad litteram*, Book V, Ch. 4: It is, therefore, causally (*causaliter*) that scripture has said that earth brought forth the crops and the trees, in the sense that it received the power of bringing them forth. In the earth from the beginning, in what we may call the roots of time, God created what was to be in times to come. For God later planted a paradise in the East, and there "from the earth He made every tree to grow, beautiful to the sight and good for food". But we must not say that He then added to creation something He had not previously made, something that was afterwards to be added to the completeness in which He had finished all that was very good on the sixth day. LMG, Vol. 1, 153

St. Lawrence of Brindisi, *Explanatio in Genesim*, Ch. 1: many such plants are benefits, although they seem useless and harmful to us, who are ignorant of their natures, and they are needed for the beauty of the universe. CF, 64

St. Ambrose, *Hexameron*, Book 3, Ch. 9: Each and every thing which is produced from the earth has its own reason for existence, which, as far as it can, fulfills the general plan of creation. Some things, therefore, are created for our consumption; other things serve other uses. There is nothing without a purpose; there is nothing superfluous in what germinates from the earth. FCAm, 96

St. Basil, *On the Hexameron*, Homily 5:1: Since some think that the sun, drawing the productive power from the center of the earth to the surface with its rays of heat, is the cause of plants growing from the earth, it is for this reason that those who had been misled may cease worshipping the sun as the origin of life. If they are persuaded that before the sun's generation all the earth had been adorned, they will retract their unbounded admiration for it, realizing that the sun is later than the grass and plants in generation. FCB, 67-68

St. Anthony of Padua, *Sermon on Septuagesima*, 7: On the third day God said: "Let the earth bring forth the green herb". The earth or ground (which derives its name from the word 'grind') is the body of Christ, which according to Isaiah was "ground down for our sins" [cf. Is. 53:5]. This ground was dug and ploughed with the nails and the spear. As someone has said, "The earth when it has been dug will give its fruits in due season. The flesh of Christ when dug gave heavenly kingdoms." It brought forth the growing herb in the Apostles, it made the seed of preaching in the martyrs, and the fruit tree bearing fruit in the confessors and virgins. In the primitive Church faith was like a tender plant, so that the Apostles might have said, in the words of Canticles, "Our sister" (the infant Church) "is little" (in the number of the faithful), "and has no breasts" (wherewith she may nourish her children) [cf. Cant. 8:8]. She had not yet been made pregnant by the Holy Spirit, and so they said, "What shall we do with our sister on the day" (of Pentecost) "when she is to be spoken to" (by the speaking of the Holy Spirit)? Concerning this, the Lord said in the Gospel: "He will teach you all things, and bring all things to your mind", [Jn. 14:26] (that is, He will supply assistance). SSA, 15-16

St. Anthony of Padua, *Sermon on Septuagesima*, 18: Note that by the third day is denoted the satisfaction of penance, which comprises three forms: prayer, fasting, and almsgiving, which are signified by the three aforementioned things. SSA, 25

St. Anthony of Padua, *Sermon on Septuagesima,* 18-19: It is written, then, "Let the earth bring forth the herb." The herb that grows signifies prayer . . . There follows, "and producing seed", by which fasting is signified . . . There follows thirdly: "The fruit tree yielding fruit after its kind". In the fruit-tree almsgiving is signified, which bears fruit among the needy, and by their hands is carried back into heaven. Notice the words: "yielding fruit according to its kind". The 'kind' of man is the 'other man', created of the ground and quickened by the soul. One should therefore give alms, the "fruit according to one's kind", because the soul is refreshed by spiritual, and the body by corporeal, bread. SSA, 25-27

The Sun, Moon and Stars

Genesis 1:14: *And God said: Let there be lights made in the firmament of heaven, to divide the day and the night, and let them be for signs, and for seasons, and for days and years:*

St. Ambrose, *Hexameron*, Book 4, Ch. 1: We have now passed the first day without a sun, and the second and the third days we have completed still without a sun. On the fourth day God bade the luminaries of the heavens to be created: the sun, the moon, and stars. FCAm, 125-26

St. Theophilus of Antioch, *To Autolycus*, Book 2, Ch. 15: In like manner also the three days which were before the luminaries, are types of the Trinity; of God, and His Word, and His wisdom. ANF, Vol. 2, 100-1

St. Thomas Aquinas, *Summa Theologiae*, I, Q 70, Art 1: In the first work, that of 'creation', the heaven and the earth were produced, but as yet without form. In the second, or work of 'distinction', the heaven and the earth were perfected, either by adding substantial form to formless matter, as Augustine holds, or by giving them the order and beauty due to them, as other holy writers suppose. To these two works is added the work of 'adornment', which differs from perfection. For the perfection of the heaven and the earth appears to be concerned with those things that belong to them intrinsically, but the adornment, those that are extrinsic. ST, 654

St. Ambrose, *Hexameron*, Book 4, Ch. 2: Who says this? God says it. And to whom is He speaking, if not to His Son. Therefore, God the Father says: "Let the Sun be made," and the Son made the sun, for it was fitting that the "Sun of Justice" should make the sun of the world.[50] FCAm, 129

[50] Mal. 4:2: "But unto you that fear my name, the Sun of justice shall arise, and health in his wings."

St. Thomas Aquinas, *Summa Theologiae*, I, Q 70, Art 1: It must also be noted that Augustine's opinion on the productions of the luminaries is not at variance with that of other holy writers. For he says that they were made actually and not merely virtually, since the firmament has not the power of producing luminaries, as the earth has of producing plants. Therefore Scripture does not say: "Let the firmament produce lights", though it says: "Let the earth bring forth the green herb". ST, 654

St. Lawrence of Brindisi, *Explanatio in Genesim*, Ch. 1: In this verse, the firmament is not understood to be the atmosphere . . . we understand that the word firmament used here means the heavens divided into eight parts, *i.e.* the eighth sphere with the orbits of the planets. CF, 72

St. Basil, *On the Hexameron*, Homily 6:2: In fact, at that time, the actual nature of light was introduced, but now this solar body has been made ready to be a vehicle for that first-created light. [51] FCB, 86

St. Lawrence of Brindisi, *Explanatio in Genesim*, Ch. 1: Nevertheless, I explain this passage in a manner that does not deviate from the path of the Holy Fathers: "Let the lights in the firmament of the heavens be made", i.e. the bodies of the sun and the moon, and the stars that are the vehicles of that primary light established on the first day, for as we explained above from the works of St. Basil and St. John Damascene, it is the light of the light and the vehicle of illumination. CF, 67

---

[51] Ecclus. 43:1-5: "The firmament on high is his beauty, the beauty of heaven with its glorious shew. The sun when he appeareth shewing forth at his rising, an admirable instrument, the work of the most High. At noon he burneth the earth, and who can abide his burning heat? As one keeping a furnace in the works of heat: The sun three times as much, burneth the mountains, breathing out fiery vapours, and shining with his beams, he blindeth the eyes. Great is the Lord that made him, and at his words he hath hastened his course."

St. Thomas Aquinas, *Summa Theologiae*, I, Q 70, Art 2: Secondly, as regards the changes of seasons, which prevent weariness, preserve health, and provide for the necessities of food; all of which could not be secured if it were always summer or winter. In reference to this he says: "Let them be for seasons, and for days, and years." ST, 657

St. Basil, *On the Hexameron*, Homily 6:8: "Let them serve," He says, "for the fixing of days," not for making days, but for ruling the days. For day and night are earlier than the generation of the luminaries. This the psalm declares to us when it says: "He placed the sun to rule the day, the moon and stars to rule the night" [Ps. 135:8-9]. FCB, 97

St. Basil, *On the Hexameron*, Homily 6:8: Therefore, one would not err if he would define the day as air, lighted by the sun, or as the measure of time in which the sun tarries in the hemisphere above the earth. FCB, 97

St. Lawrence of Brindisi, *Explanatio in Genesim*, Ch. 1: Nevertheless, fidelity to the original Hebrew seems to entail another understanding of this passage. For where our translation reads "for the seasons", the Hebrew reads *ulimoadim*. This word does not signify the seasonal time, as above, rather this seasonal notion is explained further on in the text as "for days and years". In this passage, fixed and solemn days are called *moadim*, which the Jews so name out of testimony and warning or rather from the gathering of a group to celebrate divine solemnities, from the word *yaad*, which designates an assembly and the arrangement of time to celebrate sacred assemblies. CF, 69

St. Ephrem, *Commentary on Genesis*, Part 1:23: That [God] said, "Let them be for signs," [refers to] measures of time, and "let them be for seasons," clearly indicates summer and winter. "Let them be for days," are measured by the rising and setting of the sun, and "let them be for years," are comprised of the daily cycles of the sun and the monthly cycles of the moon. FCE, 90

St. Basil, *On the Hexameron*, Homily 6:8: But, the sun and the moon were appointed to be for the years. FCB, 97

St. Ambrose, *Hexameron*, Book 4, Ch. 5: The sun and the moon, too, were designed "to fix the years." The moon in twelve times thirty days, according to the Hebrews, completes the year with the addition of a few days, and according to the Romans with an intercalary day added every fourth year. The solstitial year is that portion of time which corresponds to the completion of a period in which the sun makes a circuit through all the signs and then returns to the point of its departure. FCAm, 148

St. Ambrose, *Hexameron*, Book 4, Ch. 7: On the occasion of the moon's rise, according to report, clear indications of change make their appearance. To be more precise, the western sea, towards which the ebb tide directs itself, rises and falls with greater force, as if it were driven backward and forward by the same lunar exhalations, until it ultimately falls back into its normal and accustomed channel. FCAm, 153

St. Ambrose, *Hexameron*, Book 6, Ch. 2: He did not discuss how the lunar orb is brought into eclipse in this part of the world, since in his account these phenomena were passed over as of no significance to us. FCAm, 232

St. Basil, *On the Hexameron*, Homily 6:8: We think that 'seasons' means the changes of the periods of time—winter, spring, summer, and autumn—which, due to the regularity of the movement of the luminaries, are made to pass by us periodically. FCB, 95

St. John Damascene, *De Fide Orthodoxa*, Book 2, Ch. 7: The first of these is the spring solstice, for it was at the spring solstice that God made all things, which is evident from the fact that even down to the present time the budding of flowers takes place then. FCD, 217

St. Thomas Aquinas, *Summa Theologiae*, I, Q 70, Art 2: Thirdly, as regards the convenience of business and work, in so far as from the luminaries in the heavens is indicated fair or rainy weather, favorable to various occupations. And in this respect he says, "Let them be for signs". ST, 657

St. Basil, *On the Hexameron*, Homily 6:5: But some who go beyond the bounds interpret the divine utterance as a defense of astrology and say that our life depends on the movement of the heavenly bodies and that, for this reason, the Chaldeans take the signs of what happens to us from the stars. And they understand the simple words of scripture, "Let them serve as signs," not of the conditions of the air, nor of the changes in season, but, as it seems to them, in respect to our lot in life. FCB, 90-91

St. Thomas Aquinas, *Summa Theologiae*, I, Q 70, Art 2 ad 1: The luminaries in the heavens are set for signs of changes effected in corporeal creatures, but not of those changes which depend upon free choice. ST, 657

St. Lawrence of Brindisi, *Explanatio in Genesim,* Ch. 1: Man cannot always work, but sometimes it is necessary for him to rest, and night offers this time in which the limbs of the body are relieved and the senses renewed by pleasant sleep after day has granted the time for working. Therefore, this is first duty of the lights. CF, 68

St. Lawrence of Brindisi, *Explanatio in Genesim,* Ch. 1: The second, however, is this: The passage reads "Let them serve as signs", since very often many things are signaled by these lights, such as rain, fair skies, heat, wind, and other things of this kind, which are brought about by them and which farmers, sailors, and physicians commonly know and experience. CF, 68

St. Lawrence of Brindisi, *Explanatio in Genesim,* Ch. 1: The third purpose is that of the seasons, as the lights bring in variations, wherefore scripture says "And let them be for seasons . . ." Thus a seasonal time demands are variation, such as morning and evening, and so one day then another, one month, then another, a waxing, then a waning moon. By these changes, the year is divided into spring, summer, fall, and winter. CF, 68

St. Bonaventure, *Breviloquium*, Part II, Ch. 4:4: And because the human soul strives to its end through free will, by virtue of this freedom it excels every power of corporeal beings. That is why all things are born to serve the soul, for nothing can rule it except God alone—neither fate nor any power of the stars' position. Brev, 71

St. Basil, *On the Hexameron*, Homily 6:4: The Lord has already foretold that the signs of the dissolution of the universe will appear in the sun and moon and stars; "The sun shall be turned into blood, and the moon will not give her light" [Joel 2:31, Mt. 24:9]. These are the signs of the consummation of the world. FCB, 90

St. Ambrose, *Hexameron*, Book 4, Ch. 4: And when the Apostles asked for a sign of His coming, He replied: "The sun will be darkened and the moon will not give her light and the stars will fall from heaven." FCAm, 135

Genesis 1:15: *To shine in the firmament of heaven, and to give light upon the earth. And it was so done.*

St. Thomas Aquinas, *Summa Theologiae*, I, Q 70, Art 2: Now, he explains this service at the beginning of *Genesis* as threefold. First, the luminaries are of service to man, in regard to sight, which directs him in his works, and is most useful for perceiving things. In reference to this he says, "Let them shine in the firmament and give light to the earth." ST, 657

St. Ambrose, *Hexameron*, Book 4, Ch. 3: But let us reflect on the fact that the light of day is one thing and the light of the sun and moon and stars another, for the reason that the sun itself with its rays appears to add brilliance to the light of day. This can be seen at the dawn of the day or at its setting. There is daylight, in fact, before the rising of the sun, but it is far from being brilliant. FCAm, 132

St. Basil, *On the Hexameron,* Homily 6:3: I certainly do not say that the separation of light from the solar body is possible for you and me, but that that which we are able to separate in thought can also be separated in actuality by the creator of its nature. It is also inconceivable for you to separate the burning property of fire from its brilliancy; yet God, wishing to turn His servant back by an incredible spectacle, placed fire in a bush, which was active only in its brilliance and had its power of burning inactive. FCB, 86-87

St. Lawrence of Brindisi, *Explanatio in Genesim,* Ch. 1: Therefore the lights from that first light, which made day and night, were determined on the fourth day from the nature of their own sphere, with their parts reduced into a kind of greater density; the star is the densest part of its sphere. It was made by the divine Hand, i.e. by its power, in the manner of a primary receptive vessel of light. CF, 67

Genesis 1:16-17: *And God made two great lights: a greater light to rule the day; and a lesser light to rule the night: and the stars. And he set them in the firmament of heaven to shine upon the earth.*

St. Thomas Aquinas, *Summa Theologiae,* I, Q 70, Art 1 ad 5: As Chrysostom says, the two luminaries are called great, not so much with regard to their dimensions as to their influence and power. ST, 656

St. John Chrysostom, *Homilies on Genesis,* Homily 6:10: You see, it calls this light great and says it was brought into existence for governing the day. In other words, the sun renders the day brighter, shedding its rays like flashing lights and day by day revealing its own beauty in full bloom: as soon as it appears at dawn, it awakes the whole human race to the discharge of their respective duties. FCC, 83

St. Lawrence of Brindisi, *Explanatio in Genesim*, Ch. 1: the Sun and Moon are called "the great lights" by no means just because they are of an almost immense size and because they shine brighter than other stars but especially relative to their appearance, because they appear larger than the others. CF, 72

St. Thomas Aquinas, *Summa Theologiae*, I, Q 70, Art 1 ad 5: For though the stars be of greater bulk than the moon, yet the influence of the moon is more perceptible to the senses in this lower world. Moreover, as far as the senses are concerned, its size is greater. ST, 656

St. John Damascene, *De Fide Orthodoxa*, Book 2, Ch. 7: However, when the sun is shining at the same time as the stars and the moon, it dims them by its brighter radiance and keeps them from showing. FCD, 216

Genesis 1:18: *And to rule the day and the night, and to divide the light and the darkness. And God saw that it was good.*

St. Thomas Aquinas, *Summa Theologiae*, I, Q 71, Art 1: Hence, just as Moses makes mention of the lights and light on the fourth day, to show that the fourth day corresponds to the first day on which he had said that the light was made, so on this fifth day he mentions the waters and the firmament of heaven to show that the fifth day corresponds to the second. ST, 662-63

St. Thomas Aquinas, *Summa Theologiae*, I, Q 70, Art 1 ad 1: As to the fact that the luminaries are not mentioned as existing from the beginning, but only as made on the fourth day, Chrysostom explains this by need of guarding the people from the danger of idolatry; since the luminaries are proved not to be gods, by the fact that they were not from the beginning. ST, 655

St. John Chrysostom, *Homilies on Genesis*, Homily 6:12: Pagan peoples, however, in their wonder and stupor at this heavenly body were unable to look beyond it to praise its creator; instead they sang its praises and treated it as a deity.[52] FCC, 83

St. Ambrose, *Hexameron*, Book 3, Ch. 6: The sun is younger than the green shoot, younger than the green plant! FCAm, 87

St. Basil, *On the Hexameron*, Homily 6:10: And there is a certain hidden reason of the wise artificer for this varied interchange of shapes. In truth, it is so as to provide for us a clear example of our nature. For, nothing human is stable, but some things advance from non-being to perfection, and other, having attained their proper strength and increased to their highest limit, again, through gradual deterioration, decline and perish, and after having decreased, are completely destroyed.[53] FCB, 100

St. Ambrose, *Hexameron*, Book 4, Ch. 8: From this, let men deduce the lesson that nothing can exist in the universe, be it human or any other created thing, which shall not at some point pass away. Even the moon, to which the Lord has granted the important office of illuminating the whole world, goes through the process of waxing and waning. All things, which spring from nothing, reach their perfection and again diminish in perfection, being subject to decline. Hence we are told: "Heaven and earth shall pass away" [Mt. 24:35]. FCAm, 154

---

[52] Deut. 4:19: "Lest perhaps lifting up thy eyes to heaven, thou see the sun and the moon, and all the stars of heaven, and being deceived by error thou adore and serve them, which the Lord thy God created for the service of all the nations, that are under heaven."

[53] Ecclus. 27:12: "A holy man continueth in wisdom as the sun: but a fool is changed as the moon." Job 15:15: "Behold among his saints none is unchangeable."

St. Anthony of Padua, *Sermon on Septuagesima,* 8: On the fourth day God said: "Let there be two lights in the firmament" [Gen. 1:14]. In the firmament which is Christ, now glorified through the Resurrection, there are two lights—namely the brightness of the Resurrection, which is signified by the sun, and the incorruptibility of the flesh, which is signified by the moon. This refers to the state of the sun and moon before our first parent's fall. After his disobedience all creatures suffer some loss. That is why the Apostle says: "Every creature groaneth and travaileth in pain, even till now". [Rom. 8:22] SSA, 16

St. Ambrose, *Hexameron*, Book 4, Ch. 8: Deservedly is the moon compared to the Church, who has shone over the entire world and says as she illuminates the darkness of the world: "The night is far advanced, the day is at hand" [Rom. 13:12]. FCAm, 156

St. Ambrose, *Hexameron*, Book 4, Ch. 8: This is the real moon which from the perpetual light of her own brother has acquired the light of immortality and grace. Not from her own light does the Church gleam, but from the light of Christ. From the Sun of Justice has her brilliance been obtained, so that it is said: "It is now no longer I that live, but Christ lives in me" [Gal. 2:20]. FCAm, 156

St. Anthony of Padua, *Sermon on Septuagesima*, 20: On the fourth day God said, "Let there be two great lights in the firmament" [Gen. 1:14]. The fourth virtue is the love of God and of neighbour: the love of God being signified by the brightness of the sun, and the love of neighbour by the changeableness of the moon. Does it not seem to you that there is a certain changeableness, "to rejoice with those who rejoice, and weep with those who weep" [Rom. 12:15]? It is of these two things that there is said, towards the end of Deuteronomy, "The land of Joseph shall be filled with the fruits of the sun and the moon" [Deut. 33:14]. SSA, 28

St. Ambrose, *Hexameron*, Book 4, Ch. 2: Most authors seem, indeed, to interpret this passage mystically of Christ and the Church, maintaining that Christ had knowledge of His passion in the body when He said: "Father, the hour is come! Glorify thy Son," so that by this His setting He might grant eternal life to all men who were threatened with eternal death, and that the Church may have her seasons, namely, of persecution and peace. FCAm, 131

St. Ambrose, *Hexameron*, Book 4, Ch. 2: The Church, like the moon, seems to lose light, but she does not. She can cast as shadow, but she cannot lose her light. For example, the Church is weakened by the desertion of some in the time of persecution, but is replenished by the witness of her martyrs. FCAm, 131

The Birds and Fish

Genesis 1:20: *God also said: Let the waters bring forth the creeping creature having life, and the fowl that may fly over the earth under the firmament of heaven.*

St. Basil, *On the Hexameron*, Homily 7:1: After the creation of the lights, then the waters were filled with living creatures, so that this portion of the world also was adorned. FCB, 105

St. Basil, *On the Hexameron*, Homily 7:1: The command came. Immediately rivers were productive and marshy lakes were fruitful of species proper and natural to each; the sea was in travail with all kinds of swimming creatures, and not even the water which remained in the slime and ponds was idle or without its contribution in creation. FCB, 105

St. Basil, *On the Hexameron*, Homily 7:1: Thus all water was in eager haste to fulfill the command of its creator, and the great and ineffable power of God immediately produced an efficacious and active life in creatures of which one would not even be able to enumerate the species, as soon as the capacity for propagating living creatures came to the waters through His command. FCB, 105

St. Ambrose, *Hexameron*, Book 5, Ch. 1: At this command the waters immediately poured forth their offspring. The rivers were in labor. The lakes produced their quota of life. The sea itself began to bear all manner of reptiles and to send forth according to its kind whatever was there created. FCAm, 160

St. Ambrose, *Hexameron*, Book 5, Ch. 1: The tiny creeks and the muddy marshes were not without exercising the power of creation granted to them. Fish leaped from the rivers. Dolphins frolicked in the waves. Shell-fish clung to the rocks. Oysters adhered to the depths and the sea-urchins waxed strong. FCAm, 160

Genesis 1:21-23: *And God created the great whales, and every living and moving creature, which the waters brought forth, according to their kinds, and every winged fowl according to its kind. And God saw that it was good. And he blessed them, saying: Increase and multiply, and fill the waters of the sea: and let the birds be multiplied upon the earth. And the evening and morning were the fifth day.*

St. Bede, *In principium Genesis*, Book I: Since there are creatures of the waters that do not move by swimming, but by creeping or by walking on their feet, and since there are among the birds those that have so many feathers yet are unable to fly, so that no one should think there is any type of winged or aquatic animal being overlooked in this word of the Lord, the following words are carefully chosen: "So God created the great sea monsters and every living creature that moves, with which the waters swarm, according to their kinds, and every winged bird according to its kind". OG, 126

St. Thomas Aquinas, *Summa Theologiae*, I, Q 71, Art 1: It must, however, be observed that Augustine differs from other writers in his opinion about the production of fishes and birds, just as he differs about the production of plants. For while others say that fishes and birds were produced actually on the fifth day, he holds that the nature of the waters produced them on that day potentially. ST, 663

St. Augustine, *De Genesi ad litteram*, Book V, Ch. 5: On the fifth day the waters, being joined to sky and air, at God's command brought forth their inhabitants, all the fishes and birds; and they produced them potentially in the numbers which would come forth under appropriate influences in the course of time.[54] LMG, Vol. 1, 155

St. Thomas Aquinas, *Summa Theologiae*, I, Q 71, Art 1 ad 1: Not as though water or earth has in itself the power of producing all animals, as Avicenna held; rather it is from the power originally placed in the elements that they are able to produce animals either from elemental matters by the power of seed or the influence of the stars. ST, 663

St. Thomas Aquinas, *Summa Theologiae*, I, Q 71, Art 1 ad 1: Those things that are naturally generated from seed cannot be generated naturally in any other way. ST, 663

St. Ambrose, *Hexameron*, Book 5, Ch. 1: But we are unable to record the multiplicity of the names of all those species which by divine command were brought forth to life in a moment of time. FCAm, 160

St. Ambrose, *Hexameron*, Book 5, Ch. 1: At the same instant, substantial form and the principle of life were brought forth into existence; associated was a sort of vital vigor and power. FCAm, 160-61

St. Thomas Aquinas, *Summa Theologiae*, I, Q 71, Art 1 ad 1: But at the first beginning of the world the active principle was the Word of God, which produced animals from material elements, either in act, as some holy writers say, or virtually, as Augustine teaches. ST, 663

St. Basil, *On the Hexameron*, Homily 8:1: No, when He said: "Let it bring forth," it did not produce what was stored up in it, but He who gave the command also bestowed upon it the power to bring forth. FCB, 117

---

[54] Ps. 103:25: "So is this great sea, which stretcheth wide its arms: there are creeping things without number: Creatures little and great."

St. Lawrence of Brindisi, *Explanatio in Genesim*, Ch. 1: As soon as the divine command is issued, the waters are filled up with fishes and, after the earth and the sky, they received their characteristic and singular furnishing. CF, 74

St. Ambrose, *Hexameron*, Book 5, Ch. 2: The whale, as well as the frog, came into existence at the same time by the creative power. FCAm, 162

St. Ambrose, *Hexameron*, Book 5, Ch. 2: Take note of the fact that there are far more animals in the sea than on land. Count, if you can, all the species of fish from the smallest to the greatest. FCAm, 162

St. Basil, *On the Hexameron*, Homily 7:1: Now, for the first time, an animal was created which possessed life and sensation. FCB, 106

St. Thomas Aquinas, *Summa Theologiae*, I, Q 71, Art 1 ad 3: The air, as not being so apparent to the senses, is not enumerated by itself, but with other things: partly with water, because the lower region of air is thickened by watery exhalations; partly with the heaven as to the higher region. But the birds move in the lower part of the air, and so are said to fly "beneath the firmament", even if the firmament be taken to mean the region of the clouds. Hence the production of the birds is ascribed to the water. ST, 663-64

St. Ambrose, *Hexameron*, Book 5, Ch. 22: But why, "below the firmament"? Eagles fly above all other birds, yet they do not fly "below the firmament of heavens." The word for 'heaven' in Greek is οὐρανός, derived from the Greek word 'to see,' for the reason that the air is clear and transparent and so living species are said to fly through the air. FCAm, 216

St. Ambrose, *Hexameron*, Book 5, Ch. 22: One should not be disturbed by the phrase "below the firmament of the heavens." The word 'firmament' is used, not in its proper, but in its derivative sense. The air which we perceive with our eyes is, in comparison with that ethereal substance, the firmament, of greater thickness and density. FCAm, 216-17

St. Ambrose, *Hexameron*, Book 5, Ch. 14: Not without reason, therefore, do both species have the innate faculty of swimming, since both have their origin in water. FCAm, 198

St. Lawrence of Brindisi, *Explanatio in Genesim*, Ch. 1: But God causes the way in which even the birds originate from the waters, although they are not animals belonging to the water, but rather to the air, since they are seen to live in the air . . . Indeed, the original Hebrew version resolves any doubt: it reads: "*Weuph yeuphe al-haareç:* And let the flying thing fly over the earth". Therefore, flying things are not mixed among the things that have been produced from the waters; but they are mentioned in the verse where these things have been made, namely over the earth; for later on in Genesis birds are numbered among the living things of the earth. CF, 74

St. Ambrose, *Hexameron*, Book 5, Ch. 22: It is clear that "above the earth" is said because they search for their food on the earth. FCAm, 216

St. Basil, *On the Hexameron*, Homily 8:2: But, none of the winged creatures is without feet, because food for all of them comes from the earth and all necessarily require the assistance of feet. FCB, 121

St. Basil, *On the Hexameron*, Homily 7:5: If the fish knows what it should choose and what avoid, what shall we say who have been honored with reason, taught by the law, encouraged by the promises, made wise by the Spirit, and who have handled our own affairs more unreasonably than the fish? FCB, 113

St. Anthony of Padua, *Sermon on Septuagesima*, 9: On the fifth day, God made the birds in the sky, to which there appropriately corresponds the fifth article of faith, the Ascension. In the Ascension the

Son of God flew like a bird up to the right hand of the Father, with the flesh he had assumed. So he himself says in Isaiah: "who call a bird from the east, and from a far country the man of my own will" [Isa. 46:11]. SSA, 16

St. Anthony of Padua, *Sermon on Septuagesima,* 21: On the fifth day, God made the fishes in the sea and the birds above the earth. The fifth virtue is the exercise of the active and the contemplative life. The active man, like a fish, traverses the paths of the sea (the world) so as to be able to come to the aid of his neighbor who suffers need. Meanwhile the contemplative, like a bird, is lifted into the air upon the wings of contemplation and according to his capacity "gazes upon the King in his beauty" [Isa. 33:17]. As Job says, "Man is born to labor and the bird to fly". [Job 5.7] 'Labor' is the active life, 'flight' the contemplative life. SSA, 29

St. Ambrose, *Hexameron*, Book 5, Ch. 6: We are justified, therefore, in comparing man to a fish. Listen to the reason for this statement: "And the kingdom of heaven is like to a net cast into the sea that gathered in fish every kind. When it was filled, they hauled it out and sitting down on the beach, they gathered the good fish into vessels, but threw away the bad. So will it be at the end of the world. The angels will go out and separate the wicked from the just and will cast them into the furnace of fire" [Mt. 13:47-50]. FCAm, 170

St. Ambrose, *Hexameron*, Book 5, Ch. 6: Fish, then, are either good or bad. The good are preserved for their reward; the bad are straightaway burned. FCAm, 170

St. Ambrose, *Hexameron*, Book 5, Ch. 7: The Gospel is the sea in which the apostles fish, into which is cast the net which is like the kingdom of heaven. FCAm, 172

St. Ambrose, *Hexameron*, Book 5, Ch. 7: Since the example of the cunning serpent has been offered, let us be cunning, also, in regard to entrance into the state of matrimony and to remaining therein.[55] FCAm, 172

The Animals

Genesis 1:24: *And God said: Let the earth bring forth the living creature in its kind, cattle and creeping things, and beasts of the earth, according to their kinds. And it was so done.*

St. Basil, *On the Hexameron*, Homily 8:1: "Let the earth bring forth"; not, let it put forth what it has, but, let it acquire what it does not have, since God is enduing it with the power of active force. FCB, 117

St. Basil, *On the Hexameron*, Homily 9:3: Therefore, the soul of brute beasts did not emerge after having been hidden in the earth, but it was called into existence at the time of the command. FCB, 138

St. Ambrose, *Hexameron*, Book 6, Ch. 3: The Word of God permeates every creature in the constitution of the world. Hence, as God had ordained, all kinds of living creatures were quickly produced from the earth. FCAm, 232

St. Bede, *In principium Genesis*, Book I: It must be understood that by His command everything He willed swiftly came to be. OG, 128

St. Thomas Aquinas, *Summa Theologiae*, I, Q 72, Art 1: And here again Augustine says that the production was potential, and other holy writers that it was actual. ST, 665

St. Augustine, *De Genesi ad litteram*, Book V, Ch. 5: On the sixth day, the animals of the earth were made, the last beings from the last

[55] Mt. 10:16: "Be therefore wise as serpents."

element of the world. They too were created potentially, for time would bring them into view in the ages to come. LMG, Vol. 1, 155

St. Ephrem, *Commentary on Genesis,* Part 1:25: Just as the trees, the vegetation, the animals, the birds, and even mankind were old, so also were they young. They were old according to the appearance of their limbs and their substances, yet they were young because of the hour and moment of their creation. FCE, 91

Genesis 1:25: *And God made the beasts of the earth according to their kinds, and cattle, and every thing that creepeth on the earth after its kind. And God saw that it was good.*

St. Lawrence of Brindisi, *Explanatio in Genesim,* Ch. 1: We explain this verse in the following manner. "Let the earth bring forth", that is, let it receive the power of bringing forth, with other elements joining together for a material beginning. CF, 77

St. Lawrence of Brindisi, *Explanatio in Genesim,* Ch. 1: And immediately the earth brought forth that which God commanded it, by its own directing and producing power, namely livestock and crawling things; "and beasts", which are called terrestrial animals. CF, 77

St. Thomas Aquinas, *Summa Theologiae,* I, Q 72, Art 1 ad 2: By 'cattle', domestic animals are signified, which in any way are of service to man; but by 'beasts', wild animals such as bears and lions are designated. By 'creeping things' those animals are meant which either have no feet and cannot rise from the earth, as serpents, or those whose feet are too short to lift them far from the ground, as the lizard and tortoise. But since certain animals, as deer and goats, seem to fall under none of these classes, the word 'quadrupeds' is added. ST, 666

St. Lawrence of Brindisi, *Explanatio in Genesim,* Ch. 1: Animals designated for the use of men are called 'cattle', as if for assisting human uses. This term includes all types of livestock in herds.

The term 'crawling creatures' denotes all animals with bodies low to the ground, which move themselves not by a thrust but by dragging and which are completely deprived of feet or have feet so small that they cannot lift themselves up on the earth while they walk. Finally, the term 'wild beasts' describes those animals which travel with a thrust and progressive motion; they are untamable and always fierce, and by their very nature they do not know how to be tame, but they spend time and dwell in large forests and rage with the claws and mouth. CF, 77-78

St. Ephrem, *Commentary on Genesis*, Part 1:27: [The earth] also brought forth the beasts of the field as companions to the wild beasts, and it brought forth as many beasts as would be suitable for the service of that one who, on that very day, was to transgress the commandment of his Lord. FCE, 93

St. Basil, *On the Hexameron*, Homily 9:1: When I hear 'grass,' I think of grass, and in the same manner I understand everything as it is said, a plant, a fish, a wild animal, and an ox. FCB, 135

St. Basil, *On the Hexameron*, Homily 9:2: Consider the word of God moving through all creation, having begun at that time, active up to the present, and efficacious until the end, even to the consummation of the world. As a ball, when pushed by someone and then meeting with a slope, is borne downward by its own shape and the inclination of the ground and does not stop before some level surface receives it, so, too, the nature of existing objects, set in motion by one command, passes through creation, without change, by generation and destruction, preserving the succession of the species through resemblance, until it reaches the very end. It begets a horse as the successor of a horse, a lion of a lion, and an eagle of an eagle; and it continues to preserve each of the animals by uninterrupted successions until the consummation of the universe. FCB, 136-37

St. Ambrose, *Hexameron*, Book 6, Ch. 3: In compliance with a fixed law they all succeed each other from age to age according to their aspect and kind. The lion generates a lion; the tiger, a tiger; the ox, an ox; the swan, a swan; and the eagle, an eagle. What was once enjoined became in nature a habit for all time. FCAm, 232

St. Ambrose, *Hexameron*, Book 6, Ch. 3: The original species of living creatures is produced for future ages by successive generations of its kind. FCAm, 232

St. Ambrose, *Hexameron*, Book 3, Ch. 11: For nature maintained in every case through future ages the prerogatives which had been impressed on it at the moment of creation. FCAm, 102

St. Ambrose, *Hexameron*, Book 6, Ch. 5: But let us return to the creation of the different species, and reflect on the reason why the Lord formed some beasts, such as lions, tigers, and bears, with shorter necks, whereas other animals, such as elephants and camels, were created with longer necks. Do we not find clear reason for this in that fact that animals which are carnivorous do not need long necks? They bend down their necks and jaws to the earth in the act of feeding. They use them for waylaying a deer or for dismembering an ox or a sheep. FCAm, 246

St. Ambrose, *Hexameron*, Book 6, Ch. 5: On the other hand, the camel, a taller animal, would be unable to feed on the smallest plants unless in the process of feeding he was able it extend his long neck to the ground. Accordingly, to the camel there has been allotted a neck that is longer in proportion to his stature. This is true, also, in the case of such herbivorous animals as the horse and the ox. The elephant, too, has a prominent trunk; otherwise he would be unable, because of his surpassing size, to reach the ground in order to find pasturage. FCAm, 246

St. Thomas Aquinas, *Summa Theologiae*, I, Q 96, Art 1 ad 2: In the opinion of some, those animals which now are fierce and kill others, would, in that state, have been tame, not only in regard to man, but also in regard to other animals. But this is quite unreasonable. For the nature of animals was not changed by man's sin, as if those whose nature now it is to devour the flesh of others, would then have lived on herbs, as the lion and falcon. Nor does Bede's gloss on Gen. 1:30, say that trees and herbs were given as food to all animals and birds, but to some. Thus there would have been a natural antipathy between some animals. ST, 918

St. Thomas Aquinas, *Summa Theologiae*, I, Q 72, Art 1 ad 6: And since before he sinned man would have used the things of this world conformably to the order designed, poisonous animals would not have injured him. ST, 667

St. Ambrose, *Hexameron*, Book 6, Ch. 3: Take care not to be bent over like cattle. See that you do not incline—not so much physically as they do, but morally. Have regard for the conformation of your body and assume in accordance with it the appearance of loftiness and strength. Leave to animals the sole privilege of feeding in a prone position. FCAm, 233

St. Ambrose, *Hexameron*, Book 6, Ch. 4: There is in the nature of quadrapeds something which the language of the prophetical books exhorts us to imitate. We should follow their example and avoid slothfulness. Neither because of size nor bodily weakness should we desist from our eagerness to carry into effect the lofty aims of a virtuous life.[56] FCAm, 235-36

St. Ambrose, *Hexameron*, Book 6, Ch. 4: The puppy does not yet have his teeth, yet in defense he acts as if he had. FCAm, 244

[56] Ecclus. 43:36-37: "There are many things hidden from us that are greater than these: for we have seen but a few of his works. But the Lord hath made all things, and to the godly he hath given wisdom."

God's Rest

Genesis 2:1: *So the heavens and the earth were finished, and all the furniture of them.*

St. Thomas Aquinas, *Summa Theologiae*, I, Q 73, Art. 1: Now the final perfection, which is the end of the whole universe, is the perfect beatitude of the saints at the consummation of the world. But the first perfection is the completeness of the universe at its first founding and, this, what is ascribed to the seventh day. ST, 669

St. Thomas Aquinas, *Summa Theologiae*, I, Q 73, Art 1 ad 1: So, then, on the seventh day was the consummation of nature, in Christ's Incarnation the consummation of grace, and at the end of the world will be the consummation of glory. ST, 669

St. Irenaeus, *Adversus Haereses*, Book V, Ch. 28:3: For in as many days as this world was made, in so many thousand years shall it be concluded. And for this reason the scripture says: "Thus the heavens and the earth were finished, and all their adornment. And God brought to a conclusion upon the sixth day the works that He had made; and God rested upon the seventh day from all His works" [Gen. 2:2]. This is an account of the things formerly created, as also it is a prophecy of what is to come. "For the day of the Lord is as a thousand years;" [2Pet. 3:8] and in six days created things were completed: it is evident, therefore, that they will come to an end at the sixth thousanth year. WI, Vol. 2, 132

Genesis 2:2: *And on the seventh day God ended his work which he had made: and he rested on the seventh day from all his work which he had done.*

St. Ephrem, *Commentary on Genesis*, Part 1:32: From what toil did God rest? . . . What toil is there for us when we speak one word, that there should be toil for God due to the one word a day that He spoke? FCE, 96

St. Augustine, *City of God*, Book XI, Ch. 8: When it is said that God rested on the seventh day from all His works, and hallowed it, we are not to conceive of this in a childish fashion, as if the work were a toil to God, who "spake and it was done"—spake by the spiritual and eternal, not audible and transitory word. SA, Vol. 2, 209

St. Bonaventure, *Breviloquium*, Part II, Ch. 2:1: On the seventh day, God rested, not from activity and work, since he continues to work to this very hour, but from the production of any new species. For God made all things then [during the six days of the Genesis account]—either in their prototypes, as is the case with those that propagate themselves, or in a seminal reason, as with other things that come into existence in a different way. Brev, 63

St. Thomas Aquinas, *Summa Theologiae*, I, Q 73, Art 1 ad 2: God did not act on the seventh day, not by creating new creatures, but by directing and moving His creatures to the work proper to them; and thus He made some beginning of the *second* perfection. ST, 669

St. Thomas Aquinas, *Summa Theologiae*, I, Q 73, Art 1 ad 2: Now God might have made many other creatures besides those which He made in the six days; and hence, by the fact that He ceased making them on the seventh day, He is said on that day to have consummated His work. ST, 669

St. Lawrence of Brindisi, *Explanatio in Genesim*, Ch. 2: Why is it that *He rested*? Was he wearied from working? Rather He rested because He ceased making any new creature. CF, 101

St. Augustine, *De Genesi ad litteram*, Book V, 23: God, then, creates no new creatures, but He directs and rules by His governance of the world all the things He made together, and thus He works without ceasing, resting and working at the same time. LMG, Vol. 1, 176

St. Lawrence of Brindisi, *Explanatio in Genesim*, Ch. 2: Therefore *He rested* on the seventh day, in order that he might not make a new creature, and He *works until now*, in order that He might not cease to control and govern that which he created. CF, 101

St. Thomas Aquinas, *Summa Theologiae*, I, Q 73, Art 2: God is said to have rested on the seventh day. First, because He ceased from creating new creatures on that day, for as was said above, He made nothing afterwards that had not existed previously, in some degree, in the first works; secondly, because He Himself has no need of the things that He had made, but was happy in the fruition of Himself. Hence, when all things were made He is not said to have rested *in* His works, as though needing them for His own happiness, but to have rested *from* them, as in fact resting in Himself, since He suffices for Himself and fulfills His own desire. ST, 671

St. Augustine, *De Genesi ad litteram*, Book IV, Ch. 15: God has never, of course, lacked this rest, but He has shown it to us by means of the seventh day. Hence He has at the same time shown us that rest in Him is not enjoyed except by the perfect, since in revealing His rest to us He chose only the day that followed the perfecting of all creation. LMG, Vol. 1, 121

St. Augustine, *De Genesi ad litteram*, Book IV, Ch. 15: For God, who is always in a state of tranquility, has rested, as far as we are concerned, at that time when He has revealed Himself to us as resting. LMG, Vol. 1, 121

St. Thomas Aquinas, *Summa Theologiae*, I, Q 74, Art 2 ad 3: On the seventh day God ceased from making new beings, but not from providing for their increase, and to this latter work belongs that the first day is succeeded by other days. ST, 677

St. Ambrose, *Hexameron*, Book 6, Ch. 8: Moreover, He did not find rest when He had created such irrational creatures as fish and the various species of wild beasts. He found rest, however, after He had created man to His own image. FCAm, 261

St. Ambrose, *Hexameron*, Book 6, Ch. 8: He who does not find rest in the beasts of the field will much less find repose in his bestial heart. FCAm, 262

St. Ambrose, *Hexameron*, Book 6, Ch. 10: He found repose in the deep recesses of man, in man's mind and purpose, for He had made man with the power of reasoning, an imitator of Himself, a striver after virtue, and one eager for heavenly grace. FCAm, 282

St. Ambrose, *Hexameron*, Book 6, Ch. 10: But I do read that He made man and then found rest in one whose sins He would remit. It may well be that He had given a symbolic picture then of the future Passion of the Lord, thus revealing that in man one day Christ would find repose. FCAm, 282

St. Ambrose, *Hexameron*, Book 6, Ch. 10: He anticipated for Himself repose [of death] in the body for the redemption of mankind, as He declares in His own words: "I have slept and taken my rest and I have risen up, because the Lord hath protected me" [Ps. 3:6]. FCAm, 282-83

Genesis 2:3: *And he blessed the seventh day, and sanctified it: because in it he had rested from all his work which God created and made.*

St. Lawrence of Brindisi, *Explanatio in Genesim*, Ch. 2: God desired man to sanctify this day by worshipping God. CF, 102

St. Ephrem, *Commentary on Genesis*, Part 1:33: For it was given to them in order to depict by a temporal rest, which He gave to a temporal people, the mystery of the true rest which will be given to the eternal people in the eternal world. FCE, 96

St. Thomas Aquinas, *Summa Theologiae*, I, Q 73, Art 3 ad 3: The good mentioned in the works of each day belongs to the first institution of nature; but the blessing attached to the seventh day, to its propagation. ST, 672

St. Augustine, *Contra Faustum*, Book XVI, 29: Unless Christ had considered this Sabbath—which in your want of knowledge and of piety you laugh at—one of the prophecies written of Himself, He would not have borne such a testimony to it as He did. For when, as you say in praise of Christ, He suffered voluntarily, and so could choose His own time for suffering and for resurrection, He brought it about that His body rested from all its works on the Sabbath in the tomb, and that His resurrection on the third day, which we call the Lord's day, the day after the Sabbath, and therefore the eighth, proved the circumcision of the eighth day to be prophetical of Him. MH, 309

St. Augustine, *Contra Faustum*, Book XIX, 9: For we have our Sabbath in Him who said, "Come unto me, all ye that labor and are heavy laden, and I will give you rest. Take my yoke upon you and learn of me; for I am meek and lowly in heart, and ye shall find rest unto your souls" [Mt. 11:28-29]. MH, 334-35

St. Augustine, *City of God*, Book XI, Ch. 8: But God's rest signifies the rest of those who rest in God, as the joy of a house means the joy of those in the house who rejoice, though not the house, but something else, causes the joy. SA, Vol. 2, 209

St. Augustine, *City of God*, Book XI, Ch. 8: Most appropriately, therefore, the sacred narrative states that God rested, meaning thereby that those rest who are in Him and whom He makes to rest. And this the prophetic narrative promises also to the men to whom it speaks, and for whom it is written, that they themselves, after those good works which God does in and by them, if they have managed by faith to get near to God in this life, shall enjoy in Him eternal rest. SA, Vol. 2, 209

St. Anthony of Padua, *Sermon on Septuagesima*, 11: On the seventh day, God rested from all his works. Even so the Church rests in the seventh article of faith from all her labor and sweat. Then "God shall wipe every tear from her eyes" [Apoc. 21:4], that is to say, every cause of weeping. Then she will be praised by her Spouse, and be found worthy to hear the words: "Give her of the fruit of her hands, and let her works praise her in the gates" [Prov. 31:31]. SSA, 17

St. Augustine, *City of God*, Book XI, Ch. 8: This was pre-figured to the ancient people of God by the rest enjoined in their sabbath law. SA, Vol. 2, 209

The Second Account

Genesis 2:4: *These are the generations of the heaven and the earth, when they were created, in the day that the Lord God made the heaven and the earth: . . .*

St. Lawrence of Brindisi, *Explanatio in Genesim*, Ch. 2: In the generation of heaven and earth, this verse comprehends whatever was said and written above as a kind of epilogue and summary. . . generation must be understood as creation, again after we find the words "When they were created"—produced *ex nihilo* by the infinite power of the Artisan "In the day He created", or as it reasons in the original, "In the day the Lord God made the heaven and the earth". CF, 104

St. Augustine, *De Genesi ad litteram*, Book V, Ch. 11: In the first instance, God made everything together without any moments of time intervening, but now He works within the course of time, by which we see the stars move from their rising to their setting, the weather change from summer to winter, and in a fixed number of days the seeds sprout forth, grow, flourish, and wither away. LMG, Vol. 1, 162

St. Augustine, *De Genesi ad litteram*, Book V, Ch. 11: Hence, between the things made by God from which He rested on the seventh day and those which He now works, scripture has placed a division in the narrative and has told us that God has finished the first works of creation and has now begun to produce the later works. This is made clear in the words, "This is the book of the creation of heaven and earth . . ." [Cf. Gen. 2:4–5]. LMG, Vol. 1, 162-63

St. Ephrem, *Commentary on Genesis*, Part 2:1: After Moses spoke of the sabbath rest, of how God blessed and sanctified this day, he returned to the account of how Creation was first fashioned, briefly passing over those things of which he had already spoken, while recounting in detail those things he had left out. He then began to write about the creation a second time, saying, "These are the generations..." FCE, 97

Genesis 2:5: *And every plant of the field before it sprung up in the earth, and every herb of the ground before it grew: for the Lord God had not rained upon the earth.*

St. Ephrem, *Commentary on Genesis*, Part 2:2: This is the account of the fashioning of heaven and earth for as yet "no tree of the field existed and no vegetation had sprouted". FCE, 97

St. Thomas Aquinas, *Summa Theologiae*, I, Q 74, Art 2 ad 1: He created also every plant of the field, not indeed, actually, but "before it sprung up in the earth", that is, potentially. And this work Augustine ascribes to the third day, but other writers to the first establishment of the world. ST, 677

St. Augustine, *De Genesi ad litteram*, Book VIII, Ch. 3: For when scripture says that on the third day earth produced these trees, this was done in causes in the earth, that is, earth in the hidden recesses of its being had then received the power of producing them, and by this power even now earth puts forth similar trees to be seen in their own time. LMG, Vol. 2, 37

St. Augustine, *De Genesi ad litteram*, Book VIII, Ch. 3: But since the trees planted in paradise are of the kinds which earth had already produced on the third day, it again produced them in its own time. LMG, Vol. 2, 37

St. John Damascene, *De Fide Orthodoxa*, Book 2, Ch. 10: At that time, the earth brought forth of itself fruits for the use of the animals that were subject to man, and there were neither violent rains upon the earth nor wintry storms. FCD, 229

Genesis 2:5: . . . *and there was not a man to till the earth.*

St. Ephrem, *Commentary on Genesis*, Part 2:4: After [Moses] spoke about those things that had been omitted and that had not been recounted on the first day, he turned to write about how Adam was fashioned saying, "Adam was not there to till the earth". Obviously Adam did not exist in the days that preceded the sixth day, since he was created on the sixth day. FCE, 98-99

St. Augustine, *De Genesi ad litteram*, Book VIII, Ch. 3: Then Scripture recapitulates in order to show how God did what has been mentioned very briefly, that is, how He planted paradise and put there man whom He had formed. LMG, Vol. 2, 36

St. Augustine, *City of God*, Book XII, Ch. 10: For some hold the same opinion regarding men that they hold regarding the world itself, that they have always been. SA, Vol. 2, 232

St. Augustine, *City of God*, Book XII, Ch. 12: For the past and boundless eternity during which God abstained from creating man is so great that, compare it with what vast and untold number of ages you please, so long as there is a definite conclusion of this term of time, it is not even as if you compared the minutest drop of water with the ocean that everywhere flows around the globe. SA, Vol. 2, 233

St. Ambrose, *Hexameron*, Book 1, Ch. 8: Correctly, then was the land called unformed which was devoid of ornament and which did not present to view the linked rows of budding vine shoots. God wished to show us that the world itself would have no attraction unless a husbandman had improved it with varied culture. FCAm, 31

St. Ambrose, *Hexameron*, Book 3, Ch. 10: Of itself the earth brought forth profusely all kinds of fruits. Although it could not be ploughed in the absence of a cultivator—for the farmer had not yet been created—the earth, though unplowed, teemed with rich harvests, inasmuch as an indolent husbandman did not have occasion to defraud the earth of its abundance. FCAm, 100-1

St. John Damascene, *De Fide Orthodoxa*, Book 2, Ch. 11: Since God intended to fashion man after His own image and likeness from the visible and invisible creation to be a sort of king over the whole earth and the things in it, He prepared a sort of kingdom for him, in which he might dwell and lead a blessed and blissful life. FCD, 230

St. John Damascene, *De Fide Orthodoxa*, Book 2, Ch. 11: And this divine paradise prepared in *Eden* by the hands of God was a treasure-house of every joy and pleasure. FCD, 230

Genesis 2:6: *But a spring rose out of the earth, watering all the surface of the earth.*

St. Augustine, *De Genesi ad litteram*, Book V, Ch. 11: From the mention of this spring and subsequently throughout the narrative that follows, creatures are made in intervals of time, not all together. LMG, Vol. 1, 163

St. Lawrence of Brindisi, *Explanatio in Genesim*, Ch. 2: the Hebrew original has, "And a mist will rise up and will water all the surface of the earth". As a result, it does not refer to the production of the plants and fruits that took place on the third day, but to the production that will afterwards take place by the power of Nature. CF, 108

St. Lawrence of Brindisi, *Explanatio in Genesim*, Ch. 2: A mist will ascend, and, condensed into water in the clouds of heaven, rain will be made, and it will water the entire surface of the earth. Infusing the earth with watery moisture, the rain will make it fruitful. CF, 108

Chapter Two
The Creation of Man and Woman

The Special Creation of Man

St. Ephrem, *Commentary on Genesis*, Prologue: 5: And after [Moses] said, "This is the book of the generations of heaven and earth," he turned back and recounted those things that he had left out and not written about in the first account. FCE, 69

St. John Chrysostom, *Homilies on Genesis*, Homily 12:4: What I refer to is this: notice sacred scripture taught us in detail in the preceding verses the creation of everything, but now, instead of mentioning them all, it says: "This is the book about the origins of heaven and earth when they were created, on the day God made heaven and earth," and so on. FCC, 158

St. Augustine, *De Genesi contra Manichaeos,* Book 2, Ch. 7: After mentioning all creation both visible and invisible and the universal gift of the divine spring with regard to the invisible creature, let us see what it says of man in particular, for this especially pertains to us. FCA, 102

St. John Chrysostom. *Homilies on Genesis*, Homily 12:11: Since he had briefly said above, "God made the human being; in God's image he made them," he now says, "God shaped the human being from the dust of the earth, and breathed into him the breath of life; the human being became alive." FCC, 163

St. Bede, *In principium Genesis*, Book I: In this verse, the creation of man who was indeed made on the sixth day is more fully described. OG, 140

St. Irenaeus, *Adversus Haereses*, Book IV, Ch. 14:1: In the beginning, therefore, did God form Adam, not as if He stood in need of man, but that He might have [someone] upon whom to confer His benefits. For not alone antecedently to Adam, but also before all creation, the Word glorified His Father, remaining in Him; and was Himself glorified by the Father, as He did Himself declare, "Father, glorify Me with the glory which I had with You before the world was" [Jn. 17:5]. WI, Vol. 1, 416

The First Man

Genesis 1:26: *And he said: Let us make man to our image and likeness . . .*

St. Ambrose, *Hexameron*, Book 6, Ch. 7: To whom does He speak? Surely not to Himself, because He does not say: "I shall make," but "let us make." He does not speak to the angels, because they are servers, and servants cannot have a part in the work along with their master and creator. FCAm, 253

St. Irenaeus, *Adversus Haereses*, Book IV, Ch. 20:1: It was not angels, therefore, who made us, nor who formed us, neither had angels power to make an image of God, nor any one else, except the Word of the Lord, nor any power remotely distant from the Father of all things. WI, Vol. 1, 439

St. Ephrem, *Commentary on Genesis*, Part 1:28: But to whom was God speaking? Here, as in every place where he creates, it is clear that He was speaking to His Son. FCE, 93-94

St. Thomas Aquinas, *Summa Theologiae*, I, Q 91, Art 4 ad 2: We must not imagine that when God said "Let us make man", He spoke to the angels, as some perversely thought. But by these words is signified the plurality of the divine persons, Whose image is more clearly expressed in man.[57] ST, 877

St. Irenaeus, *Adversus Haereses*, Book IV, Ch. 20:1: For with Him were always present the Word and Wisdom, the Son and the Spirit, by whom and in whom, freely and spontaneously, He made all things, to whom also He speaks, saying "Let us make man after our image and likeness;" [Gen. 1:26] He taking from Himself the substance of the creatures [formed], and the pattern of things made, and the type of all adornments in the world. WI, Vol. 1, 439

St. Lawrence of Brindisi, *Explanatio in Genesim*, Ch. 1: This phrase, as the holiest men and most learned commentators have asserted, references the plurality of the divine persons and is the utterance of the Father to the Son and the Holy Ghost inasmuch as the outward operation of all the divine Persons is one and undivided. CF, 83

St. Ambrose, *Hexameron*, Book 6, Ch. 7: He speaks, rather, to the Son, although the Jews are unwilling to accept this and the Arians object to it. FCAm, 253

St. Ambrose, *Hexameron*, Book 6, Ch. 7: When He says "let us make," how can there be inequality? FCAm, 254

St. Basil, *On the Hexameron*, Homily 9:6: What coppersmith or carpenter or shoemaker, sitting down alone among the tools of his craft,

[57] 2Cor. 4:4: "Christ, who is the image of God."

with no one helping him, says to himself; "Let us make a sword," or "Let us construct a plow," or "Let us make a shoe"? Does he not rather accomplish the work undertaken in silence? Truly, it is utter nonsense for anyone to sit down and command and watch over himself, and imperiously and vehemently urge himself on. FCB, 147

St. Lawrence of Brindisi, *Explanatio in Genesim*, Ch. 1: This referred to Christ, who is God, in whose image man was especially created so that He might form man to that image which the Lord had created by His predetermination, as it is written, "From the beginning, and before the world, was I created" [Prov. 8:22–23], and Christ Himself was the archetype of human nature. CF, 90

St. Lawrence of Brindisi, *Explanatio in Genesim*, Ch. 1: However, the Christ was determined, not according to divine nature, but human nature, because the divine mind before everything else conceived the form that the Word-to-be-Incarnate would receive. CF, 90

St. Irenaeus, *Adversus Haereses*, Book V, Ch. 16:2: And then, again, this Word was manifested when the Word of God was made man, assimilating Himself to man, and man to Himself, so that by means of his resemblance to the Son, man might become precious to the Father. For in times long past, it was *said* that man was created after the image of God, but it was not [actually] *shown*; for the Word was as yet invisible, after whose image man was created, wherefore also he did easily lose the similitude. When, however, the Word of God became flesh, He confirmed both these: for He both showed forth the image truly, since He became Himself what was His image; and He re-established the similitude after a sure manner, by assimilating man to the invisible Father through means of the visible Word. WI, Vol. 2, 99

St. John Damascene, *De Fide Orthodoxa*, Book 2, Ch. 12: From the earth He formed His body, and by His own inbreathing gave him a rational and understanding soul, which last we say is the divine image—for the "according to His image" means the intellect and free will, while the "according to His likeness" means such likeness in virtue as is possible. FCD, 235

St. Ambrose, *Hexameron*, Book 6, Ch. 7: But let the Jews preserve silence and let the Arians with their progenitors be mute, who, while they exclude the One from sharing in the divine work, introduce more participants and grant to underlings a privilege which they deny to the Son. FCAm, 253

St. Ambrose, *Hexameron*, Book 6, Ch. 7: The 'image' of God is virtue, not infirmity. The 'image' of God is wisdom. The 'image' of God is He alone who has said: "I and the Father are one," thus possessing the likeness of the Father so as to have a unity of divinity and of plenitude. FCAm, 254

St. Ambrose, *Hexameron*, Book 6, Ch. 7: Adam before he sinned conformed to this image. But after his fall he lost that celestial image and took on one that is terrestrial. FCAm, 255

Body and Soul Together

St. Irenaeus, *Adversus Haereses*, Book IV, Preface: Now man is a mixed organization of soul and flesh, who was formed after the likeness of God, and moulded by His hands, that is, by the Son and the Holy Spirit, to whom also He said, "Let us make man." WI, Vol. 1, 377

St. Lawrence of Brindisi, *Explanatio in Genesim*, Ch. 1: When He came to man, he did not say, "Let the earth bring forth" but "let us make". Even if the body of man came from original matter, nevertheless his soul, which is the noblest of forms, was not produced from there but by its very nature was created by God. In so far as man is man, he is endowed with a rational soul, and he lives by sense and reason. For this reason, scripture says, "Let us make man". CF, 83

St. Thomas Aquinas, *Summa Theologiae*, I, Q 91, Art 4 ad 3: Some have thought that man's body was formed first in priority of time, and that afterwards a soul was infused into an already formed body. ST, 877

St. John Damascene, *De Fide Orthodoxa*, Book 2, Ch. 12: The body and soul were formed at the same time—not one before and the other afterwards, as the ravings of Origen would have it. FCD, 235

St. Irenaeus, *Adversus Haereses*, Book V, Ch. 6:1: For that flesh which has been moulded is not a perfect man in itself, but the body of a man, and part of a man. Neither is the soul itself, considered apart by itself, the man; but it is the soul of a man, and part of a man. Neither is the spirit a man, for it is called the spirit, and not a man; but the commingling and union of all these constitutes the perfect man. WI, Vol. 2, 68-69

St. Thomas Aquinas, *Summa Theologiae*, I, Q 91, Art 4 ad 3: But it is inconsistent with the perfection of the first production of things that God should have made either the body without the soul, or the soul without the body, since each is a part of human nature. ST, 877

St. John Damascene, *De Fide Orthodoxa*, Book 2, Ch. 12: "But, as a mark of greater wisdom and if His munificence toward created natures, it was also necessary that a combination of both substances should be made," as the inspired Gregory says, "as a sort of bond between the visible and invisible natures." FCD, 234

St. John Damascene, *De Fide Orthodoxa*, Book 2, Ch. 12: Since this was the case, with His own hands He created *man* after His own image and likeness from the visible and invisible natures. FCD, 234-35

St. Thomas Aquinas, *Summa Theologiae*, I, Q 91, Art 4 ad 3: This is especially unfitting as regards the body, for the body depends on the soul, and not the soul on the body. ST, 877

St. John Damascene, *De Fide Orthodoxa*, Book 2, Ch. 12: Now, a soul is a living substance, simple and incorporeal, of its own nature invisible to bodily eyes, activating an organic body in which it is able to cause life, growth, sensation, and reproduction. It does not have the mind as something distinct from itself, but as its purest part, for, as the eye is to the body, so is the mind to the soul. It is free, endowed with will and the power to act, and subject to change, that is, subject to change of will, because it is also created. FCD, 236

St. John Damascene, *De Fide Orthodoxa*, Book 2, Ch. 12: One should note that man has something in common with inanimate things, that he shares life with the rational living beings, and that he shares understanding with the rational. In common with inanimate things, he has his body and its composition from the four elements. In common with the plants, he has these same things plus the power of assimilating nourishment, of growing and of semination of generation. In common with the brute beasts, he has all these plus appetite—that is to say, anger and desire—sensation, and spontaneous movement. FCD, 237

St. Thomas Aquinas, *Summa Theologiae*, I, Q 91, Art 4 ad 5: According to St. Augustine . . . on the sixth day itself both the soul of the first man was made actually, and his body was made in its caussal principles. But other doctors hold that on the sixth day both the body and soul of man were made actually. ST, 877–78

St. Augustine, *De Genesi ad litteram*, Book VII, Ch. 24: Let us assume that man was made on the sixth day in the sense that the causal reason of his body was created in the elements of the world, but that his soul in its own proper being was already created with the making of the first day, and that thus created it lay hidden in the works of God until at the proper time He would breathe it into the body He would form from the slime of the earth. LMG, Vol. 2, 26

St. Augustine, *De Genesi ad litteram*, Book VI, Ch. 6: Later visibly, in the form of the human body familiar to us; not, however, generated by parents, but man formed from the slime of the earth and the woman from his rib. LMG, Vol. 1, 184–85

St. Gregory of Nyssa, *On the Making of Man*, Ch. 29:2: For as our nature is conceived as twofold, according to the apostolic teaching made up of the visible and the hidden man, if the one came first and the other supervened, the power of Him who made us will be shown to be in some way imperfect, as not being completely sufficient for the whole task at once, but dividing the work, and busying itself with each of the halves in turn. NPNF, Vol. V, 421

St. Gregory of Nyssa, *On the Making of Man*, Ch. 29:3: So it is not true to say either that the soul exists before the body or that the body exists without the soul, but there is one beginning of both, which according to the heavenly view was laid as their foundation in the will of God; according to the other, came into existence on the occasion of generation. NPNF, Vol. V, 421

St. Augustine, *City of God*, Book XII, Ch. 27: These works of God do certainly seem extraordinary, because they are the first works. They who do not believe them, ought not to believe any prodigies; for these would not be called prodigies did they not happen out of the ordinary course of nature. SA, Vol. 2, 244

Genesis 1:26: *And let him have dominion over the fishes of the sea, and the fowls of the air, and the beasts, and the whole earth, and every creeping creature that moveth upon the earth.*

St. Ephrem, *Commentary on Genesis*, Part 1:29: It is the dominion that Adam received over the earth and over all that is in it that constitutes the likeness of God Who has dominion over the heavenly things and the earthly things. FCE, 94

St. John Damascene, *De Fide Orthodoxa*, Book 2, Ch. 10: Before the fall, all things were subject to the control of man, because God made him ruler over all the things on the earth and in the water. FCD, 228-29

St. Lawrence of Brindisi, *Explanatio in Genesim*, Ch. 1: Nevertheless, I say that dominion of this sort is natural to man. Man is by his nature more eminent, more noble, and more perfect. The more imperfect things are always directed and ordered to the more perfect, as to the purposes and the things they serve: the earth serves plants, plants serve animals, and all these things serve man.[58] CF, 89

St. Lawrence of Brindisi, *Explanatio in Genesim*, Ch. 1: Even though in virtue of that first fault, the source of everything else that followed, man actually was stripped of the power to have dominion over a number of animals that rage against man and threaten men's lives, he nonetheless never lost the right of having dominion over all things. CF, 89

St. Ambrose, *Hexameron*, Book 6, Ch. 7: This is the means by which men lord it over other living things, wild beasts, and birds. Your soul is made to the image of God, whereas your body is related to the beasts. In one there is the holy seal of imitation of the divine. In the other there is found base association with beasts and wild animals. FCAm, 256

St. Augustine, *De Genesi ad litteram*, Book III, Ch. 20: From this we are to understand that man was made to the image of God in that part of his nature wherein he surpasses the brute beasts. This is, of course, his reason, or mind, or intelligence, or whatever we wish to call it. LMG, Vol. 1, 96

---

[58] Jas. 3:7: "For every nature of beasts and of birds and of serpents and of the rest is tamed by and hath been tamed by the nature of man."

St. Thomas Aquinas, *Summa Theologiae*, I, Q 3, Art. 1 ad 2: Man is said to be in the image of God, not as regards his body, but as regards that whereby he excels other animals. Hence, when it is said, "Let us make man to our image and likeness", it is added, "And let him have dominion over the fishes of the sea" (Gen. 1:26). Now man excels all animals by his reason and intellect; hence it is according to his intellect and reason, which are incorporeal, that man is said to be in the image of God. ST, 27

St. Gregory of Nyssa, *On the Making of Man*, Ch. 7:1: But what means the uprightness of his figure? and why is it that these powers which aid life do not naturally belong to his body? but man is brought into life bare of natural covering, an unarmed and poor being, destitute of all things useful, worthy, according to appearances, of pity rather than of admiration, not armed with prominent horns or sharp claws, nor with hoofs nor with teeth, nor possessing by nature any deadly venom in a sting—things such as most animals have in their own power for defence against those who do them harm: his body is not protected with a covering of hair: and yet possibly it was to be expected that he who was promoted to rule over the rest of creatures should be defended by nature with arms of his own so that he might not need assistance from others for his own security. NPNF, Vol. V, 392

St. Thomas Aquinas, *Summa Theologiae*, I, Q 76, Art. 5 ad 4: Instead of all these, man has by nature his reason and his hands, which are *the organs of organs*, since by their means man can make for himself instruments of an infinite variety, and for any number of purposes. ST, 712

St. Gregory of Nyssa, *On the Making of Man*, Ch. 7:2: Well, I think it would not be at all hard to show that what seems to be a deficiency of our nature is a means for our obtaining dominion over the subject creatures. NPNF, Vol. V, 392

Genesis 1:27: *And God created man to his own image: to the image of God he created him: male and female he created them.*

St. Thomas Aquinas, *Summa Theologiae*, I, Q 93, Art. 6 ad 2: Therefore we must observe that when Scripture had said, "to the image of God He created him", it added, "male and female He created them", not to imply that the image of God came through the distinction of sex, but that the image of God belongs to both sexes, since it is in the mind, wherein there is no distinction of sexes. ST, 894

St. Augustine, *De Genesi ad litteram*, Book III, Ch. 22: Scripture says merely, "God made man to the image of God". And, lest anyone think that this refers only to the creation of man's spirit, although it was only according to the spirit that he was made to the image of God, Scripture adds, "Male and female He made them", to indicate that the body was also now made. LMG, Vol. 1, 99

St. Ephrem, *Commentary on Genesis*, Part 1:29: Then [Moses] said, "male and female He created" them, to make known that Eve was inside Adam, in the rib that was drawn out from him. Although she was not in his mind, she was in his body, and she was not only in his body with him, but she was also in soul and spirit with him, for God added nothing to that rib that He took out except the structure and adornment. FCE, 94

Genesis 2:7: *And the Lord God formed man of the slime of the earth: and breathed into his face the breath of life, and man became a living soul.*

St. Lawrence of Brindisi, *Explanatio in Genesim*, Ch. 1: I affirm that when the Lord said "Let us make man", by 'man' He understood the first man, and in him all human nature was altogether, as if we were all contained in him, from whom we were to be propagated afterwards. CF, 84

St. Ambrose, *Hexameron*, Book 5, Ch. 7: At the beginning, God formed two creatures, Adam and Eve; that is, man and his wife. He formed woman from the man; that is, from the rib of Adam. He bade them both to live in one body and in one spirit. FCAm, 175

St. Bede, *In principium Genesis*, Book I: Plainly in this statement any carnal interpretation should be avoided, lest by chance we would think that God had formed the body of man from the dust of the earth with corporeal hands or that He had breathed into his nostrils with His mouth or lips so that man could live and have the breath of life. OG, 140

St. Ambrose, *Hexameron*, Book 6, Ch. 7: But let us consider the precise order of our creation. "Let us make mankind," He said, "in our image and likeness." FCAm, 253

St. Irenaeus, *Adversus Haereses*, Book IV, Ch. 20:1: For God did not stand in need of these [beings], in order to the accomplishing of what He had Himself determined with Himself beforehand should be done, as if He did not possess His own hands. For with Him were always present the Word and Wisdom, the Son and the Spirit, by whom and in whom, freely and spontaneously, He made all things, to whom also He speaks, saying, "Let Us make man after Our image and likeness;" [Gen. 1:26] He taking from Himself the substance of the creatures [formed], and the pattern of things made, and the type of all the adornments in the world. WI, Vol. 1, 439

St. Lawrence of Brindisi, *Explanatio in Genesim*, Ch. 1: "Therefore, God created man in the image of the God" the Christ, namely in that form and figure which had been predetermined for the Christ, the Son of God, before the formation of all the creatures, Whom St. Paul calls "the firstborn of every creature, in whom were created all things". Man, the noblest creature of the world, was formed and produced according to that pre-formed semblance in the divine mind, which the Word would assume. CF, 90-91

Man's Soul

St. Thomas Aquinas, *Summa Theologiae*, I, Q 91, Art 4 ad 4: Since vital operations are more clearly seen in man's face, because of the senses which are there found, therefore scripture says that the breath of life was breathed into man's face. ST, 877

St. Augustine, *De Genesi ad litteram*, Book VII, Ch. 17: Thus, the face along with the rest of the body has the sense of touch, but the senses of sight, hearing, smell, and taste are found only in the face. LMG, Vol. 2, 18

St. Lawrence of Brindisi, *Explanatio in Genesim* Ch. 2: God breathed "into his face" the breath of life because all the senses are perceived to flourish in the face and from there reason and intellect are noted, and, in the face, internal emotions are manifested. CF, 111

St. Thomas Aquinas, *Summa Theologiae*, I, Q 94, Art 2: For in the state of innocence, man's soul was adapted to the work of perfecting and governing the body, even as now. Hence, the first man is said to have been made into a "living soul" (Gen. 2:7), that is, a soul giving life to the body—namely, animal life. ST, 905

St. Thomas Aquinas, *Summa Theologiae*, I, Q 91, Art 4 ad 3: For we read further on, "And man was made into a living soul"; which words the Apostle (I Cor. 14:45) refers not to spiritual life, but to animal life. Therefore, by the "breath of life" we must understand the soul, so that the words, "He breathed into his face the breath of life", are a sort of exposition of what had gone before; for the soul is the form of the body. ST, 877

St. Lawrence of Brindisi, *Explanatio in Genesim*, Ch. 2: Perhaps "Man became a living being" may mean he became a "living animal", since after breath was put into his lifeless body that had already been formed, man became a living animal: Neither the body nor the soul is an animal but from the soul and body together (for the former informing and the latter capable of being informed, so to speak), this rational animal, man, exists. CF, 111

St. Lawrence of Brindisi, *Explanatio in Genesim*, Ch. 2: In sacred scripture it is very usual for the word 'soul' to be taken for the entire body-soul composite. CF, 111-12

St. Thomas Aquinas, *Summa Theologiae*, I, Q 90, Art. 4: For it is clear that God made the first things in their perfect natural state, as their species required. Now the soul, as part of human nature, has its natural perfection only as united to the body. Therefore it would have been unfitting for the soul to be created without the body. ST, 869

St. Bonaventure, *Breviloquium*, Part IV, Ch. 3:5: Now, of the four possible ways of producing a human being, three had already been employed: first, out of neither man nor woman, as with Adam; then, out of man but not woman, as with Eve; third, out of both man and woman, as with all those born of concupiscence. And so, for the completeness of the universe, it was fitting that a fourth way be introduced: out of woman without the seed of a man, through the power of the supreme maker. Brev, 142

St. Thomas Aquinas, *Summa Theologiae*, III, Q 31, Art. 4: For the first man was produced from the slime of the earth, without man or woman; Eve, however, was produced out of man without a woman; but other men are born from man and woman. Whence this fourth manner was left as it were to Christ, that he should be produced from woman without a man.[59] STC, 2617

[59] My translation: *Nam primus homo productus est ex limo terrae sine viro et femina; Heva vero producta est ex viro sine femina; ceteri vero homines producuntur ex viro et femina. Unde hoc quartum quasi Christo proprium relinquebatur, ut produceretur ex femina sine viro.*

St. Cyril of Jerusalem, *Catecheses*, 12,29: Eve having been born from Adam's side without a mother, Jesus Christ was born from His Mother without a father. FG. 112

St. Irenaeus, *Adversus Haereses*, Book III, Ch. 21:10: And as the protoplast himself, Adam had his substance from untilled and as yet virgin soil ("for God had not yet sent rain, and man had not tilled the ground" [Gen. 2:5]), and was formed by the hand of God, that is, by the Word of God, for "all things were made by Him," [Jn. 1:3] and the Lord took dust from the earth and formed man; so did He who is the Word, recapitulating Adam in Himself, rightly receive a birth, enabling Him to gather up Adam [into Himself], from Mary, who was as yet a virgin. If, then, the first Adam had a man for his father, and was born of human seed, it were reasonable to say that the second Adam was begotten of Joseph. But if the former was taken from the dust, and God was his maker, it was incumbent that the latter also, making a recapitulation in Himself, should be formed as man by God, to have an analogy with the former as respects His origin. Why, then, did not God again take dust, but wrought so that the formation should be made of Mary? It was that there might not be another formation called into being, nor any other which should [require to] be saved, but that the very same formation should be summed up [in Christ as had existed in Adam], the analogy having been preserved. WI, Vol. 1, 358-59

St. Augustine, *De Genesi ad litteram*, Book VI, Ch. 13: The one characteristic that distinguishes Adam from other men is that he was not born of parents but made from the earth. LMG, Vol. 1, 194

St. Augustine, *De Genesi ad litteram*, Book VI, Ch. 13: Now did the Lord need a vine or earth or this passage of time when, without any aids, He changed water into wine, and such wine that even the guest who had had his fill would praise it? Did the author of time need the help of time? LMG, Vol. 1, 195

St. Augustine, *De Genesi ad litteram,* Book VI, Ch. 15: On the other hand, if in the causal reasons God placed only the potentiality for man's creation in whatever way he would be created, in one way or the other (that is, if He determined in the causal reasons that it could be either one way or the other, and if He reserved to His own will the one way in which He would subsequently create him rather than foreordaining this in nature), it is obvious that this supposition also was made in a manner contrary to what was in the first creation of causes. LMG, Vol. 1, 197

St. Augustine, *De Genesi ad litteram,* Book VI, Ch. 14: Or did He provide that through these reasons creatures would be fully formed instantaneously, as Adam is believed to have been made an adult man without any previous period of development? LMG, Vol. 1, 195

St. Augustine, *De Genesi ad litteram,* Book VI, Ch. 14: But why can we not assume that the causal reasons had both potentialities, so that from them would come whatever would have pleased the creator? For if we take the first hypothesis referred to above, certain facts present themselves to contradict our explanation of the causal reasons, such as the case of water made wine already mentioned, and all miracles that happen against the ordinary course of nature. LMG, Vol. 1, 195-96

St. Augustine, *De Genesi ad litteram,* Book VI, Ch. 14: But if we take the second hypothesis, our position will be even more absurd in that the forms and appearances of nature we observe every day would be passing through periods of time in their development contrary to the original causes governing the production of all organisms. LMG, Vol. 1, 196

St. Augustine, *De Genesi ad litteram,* Book VI, Ch. 14: We must conclude, then, that these reasons were created to exercise their causality in either one way or the other; by providing for the ordinary development of new creatures in appropriate periods of time, or by providing for the rare occurrence of a miraculous production of a creature, in accordance with what God wills proper to the occasion. LMG, Vol. 1, 196

St. Thomas Aquinas, *Summa Theologiae,* I, Q 92, Art. 2 ad 2: On the other hand, the divine power, being infinite, can produce things of the same species out of any matter, such as a man from the slime of the earth, and a woman from a man. ST, 882

St. Clement of Rome, *First Letter to the Corinthians,* Ch. 33: Above all, with His holy and undefiled hands He formed man, the most excellent [of His creatures], and truly great through the understanding given him—the express likeness of His own image.[60] AF, 30

St. Lawrence of Brindisi, *Explanatio in Genesim,* Ch. 2: Of no other creature was it described that God assisted in its formation.[61] CF, 110

St. Augustine, *De Genesi ad litteram,* Book VI, Ch. 12: and when His hand is spoken of, there is reference not to a visible member of a body, but to His creative power. [62] LMG, Vol. 1, 193

St. Irenaeus, *The Demonstration of the Apostolic Preaching,* 11: But man He formed with His own hands, taking from the earth

---

[60] Job 10:8-11: "Thy hands have made me, and fashioned me wholly round about, and dost thou thus cast me down headlong on a sudden? Remember, I beseech thee, that thou hast made me as the clay, and thou wilt bring me into dust again. Hast thou not milked me as milk, and curdled me like cheese?"

[61] Ecclus. 33:10: "And all men are from the ground, and out of the earth, from whence Adam was created."

[62] Ecclus. 33:13-14: "As the potter's clay is in his hand, to fashion and order it: All his ways are according to his ordering: so man is in the hand of him that made him, and he will render to him according to his judgment." Isa. 49:16: "Behold, I have graven thee in my hands: thy walls are always before me."

that which was purest and finest, and mingling in measure His own power with the earth. IP, 80

St. Ireneaus, *Adversus Haereses*, Book V, Ch. 3:2: But that He is powerful in all these respects, we ought to perceive from our origin, inasmuch as God, taking dust from the earth, formed man. And surely it is much more difficult and incredible, from non-existent bones, and nerves, and veins, and the rest of man's organization, to bring it about that all this should be, and to make man an animated and rational creature, than to reintegrate again that which had been created and then afterwards decomposed into earth (for the reasons already mentioned), having thus passed into those [elements] from which man, who had no previous existence, was formed. WI, Vol. 2, 62

St. Ireneaus, *Adversus Haereses*, Book V, Ch. 3:2: For He who in the beginning caused him to have being who as yet was not, just when He pleased, shall much more reinstate again those who had a former existence, when it is His will [that they should inherit] the life granted by Him. And that flesh shall also be found fit for and capable of receiving the power of God, which at the beginning received the skilful touches of God. WI, Vol. 2, 62

St. Ambrose, *Hexameron*, Book 6, Ch. 7: Who says this? Was it not God who made you? What is God: flesh or spirit? Surely not flesh, but spirit, which has no similarity to flesh. This is material, whereas the spirit is incorporeal and invisible. FCAm, 253

St. Thomas Aquinas, *Summa Theologiae*, I, Q 90, Art 1 ad 1: The term 'breathe' is not to be taken in the material sense; but as regards to the act of God, to breathe [*spirare*] is the same as to "make a spirit". ST, 865

St. Irenaeus, *Adversus Haereses*, Book V, Ch. 7:1: Now the breath of life is an incorporeal thing. And certainly they cannot maintain that the very breath of life is mortal. Therefore David says,

"My soul also shall live to Him," [Ps. 21:31] just as if its substance were immortal. WI, Vol. 1, 70-71

St. Irenaeus, *Adversus Haereses*, Book V, Ch. 12:2: For the breath of life, which also rendered man an animated being, is one thing, and the vivifying Spirit another, which also caused him to become spiritual. WI, Vol. 1, 83

St. Thomas Aquinas, *Summa Theologiae*, I, Q 93, Art 6: Hence, this image of God is not found even in the rational creatures except in the mind. In the other parts, however, which the rational creature may happen to possess, we find the likeness of a 'trace', as is the case in the other creatures to which, in reference to such parts, the rational creature can be likened. ST, 893

St. Ambrose, *Hexameron*, Book 6, Ch. 6: Not without reason is the soul comely, since it longs, not for the things of earth, but for those of heaven; not for the corruptible, but for the incorruptible, the beauty of which is not liable to perish.[63] FCAm, 252

St. Ambrose, *Hexameron*, Book 6, Ch. 8: This is true, however, of our souls, which are free to wander far and wide in acts of reflection and of counsel. FCAm, 257

St. Irenaeus, *Adversus Haereses*, Book IV, Ch. 37:1: This expression [of our Lord], "How often would I have gathered your children together, and you would not," [Mt. 23:37] set forth the ancient law of human liberty, because God made man a free [agent] from the beginning, possessing his own power, even as he does his own soul, to obey the behests (*ad utendum sententia*) of God voluntarily, and not by compulsion of God. For there is no coercion with God, but a good will [towards us] is present with Him continually. And therefore does He give good counsel to all. And in man, as well as in angels, He has placed

[63] Deut. 4:9: "Keep thyself therefore, and thy soul carefully."

the power of choice (for angels are rational beings), so that those who had yielded obedience might justly possess what is good, given indeed by God, but preserved by themselves. WI, Vol. 2, 36

St. Ambrose, *Hexameron*, Book 6, Ch. 8: That, therefore, is made to the image of God which is perceived, not by the power of the body, but by that of the mind. It is that power which beholds the absent and embraces in its vision countries beyond the horizon. Its vision crosses boundaries and gazes intently on what is hidden. In one moment the utmost bounds of the world and its remote secret places are under its ken. God is attained and Christ is approached. FCAm, 258

St. Bonaventure, *Breviloquium*, Part II, Ch. 9:5: By means of its intellective power, it discerns truth, flees from evil, and desires the good; it discerns truth through the rational power, it repels evil through the irascible appetite, and desires the good through the concupiscible appetite.[64] SB, 267

St. Augustine, *De Genesi ad litteram*, Book X, Ch. 9: The text cited above,[65] then, clearly teaches us that God made from nothing the soul which He gave to the first man, and did not form it from some creature already made, as in the case of the body made from the earth. LMG, Vol. 2, 107

St. Thomas Aquinas, *Summa Theologiae*, I, Q 93, Art 2: Augustine says: "Man's excellence consists in the fact that God made him to His own image by giving him an intellectual soul, which raises him above the beasts of the field". Therefore things without intellect are not made to God's image. ST, 887

---

[64] My translation: *Per intellectivam autem discernit verum, refugit malum, and appetit bonum: verum quidem discernit per rationale; malum repellit per irascibilem; bonum appetit per concupiscibilem.*

[65] Eccles. 12:7: "And the dust return into its earth, from whence it was, and the spirit return to God, who gave it."

St. Lawrence of Brindisi, *Explanatio in Genesim*, Ch. 1: All the holy Doctors assert that this image and likeness of God in man must be understood not according to the body but according to the mind, according to which man by his very nature surpasses non-rational beings. CF, 85

St. Thomas Aquinas, *Summa Theologiae*, I, Q 93, Art 2: Hence, some things are like God first and most commonly because they exist; secondly, because they live; and thirdly because they know or understand. ST, 887

St. Gregory of Nyssa, *On the Making of Man*, Ch. 29:1: Nor again are we in our doctrine to begin by making up man like a clay figure, and to say that the soul came into being for the sake of this; for surely in that case the intellectual nature would be shown to be less precious than the clay figure. NPNF, Vol. V, 420

St. Bonaventure, *Breviloquium*, Part II, Ch. 9:1: Regarding the soul: that it is a form endowed with existence, life, intelligence, and freedom of choice. Brev, 84

St. Bonaventure, *Breviloquium*, Part VII, Ch. 2:4: For, as the soul is united to the body in the order of nature for the sake of vivifying it, so it should be united to material fire in the order of justice for the sake of receiving punishment—for one who is to be punished must be united to a punishing agent. Brev, 271

St. Bonaventure, *Breviloquium*, Part II, Ch. 9:5: Now the soul confers not simply existence, but also life, sensation, and intelligence. It therefore possesses a vegetative power, a power of sensation, and an intellective power. Brev, 87

St. Lawrence of Brindisi, *Explanatio in Genesim*, Ch. 2: Why does the Hebrew original say the "breath of lives"? Because man certainly lives by the life of plants in which his limbs and bodily parts are invigorated; he lives the life of the sense, in which he perceives each thing whether it is received outwardly or inwardly. He lives by a life characterized by motion and progression whereby he seeks the things necessary for life, he lives by a rational life and by art whereby he is distinguished from brute animals and excels all things. But the one breath breathed into man by God brings about all these lives, for there are not four souls in man performing these effects, but these are the faculties and powers of one soul only. CF, 110-11

St. Thomas Aquinas, *Summa Theologiae*, I, Q 76, Art. 6 ad 1: For the same essential form makes man an *actual being*, a *body*, a *living being*, an *animal*, and a *man*. ST, 713

St. Gregory of Nyssa, *On the Making of Man*, Ch. 8:5: For this rational animal, man, is blended of every form of soul; he is nourished by the vegetative kind of soul, and to the faculty of growth was added that of sense, which stands midway, if we regard its peculiar nature, between the intellectual and the more material essence, being as much coarser than the one as it is more refined than the other: then takes place a certain alliance and commixture of the intellectual essence with the subtle and enlightened element of the sensitive nature. NPNF, Vol. V, 394

St. Gregory of Nyssa, *On the Making of Man*, Ch. 8:5: So that man consists in these three: as we are taught the like thing by the apostle in what he says . . . [1Thes. 5:23], praying for them that the complete grace of their "body and soul and spirit" may be preserved at the coming of the Lord; using the word 'body' for the nutritive part, and denoting the sensitive by the word 'soul,' and the intellectual by 'spirit.' NPNF, Vol. V, 394

St. Augustine, *De Genesi ad litteram*, Book VII, Ch. 16: The statement, "Man was made into a living being", in my opinion was made precisely because he began to have sensation in his body, a clear sign of animated and living flesh. LMG, Vol. 2, 17

St. Bonaventure, *Breviloquium*, Part II, Ch. 9:5: By virtue of its sensitive power, the soul apprehends sensible objects, retains what it has apprehended, and combines and sorts what it has retained. It apprehends through the five external senses that correspond to the five principal corporeal elements of the world; it retains through memory; it combines and distinguishes through imagination, which is the primary power of association. Brev, 87

St. Bonaventure, *Breviloquium*, Part II, Ch. 9:5: By virtue of its vegetative power, the soul is the principle of generation, nourishment, and growth. Brev, 87

St. Anthony of Padua, *Sermon on Septuagesima*, 10: On the sixth day God said: "Let us make man" [Gen. 1:26] and the sixth article of faith is the sending of the Holy Spirit. In this mystery the image of God which had been deformed and defiled in man is re-formed and enlightened by the inspiration of the Holy Spirit, who "breathed into the face of man the breath of life" [Gen. 2:7]. SSA, 16-17

St. Anthony of Padua, *Sermon on Septuagesima*, 22: On the sixth day God said: "Let us make man to our own image and likeness" [Gen. 1:26]. The sixth and last virtue of the soul is final perseverance, which is the tail of the sacrificial victim and the many coloured coat of Joseph. Without it the possession of the previous virtues is useless; with it their possession is profitable, and in it (as on the sixth day) the image and likeness of God is eternally imprinted upon the face of the soul. This image is never to be soiled, never obliterated, never defiled. SSA, 30

His Body

St. Thomas Aquinas, *Summa Theologiae*, I, Q 91, Art 2: The first formation of the human body could not be by the instrumentality of any created power, but was immediately from God. ST, 873

St. Thomas Aquinas, *Summa Theologiae*, I, Q 91, Art 2: Therefore, as no pre-existing body had been formed, through whose power another body of the same species could be generated, the first human body was of necessity made immediately by God. ST, 873

St. Thomas Aquinas, *Summa Theologiae*, I, Q 91, Art 2: Now God, though He is absolutely immaterial, can alone by His own power produce matter by creation: wherefore He alone can produce a form in matter, without the aid of any preceding material form. ST, 873

St. Lawrence of Brindisi, *Explanatio in Genesim*, Ch. 2: I have no doubt whatsoever that God wholly by Himself formed the body of man with absolutely no intervening cause. CF, 110

St. Gregory of Nyssa, *On the Making of Man*, Ch. 22:3: For the thing formed from the earth is called Adam, by etymological nomenclature, as those tell us who are acquainted with the Hebrew tongue—wherefore also the apostle, who was specially learned in his native tongue, the tongue of the Israelites, calls the man "of the earth" χοϊκός, as though translating the name Adam into the Greek word.[66] NPNF, Vol. V, 411

St. Ephrem, *Hymns on the Nativity*, 1:16: The virgin earth gave birth to that Adam, head of the earth; the Virgin today gave birth to [second] Adam, head of heaven. EH, 65

St. Irenaeus, *Adversus Haereses*, Book V, Ch. 15:3: As, therefore, we are by the Word formed in the womb, this very same Word formed the visual power in him who had been blind from his birth; showing openly who it is that fashions us in secret, since the Word Himself had been made manifest to men: and declaring the original formation of Adam, and the manner in which he was created, and by what hand he was

[66] 1Cor. 15:47: "The first man was of the earth, earthly: the second man, from heaven, heavenly."

fashioned, indicating the whole from a part. For the Lord who formed the visual powers is He who made the whole man, carrying out the will of the Father. And inasmuch as man, with respect to that formation which was after Adam, having fallen into transgression, needed the laver of regeneration, [the Lord] said to him [upon whom He had conferred sight], after He had smeared his eyes with the clay, "Go to Siloam, and wash" [Jn. 9:7] thus restoring to him both [his perfect] confirmation, and that regeneration which takes place by means of the laver. And for this reason when he was washed he came seeing, that he might both know Him who had fashioned him, and that man might learn [to know] Him who has conferred upon him life. WI, Vol. 2, 97

St. Irenaeus, *Adversus Haereses*, Book V, Ch. 15:4: For, from the earth out of which the Lord formed eyes for that man, from the same earth it is evident that man was also fashioned at the beginning. For it were incompatible that the eyes should indeed be formed from one source and the rest of the body from another; as neither would it be compatible that one [being] fashioned the body, and another the eyes. But He, the very same who formed Adam at the beginning, with whom also the Father spoke, [saying], "Let Us make man after Our image and likeness," [Gen. 1:25] revealing Himself in these last times to men, formed visual organs (*visionem*) for him who had been blind [in that body which he had derived] from Adam. WI, Vol. 2, 98

St. Irenaeus, *Adversus Haereses*, Book V, Ch. 15:2: To that man, however, who had been blind from his birth, He gave sight, not by means of a word, but by an outward action; doing this not without a purpose, or because it so happened, but that He might show forth the hand of God, that which at the beginning had moulded man. And therefore, when His disciples asked Him for what cause the man had been born blind, whether for his own or his parents' fault, He replied, "Neither has this man sinned, nor his parents, but that the works of God should be made manifest in him" [Jn. 9:3]. Now the work of God is the fashioning of man. For, as the scripture says, He made [man] by a kind of process: "And the Lord took clay from the earth, and formed man"

[Gen. 2:7]. Wherefore also the Lord spat on the ground and made clay, and smeared it upon the eyes, pointing out the original fashioning [of man], how it was effected, and manifesting the hand of God to those who can understand by what [hand] man was formed out of the dust. For that which the artificer, the Word, had omitted to form in the womb, [viz., the blind man's eyes], He then supplied in public, that the works of God might be manifested in him, in order that we might not be seeking out another hand by which man was fashioned, nor another Father; knowing that this hand of God which formed us at the beginning, and which does form us in the womb, has in the last times sought us out who were lost, winning back His own, and taking up the lost sheep upon His shoulders, and with joy restoring it to the fold of life. WI, Vol. 2, 96-97

St. John Chrysostom, *Homilies on Genesis*, Homily 13:6: You see, just as He brought into being the very substance of the soil when it did not exist, so now, at will, He changed the dust from soil into body. At this it is good to exclaim what was said by blessed David, "Who will speak of the wonders of the Lord, and bring to our ears all His praise?" [Ps. 106:2]—namely, that from dust He produced such a creature and elevated it to such eminence, and that He displays such marks of regard for it right from outset, revealing in all this His own loving kindness. FCC, 171

St. John Chrysostom. *Homilies on Genesis*, Homily 12:11: A mighty saying, giving rise to great wonderment, and beyond the limits of human understanding: "God shaped the human being," it says, "from the dust of the earth." Just as in the case of all the visible creatures I kept saying that the creator of all performs everything in a manner contrary to human nature so as to demonstrate his ineffable power through this as well, so too in the case of the formation of the human being we will find this taking place. FCC, 163

St. Thomas Aquinas, *Summa Theologiae*, I, Q 91, Art 2 ad 4: An effect may be said to pre-exist according to causal principles in creatures . . . in passive potentiality only, that is, that it can be produced out of pre-existing matter by God. In this sense, according to Augustine, the human body pre-existed in the works produced in their causal principles. ST, 873-74

St. Augustine, *De Genesi ad litteram*, Book VI, Ch. 15: He was not born of parents, since there were no human beings before him, but to be formed from the slime of the earth in accordance with the causal reason in which he had been originally created. LMG, Vol. 1, 196

St. Thomas Aquinas, *Summa Theologiae*, I, Q 91, Art 3: Now the proximate end of the human body is the rational soul and its operations; since matter is for the sake of the form, and instruments are for the action of the agent. I say, therefore, that God fashioned the human body in that disposition which was best, as most suited to such a form and to such operations. ST, 874

St. Augustine, *De Genesi contra Manichaeos,* Book 2, Ch. 7: For, as water gathers, glues, and holds earth together when by its mixture it makes mud, so the soul by vivifying the matter of the body forms it into a harmonious unity and does not allow it to fall into dissolution. FCA, 103-4

St. Thomas Aquinas, *Summa Theologiae*, I, Q 76, Art. 1 ad 5: The soul communicates that being in which it subsists to the corporeal matter, out of which and the intellectual soul there results one being; so that the being of the whole composite is also the being of the soul. ST, 699

St. John Chrysostom. *Homilies on Genesis*, Homily 12:12: What is that you say? Taking dust from the earth he shaped the human being? Yes, it says; it did not simply say 'earth' but 'dust,' something more lowly and substantial even than earth, so to say. You think the saying amazing and incredible; but if you recall who is the creator in this case, you will no longer withhold faith in the event but marvel at the creator's power and bow your knee to it. FCC, 164

St. John Chrysostom. *Homilies on Genesis,* Homily 12:12: Do you see that unless we take into account the creator's power and suppress our own reasoning which betrays such limitations, we will be unable to accept the sublimity of the message? After all, the words require the eyes of faith, spoken as they are with such a great considerateness and with our limitations in mind. FCC, 164

St. Thomas Aquinas, *Summa Theologiae,* I, Q 91, Art. 2 ad 1: Nevertheless, the angels could act as ministers in the formation of the body of the first man, in the same way as they will do at the last resurrection, by gathering the dust. ST, 873

St. Lawrence Brindisi, *Explanatio in Genesim,* Ch. 2: For what is there to prohibit the angels from performing, by means of their ministry, some things toward which their power and art applies? Indeed, on the last day according to Matthew, God will use the service of the angels to re-form the bodies of men; they will gather ashes and form bodies. I have absolutely no doubt that the angels themselves very much desired to assist the creation of man so that they might follow us with a greater love and more vigilantly watch over us, as if the work were in part their own. CF, 110

St. Thomas Aquinas, *Summa Theologiae,* I, Q 91, Art. 2 ad 1: Although the angels are to some extent the ministers of God, as regards what He does in bodies, yet God does something in bodies beyond the angels' power, as, for instance, raising the dead, or giving sight to the blind: and by this power He formed the body of the first man from the slime of the earth. ST, 873

St. Thomas Aquinas, *Summa Theologiae,* I, Q 91, Art 2 ad 3: Changes that surpass the order of nature and are caused by the divine power alone, as for the dead to be raised to life, or the blind to see; and the making of man was this sort of work. ST, 873

St. Thomas Aquinas, *Summa Theologiae,* I, Q 91, Art 3 ad 2: Therefore such things do not suit the nature of man. Instead of these, he has reason and hands whereby he can make himself arms and clothes, and other necessaries of life, of infinite variety. As so the hand is called by Aristotle "the organ of organs". Moreover it was more becoming to a rational nature, which is capable of conceiving an infinite number of things, to have the power of devising for itself an infinite number of instruments. ST, 875

St. Gregory of Nyssa, *On the Making of Man,* Ch. 8:2: Especially do these ministering hands adapt themselves to the requirements of the reason: indeed if one were to say that the ministration of hands is a special property of the rational nature, he would not be entirely wrong; and that not only because his thought turns to the common and obvious fact that we signify our reasoning by means of the natural employment of our hands in written characters. NPNF, Vol. V, 393

Man was Made Upright

St. Bonaventure, *Breviloquium,* Part II, Ch. 10:1: The body of the first man [Adam], formed from the slime of the earth, was created subject to the soul and yet proportioned to it in its own way. By 'proportioned', I imply a well-balanced physical constitution, a beautiful and complex structure, and an upright posture. Brev, 89

St. Ambrose, *Hexameron,* Book 6, Ch. 9: But something must be said on the subject of the human body. Who can deny that it excels all things in grace and beauty? FCAm, 268

St. Ambrose, *Hexameron,* Book 6, Ch. 9: What is man without his head, since the totality of man is in his head? When you see a head you recognize a man If the head is lacking, no recognition is possible. FCAm, 270

St. Ambrose, *Hexameron,* Book 6, Ch. 9: Those skilled in the art of medicine maintain, in fact, that the brain is placed in man's head for the sake of the eyes and that the other senses of our bodies are housed close together on account of the brain. The brain is the source of our nervous system and of all the sensations and voluntary movements. FCAm, 273

St. Ambrose, *Hexameron*, Book 6, Ch. 9: All living things have the same liberty to see, but man alone has the will to interpret what he perceives. FCAm, 276

St. Anthony of Padua, *Sermon on Septuagesima*, 14: "In the morning I will stand before you". [Ps. 5:5] that is, in the beginning of grace I shall stand as true and upright as you made me to be. For, as St Augustine says, "God, who is true and upright, made man to be true and upright, so that only the soles of his feet should touch the ground; in other words, so that he might seek from the earth only those things that are necessary." SSA, 20

St. Augustine, *De Genesi ad litteram*, Book VI, Ch. 12: Man's body, then, is appropriate for his rational soul not because of his facial features and the structure of his limbs, but rather because of the fact that he stands erect, able to look up to heaven and gaze upon the higher regions in the corporeal world. LMG, Vol. 1, 193-94

St. Augustine, *De Genesi ad litteram*, Book VI, Ch. 12: In like manner, his rational soul must be raised up to spiritual realities, which by their very nature are of far greater excellence, so that a man's thoughts may be on heavenly things, not on the things that are on the earth. LMG, Vol. 1, 194

St. Thomas Aquinas, *Summa Theologiae*, I, Q 91, Art 3 ad 3: An upright stature was becoming to man for four reasons. First, because the senses are given to man, not only for the purpose of procuring the necessaries of life, for which they are bestowed on other animals, but also for the purpose of knowledge. ST, 875

St. Thomas Aquinas, *Summa Theologiae*, I, Q 91, Art 3 ad 3: Whereas man has his face erect, in order that by the senses, and chiefly by sight, which is more subtle and reveals many different things, he may freely survey the sensible things around him, both heavenly and earthly, so as to gather intelligible truth from all things. ST, 875-76

St. Thomas Aquinas, *Summa Theologiae*, I, Q 91, Art 3 ad 3: Secondly, for the greater freedom of the acts of the interior powers, which requires that the brain, wherein these actions are, in a way performed, be not low down, but lifted up above other parts of the body. ST, 876

St. Thomas Aquinas, *Summa Theologiae*, I, Q 91, Art 3 ad 3: Thirdly, because if man's figure were prone to the ground, he would need to use his hands as fore-feet, and thus their utility for other purposes would cease. ST, 876

St. Thomas Aquinas, *Summa Theologiae*, I, Q 91, Art 3 ad 3: Fourthly, because if man's figure were prone to the ground, and he used his hands as fore-feet, he would be obliged to take hold of his food with his mouth . . . Now such a disposition would completely hinder speech which is the proper work of reason. ST, 876

St. Thomas Aquinas, *Summa Theologiae*, I, Q 91, Art 3 ad 3: For man's superior part, his head, is turned towards the superior part of the world, and his inferior part is turned towards the inferior world. ST, 876

St. Basil, *On the Hexameron*, Homily 9:2: The herds are earthy and are bent toward the earth, but man is a heavenly creature who excels them as much by the excellence of his soul as by the character of his bodily structure. FCB, 138

St. Basil, *On the Hexameron*, Homily 9:2: Your head stands erect toward the heavens; your eyes look upward, so that, if you ever dishonor yourself by the passions of the flesh, serving your belly and your lowest parts, "you are compared to senseless beasts, and are become like them" [Ps. 48:13]. FCB, 138

Paradise

Genesis 2:8: *And the Lord God had planted a paradise of pleasure from the beginning: wherein he placed man whom he had formed.*

St. Ephrem, *Commentary on Genesis*, Part 2:5: After Moses spoke of how Adam was so gloriously fashioned, he turned to write about paradise and Adam's entry therein saying, "The Lord had previously planted Paradise . . . " FCE, 99

St. Augustine, *On Christian Doctrine*, Book III, Ch. 36: Now here it seems to be indicated that the events last mentioned took place after God had formed man and put him in the garden; whereas the fact is, that the two events having been briefly mentioned, viz., that God planted a garden, and there put the man whom He had formed, the narrative goes back, by way of recapitulation, to tell what had before been omitted, the way in which the garden was planted: that out of the ground God made grow every tree that is pleasant to the sight, and good for food. SA, Vol. 2, 572

St. Augustine, *De Genesi ad litteram*, Book VIII, Ch. 1: Paradise, in which God placed him, should be understood as simply a place, that is, a land, where an earthly man would live. LMG, Vol. 2, 32-33

St. Thomas Aquinas, *Summa Theologiae*, I, Q 102, Art 4: God made man outside of paradise, and afterwards placed him in paradise to live during the whole of his animal life; and, having attained to the spiritual life, to be transferred thence to heaven. ST, 949

St. Ephrem, *Commentary on Genesis*, Part 2:5: Eden is the land of paradise and [Moses] said 'previously' because God had [already] planted it on the third day. He explains this by saying, "The Lord caused every tree . . ." FCE, 99

St. Jerome, *Hebraicae Quaestiones in Libro Geneseos*, 4: From which it is manifestly proven that before God made heaven and earth, He previously had established paradise, as it is also written in Hebrew "and the Lord God had planted paradise in Eden in the beginning".[67] CC, 4

St. Bede, *In principium Genesis*, Book I: It is understood that paradise was made on this same day in which the earth brought forth the rest of the fruit-bearing trees, as God had commanded. But by necessity here it is repeated so that we can know what type of place paradise was, especially since there was reference to the tree of life and the tree of knowledge of good and evil specifically. OG, 141

St. Ambrose, *Paradise*, Ch. 3:12: Paradise is, therefore, a land of fertility—that is to say, a soul which is fertile—planted in Eden, that is, in a certain delightful or well-tilled land in which the soul finds pleasure. FCAm, 294

St. Irenaeus, *Adversus Haereses*, Book V, Ch. 5:1: Where, then, was the first man placed? In paradise certainly, as the Scripture declares "And God planted a garden [*paradisum*] eastward in Eden, and there He placed the man whom He had formed" [Gen. 2:8]. And then afterwards when [man] proved disobedient, he was cast out thence into this world. Wherefore also the elders who were disciples of the apostles tell us that those who were translated were transferred to that place (for paradise has been prepared for righteous men, such as have the Spirit; in which place also Paul the apostle, when he was caught up, heard words which are unspeakable as regards us in our present condition [2Cor. 12:4], and that there shall they who have been translated remain until the consummation [of all things], as a prelude to immortality. WI, Vol. 2, 66

---

[67] My translation: *Ex quo manifestissime comprobatur quod prius quam caelum et terram deus faceret, paradisum ante condiderat, sicut et legitur in hebraeo plantaverat autem dominus deus paradisum in eden in principio.*

St. John Damascene, *De Fide Orthodoxa*, Book 2, Ch. 11: Some have imagined paradise to have been material, while others have imagined it to have been spiritual. However, it seems to me that, just as man was created both sensitive and intellectual, so did this most sacred domain of his have the twofold aspect of being perceptible both to the senses and to the mind. FCD, 232

St. John Damascene, *De Fide Orthodoxa*, Book 2, Ch. 11: There he had the indwelling of God as a dwelling place and wore Him as a glorious garment. He was wrapped about with His grace, and, like some one of the angels, he rejoiced in the enjoyment of that one most sweet fruit which is the contemplation of God, and by this he was nourished. FCD, 232

St. John Damascene, *De Fide Orthodoxa*, Book 2, Ch. 11: For, while in his body he dwelt in this most sacred and superbly beautiful place, as we have related, spiritually he resided in a loftier and far more beautiful place. FCD, 232

St. Ambrose, *Paradise*, Ch. 1:2: Nevertheless, we can find out who was the creator of this paradise. We read in Genesis that God planted a garden to the east and he put there the man he had formed. FCAm, 288

St. Ambrose, *Paradise*, Ch. 1:5: In this garden, therefore, God put the man He had formed. Take note that He placed man there not in respect to the image of God, but in respect to the body of man. The incorporeal does not exist in a place. He placed man in paradise, just as He placed the sun in heaven, awaiting lordship over the heavens, just as the creature expects the revelation of the sons of God. FCAm, 289

Genesis 2:9: *And the Lord God brought forth of the ground all manner of trees, fair to behold, and pleasant to eat of: the tree of life also in the midst of paradise: and the tree of knowledge of good and evil.*

St. Ambrose, *Paradise*, Ch. 1:2: Who had the power to create paradise, if not almighty God, who "spoke and they were made" [Ps. 32:9] and who was never in want of the thing which He wished to bring into being? FCAm, 288

St. Ephrem, *Commentary on Genesis*, Part 2:5: And to show he was talking about paradise, [Moses] said, "and the tree of life was in the midst of Paradise, and the tree of knowledge of good and evil". FCE, 100

St. Ambrose, *Paradise*, Ch. 2:7: There was a tree of the knowledge of good and evil in paradise. This was so because "God made to grow a tree pleasant to sight and good for food, the tree of life also in the midst of the garden and the tree of the knowledge of good and evil." We shall see later whether this tree, like the others, was pleasant to sight and good for food. FCAm, 290

St. John Damascene, *De Fide Orthodoxa*, Book 2, Ch. 11: He planted the tree of knowledge as a sort of trial, test, and exercise of man's obedience and disobedience. FCD, 231

St. John Damascene, *De Fide Orthodoxa*, Book 2, Ch. 11: It is either for this reason that it was called the tree of knowledge of good and evil, or because it gave to them that partook of it the power to know their own nature—which, while it is good for the perfect, is bad for them that are less perfect and more given to their desires. FCD, 231

St. Ambrose, *Paradise*, Ch. 1:2: He planted, therefore, that paradise of which He says in His wisdom: "Every plant which my Father has not planted will be rooted up" [Mt. 15:13]. This is a goodly plantation for angels and saints. The saints are said to live beneath the fig tree and the vine [Mich. 6:6]. In respect to this they are a type of the angels in that time of peace which is to come. FCAm, 288

St. Ambrose, *Paradise*, Ch. 2:7: In fact, we are unable, owing to human weakness, yet to know and understand the reason for the creation of each and every object. Let us, therefore, not criticize in holy Scripture something which we cannot comprehend. FCAm, 290

St. Ambrose, *Paradise*, Ch. 2:7: There are very many things which must not be subjected to the judgment of our intellect. Rather, these should be surveyed from the lofty heights of divine providence and from the intentions of God Himself. FCAm, 290

St. Ambrose, *Paradise*, Ch. 2:8: This tree grew in paradise and it was permitted by God, in order that we might know the pre-eminence of good. FCAm, 290

St. John Damascene, *De Fide Orthodoxa*, Book 2, Ch. 11: And He also wanted us to be free from care and to have but one task, that of the angels, which is unceasingly and unremittingly to sing the praises of the creator and to rejoice in contemplating Him. FCD, 231

St. Ambrose, *Paradise*, Ch. 5:29: Therefore, in the middle of paradise there was both a tree of life and a cause for death. FCAm, 306

St. John Damascene, *De Fide Orthodoxa*, Book 2, Ch. 11: The tree of life was either a tree possessing a life-giving force or a tree that was to be eaten of only by such as were worthy of life and not subject to death. FCD, 232

St. Lawrence of Brindisi, *Explanatio in Genesim*, Ch. 2: Before the Fall, it was necessary for man to eat to preserve his life and not die . . . Nevertheless, by the gift of grace he was made immortal . . . For God had provided him with remedies against the power of death so that while he remained in that state in which God had created him, he was not subject to the necessity of dying. CF, 114

St. Lawrence of Brindisi, *Explanatio in Genesim*, Ch. 2: He provided man with "every tree lovely to the sight and pleasant to eat", so that man might preserve the sense of life that food requires. God places "the tree of life in the midst of paradise . . ." From the tree's power of preservation, it was called the "tree of life", because by its nourishment it would preserve the sense of life of man forever and keep him from old age. CF, 11

Genesis 2:10: *And a river went out of the place of pleasure to water paradise, which from thence is divided into four heads.*

St. Ephrem, *Commentary on Genesis*, Part 2:6: He turned to write about the river that flowed out from paradise, and once outside of it, divided into four distinct sources. FCE, 100

St. John Damascene, *De Fide Orthodoxa*, Book 2, Ch. 9: Then there is the ocean which encircles the entire earth like a sort of river and to which it seems to me that scripture referred when it said that "a river went out of the place of pleasure." FCD, 225

St. Ambrose, *Paradise*, Ch. 3:13: There was a fount which irrigated the land of paradise. Is not this stream our Lord Jesus Christ, the Fount as well as Father of eternal life? It is written: "For with thee is the fountain of life" [Ps. 35:10]. Hence: "From within him there shall flow living waters" [Jn. 7:38]. We read of a fountain and a river which irrigates in paradise the fruit-bearing tree that bears fruit for life eternal. You have read, then, that a fount was there and that "a river rose in Eden," that is, in your soul there exists a fount. FCAm, 294-95

St. Ambrose, *Paradise*, Ch. 3:14: As wisdom is the fountain of life, it is also the fountain of spiritual grace. It is also the fountain of other virtues which guide us to the course of eternal life. Therefore the stream that irrigates paradise rises from the soul when well-tilled, not from the soul which lies uncultivated. FCAm, 295-96

St. Ambrose, *Paradise*, Ch. 3:14: The results therefrom are fruit trees of diverse virtues. There are the four principal trees which constitute the divisions of wisdom. These are the well-known four principal virtues; prudence, temperance, fortitude, and justice. FCAm, 296

St. Ambrose, *Paradise*, Ch. 3:14: Hence, wisdom acts as the source from which these four rivers take their rise, producing streams that are composed of these virtues. FCAm, 296

St. Ephrem, *Commentary on Genesis*, Part 2:6: The four rivers, then, are these: the Pishon, which is the Danube; the Gihon, which is the Nile; and then the Tigris and Euphrates, between which we dwell. FCE, 100-1

St. John Damascene, *De Fide Orthodoxa*, Book 2, Ch. 9: This ocean is divided into four heads, or rivers. The name of the first is Phison; this is the Ganges of India. The name of the second is Gehon; this is the Nile which comes down from Ethiopia into Egypt. The name of the third is Tigris, and of the fourth, Euphrates. There are also a great many other very large rivers, of which some empty into the sea, while others are absorbed into the earth. FCD, 225

St. Ambrose, *Paradise*, Ch. 3:18: In these four rivers are symbolized, therefore, the four principal virtues.[68] FCAm, 298-99

Genesis 2:11-12: *The name of the one is Phison: that is it which compasseth all the land of Hevilath, where gold groweth. And the gold of that land is very good: there is found bdellium, and the onyx stone.*

---

[68] My translation: *Ex quo manifestissime comprobatur quod prius quam caelum et terram deus faceret, paradisum ante condiderat, sicut et legitur in hebraeo plantaverat autem dominus deus paradisum in eden in principio.*

St. Ambrose, *Paradise,* Ch. 3:15: Phison, therefore, stands for prudence. Hence it has pure gold, brilliant rubies, and topaz stones. FCAm, 296

St. Ambrose, *Paradise*, Ch. 3:15: The Hebrews call it Pheoyson, which means "change of mouth," because it flows even through Lydia and not merely around one nation, for Wisdom, which is of benefit to all men, is productive and useful. Hence, if a person were to leave paradise, this river of Wisdom would be the first object he would meet. Thus he may not become inert and arid and his return to paradise may be facilitated. FCAm, 296-97

Genesis 2:13: *And the name of the second river is Gehon: the same is it that compasseth all the land of Ethiopia.*

St. Ambrose, *Paradise*, Ch. 3:16: The second river is Gehon, by which, when they were sojcurning in Egypt, was laid down the law of the Israelites that they should not depart from Egypt, and having girded their loins they should as a sign of temperance partake of lamb. It is fitting that the chaste and sanctified should celebrate the Pasch of the Lord. For that reason the observance of the Law was first carried out beside that river, the name of which signifies an opening of the earth. FCAm, 297

St. Ambrose, *Paradise*, Ch. 3:16: Therefore, just as an opening absorbs the earth and whatever defilements and refuse there be in it, in like manner chastity tends to consume all the passions of the body. Appropriately, then, the observance of the established Law first took place there, because carnal sin is absorbed by the Law. FCAm, 297

St. Ambrose, *Paradise*, Ch. 3:16: And so Gehon, which is a figure of chastity, is said to surround the land of Ethiopia in order to wash away our lowly bodies and quench the fires of our vile flesh. The meaning of

Ethiopia in Latin is "holy and vile." What is more lowly, what is more like Ethiopia, than our bodies, blackened, too, by the darkness of sin? FCAm, 297

Genesis 2:14: *And the name of the third river is Tigris: the same passeth along by the Assyrians.*

St. Ambrose, *Paradise*, Ch. 3:17: The third river is the Tigris, which flows by the Assyrian land. To this river the deceiver Israel was dragged as a prisoner. This river is the swiftest of all rivers. The Assyrian dwell by it, guarding its course—for this is the meaning of its name. Hence, those who by their fortitude hold in check the guileful vices of the body and direct themselves to higher things are thought to have something in common with this river. FCAm, 297–98

St. Ambrose, *Paradise*, Ch. 3:17: For that same reason fortitude emanated from that source in paradise. Fortitude in its rapid course tosses aside everything standing in its path and like this river is not hindered by any natural obstacle. FCAm, 298

Genesis 2:14: *And the fourth river is Euphrates.*

St. Ambrose, *Paradise*, Ch. 3:18: The fourth river is the Euphrates, which means in Latin "fecundity and abundance of fruits." It presents a symbol of justice, the nourishment of every soul. No virtue produces more abundant benefits than equity or justice, which is more concerned with others than with itself, neglecting its own advantages, and preferring the common good. FCAm, 298

St. Ambrose, *Paradise*, Ch. 3:18: Many derive Euphrates from the Greek ἀπὸ τοῦ εὔφραίνεσθαι, that is, from a "feeling of gladness," because the human race rejoices in nothing more than it does in justice and equity. FCAm, 298

Genesis 2:15: . . . *the paradise for pleasure* . . .

St. Lawrence of Brindisi, *Explanatio in Genesim*, Ch. 2: *God* therefore *planted* a sensible and corporeal *paradise*, a place abundantly full of delights, filled with all the most pleasant herbs and flowers, where most pleasant trees are found filled with every kind of abundance of fruits that beautiful to look at and very sweet to taste. CF, 113

St. John Damascene, *De Fide Orthodoxa*, Book 2, Ch. 11: In truth, it was a divine place and a worthy habitation for God in His image. And in it no brute beast dwelt, but only man, the handiwork of God. FCD, 230

St. Thomas Aquinas, *Summa Theologiae*, I, Q 102, Art 2 ad 2: Therefore, as Damascene says: "No irrational animal inhabits paradise"; although, by a certain dispensation, the animals were brought thither by God to Adam; and the serpent was able to trespass therein by the complicity of the devil. ST, 947

St. Thomas Aquinas, *Summa Theologiae*, I, Q 102, Art 2 ad 3: On the other hand, some say that Enoch and Elias still dwell in that paradise.[69] ST, 948

St. Lawrence of Brindisi, *Explanatio in Genesim*, Ch. 2: St. Augustine rightly warns with these words: "Paradise can be understood spiritually provided that we believe in the actual truth of the events narrated in the account." CF, 113

St. Augustine, *De Genesi ad litteram*, Book VIII, Ch. 4: All the events signified something other than what they were, but none the less they themselves existed in the world of material reality. LMG, Vol. 2, 38

---

[69] Ecclus. 44:16: "Henoch pleased God, and was translated into paradise, that he may give repentance to the nations."

St. Lawrence of Brindisi, *Explanatio in Genesim*, Ch. 3: It calls the Terrestrial paradise a 'garden', lest we should think that it was extended over immense tracts of land and was of a huge size in length and breadth. Next, Scripture reveals the name of the region in which this paradise or 'garden' was set, locating it in *Eden*. The region was given this name owing to the pleasantness, delights, and enjoyment, for it was the most pleasurable, delightful, and temperate region as well as one that was very much suited as a dwelling place. CF, 218

St. Lawrence of Brindisi, *Explanatio in Genesim*, Ch. 3: Therefore, if the merchants came to Tyre (which is near Israel) from Eden, namely the place of paradise, it is clear that the place was inhabited and existed not too far from the land of Israel. [70] CF, 219

St. Lawrence of Brindisi, *Explanatio in Genesim*, Ch. 3: The waters of the Flood "increased greatly on the earth" and all "the highest mountains" were "covered" which are "under the heavens". Wherefore the waters overcame that place and destroyed the lovely trees. CF, 219

St. Lawrence of Brindisi, *Explanatio in Genesim*, Ch. 3: However, some think that the place remains untouched to this day and Henoch, Elias, and the Apostle John live a blessed life there until Judgment Day. Yet nowhere is it certain that they were taken to the terrestrial paradise. CF, 220

St. Ephrem, *Commentary on Genesis*, Part 2:7: He turned to speak about Adam's entry into paradise and about the law that was laid down for him saying . . . FCE, 101

Genesis 2:15: *And the Lord God took man, and put him into the paradise of pleasure, to dress it, and to keep it.*

---

[70] Ezec. 27:23: "Haran, and Chene, and Eden were thy merchants."

St. Lawrence of Brindisi, *Explanatio in Genesim*, Ch. 2: from the beginning Adam was endowed with knowledge of the stars so that he would already have fully known the earth's potency and the seasonal changes in order to obtain produce in their seasons. CF, 120

St. Thomas Aquinas, *Summa Theologiae*, I, Q 102, Art 3: As Augustine says, these words of *Genesis* may be understood in two ways. First, in the sense that God placed man in paradise that He might work in man and guard him, by sanctifying him (for if this work cease, man at once relapses into darkness, as the air grows dark when the light ceases to shine), and by guarding man from all corruption and evil. ST, 948–49

St. Lawrence of Brindisi, *Explanatio in Genesim*, Ch. 2: Some, however, say that in this verse God forewarned man that he should keep himself from the twisted serpent Satan lest he should merit being cast out of paradise for the sin of the fall on account of its tricks and deceit. CF, 120

St. Augustine, *De Genesi ad litteram*, Book VIII, Ch. 10: Man was indeed placed in paradise to cultivate it by the art of agriculture . . . The exercise of this art did not involve wearisome toil but was filled with delights, suggesting noble and salutary thoughts to the mind of the wise man. LMG, Vol. 2, 48

St. Thomas Aquinas, *Summa Theologiae*, I, Q 102, Art 3: Secondly, that man might work and guard paradise, which working would not have involved labor, as it did after sin; but it would have been joyous because man would have experienced the power of nature. Nor would man have guarded paradise against a trespasser; but he would have striven to guard paradise for himself lest he should lose it by sin. ST, 949

St. John Damascene, *De Fide Orthodoxa*, Book 2, Ch. 12: And so God made man innocent, straightforward, virtuous, free from pain, free from care, ornamented with every virtue, and adorned with all good qualities. He made him a sort of miniature world within the larger one, another adoring angel, a compound, an eye-witness of the visible creation, lord of the things of earth, lorded over from on high, earthly and heavenly, passing and immortal, visible and spiritual, halfway between greatness and lowliness, at once spirit and flesh. FCD, 235

St. Ambrose, *Paradise*, Ch. 4:24: Note, now, the person who was taken and the land where he was formed. The virtue of God, therefore, took man and breathed into him, so that man's virtue will advance and increase. FCAm, 301

St. Ambrose, *Paradise*, Ch. 4:24: God set him apart in paradise that you may know that man was taken up, that is to say, was breathed upon by the power of God. FCAm, 301

St. Ephrem, *Commentary on Genesis*, Part 2:7: Adam had nothing to guard except the law that has been set down for him. Nor was there any other 'tilling' entrusted to him except to fulfill the commandment that had been commanded him. FCE, 102

St. Ambrose, *Paradise*, Ch. 4:24: Note the fact that man was created outside paradise, whereas woman was made within it. This teaches us that each person acquires grace by reason of virtue, not because of locality or of race. FCAm, 301

St. Ambrose, *Paradise*, Ch. 4:24: Hence, although created outside paradise, that is, in an inferior place, man is found to be superior, whereas woman, created in a better place, that is to say, in paradise, is found to be inferior. FCAm, 301

St. Ambrose, *Paradise*, Ch. 4:25: The act of tilling and the act of keeping are one and the same thing. In tilling there is a certain exercise of man's virtue, while in keeping it is understood that the work is accomplished, for protection implies something completed. FCAm, 302-3

St. Ambrose, *Paradise*, Ch. 4:25: In this way, it is generally assumed, man can seek after something new and may keep what he has acquired. FCAm, 303

St. Ambrose, *Paradise*, Ch. 11:51: Hence, many hold that by paradise is meant the soul of man and that, while man was placed there as a worker and guardian, certain seeds of virtue sprouted forth. This may be taken to mean that the mind of man, whose virtue it is to cultivate the soul intensively, not only performs its appropriate function, but also acts as a custodian of the work accomplished. FCAm, 329

St. Anthony of Padua, *Sermon on the Fifth Sunday after Easter*, 7: Solomon says, "He that breaks through a hedge (the law), a serpent shall bite him (the devil)" [Eccles. 10:8]. He that does not live according to what he says and hears, dissipates the law. He is the man of whom it is said: "If a man be a hearer of the word and not a doer, etc." [Jas. 1:22-24]. SSA, 372

Genesis 2:18: *And the Lord God said: It is not good for man to be alone: let us make him a help like unto himself.*

St. Ambrose, *Paradise*, Ch. 10:46: Recognize the fact, first of all, that, when God created man from the slime of the earth, He did not add: "God saw that it was good," as He did in the case of each of His works. If He had said at that time that the creation of man was good, then the other statement that "it is not good" would have been a contradiction in terms, although He had said that the creation of what preceded the formation of man was good.[71] FCAm, 325

St. Ambrose, *Paradise*, Ch. 10:46: The meaning is clear. The creation of both man and woman is considered to be good. FCAm, 325

---

[71] Wis. 10:1: "She preserved him, that was first formed by God, the father of the world, when he was created alone."

St. Ambrose, *Paradise*, Ch. 10:47: Accordingly, the Lord declared that it was not good for man to be alone, because the human race could not have been propagated from man alone. FCAm, 326

Genesis 2:19: *And the Lord God having formed out of the ground all the beasts of the earth, and all the fowls of the air, brought them to Adam to see what he would call them: for whatsoever Adam called any living creature the same is its name.*

St. Ephrem, *Commentary on Genesis*, Part 2:9: They were not really *formed*, for the earth brought forth the animals and the water the birds . . . That [Moses] said, "He brought them to Adam", is so that God might make known the wisdom of Adam and the harmony that existed between the animals and Adam before he transgressed the commandment. The animals came to Adam as to a loving shepherd. Without fear they passed before him in orderly fashion, by kinds and by species. FCE, 103

St. Lawrence of Brindisi, *Explanatio in Genesim*, Ch. 2: One must not think that the animals were led by God as though He were a man using hands and ropes. Also, they were not led by the ministry of the angels, as some say. CF, 124

St. Ephrem, *Commentary on Genesis*, Part 2:15: Just as Israel, without a veil, was unable to look upon the face of Moses, neither were the animals able to look upon the splendor of Adam and Eve; when the beasts passed before Adam and they received their names from him, they would cast their eyes downwards, for their eyes could not endure Adam's glory. FCE, 107

St. Ambrose, *Paradise*, Ch. 11:51: The beasts of the field and the birds of the air which were brought to Adam are our irrational senses, because beasts and animals represent the diverse emotions of the body, whether of the more violent kind or even of the more temperate.

What else are we to consider the birds of the air if not as representations of our idle thoughts, which, like winged creatures, flit around our souls and frequently lead us by their varied motions now in one direction, now in another? FCAm, 329

Genesis 2:20: *. . . And Adam called all the beasts by their names, and all the fowls of the air, and all the cattle of the field:*

St. Ephrem, *Commentary on Genesis*, Part 2:10: For God gave Adam not only rule over everything, which had been promised to him, but He also allowed him to bestow names on the animals, which had not been promised to him . . . It is possible for someone to bestow many names on many kinds of insects, animals, beasts, and birds, but never to name one kind by the name of another belongs either to God or to someone to whom it has been granted by God. FCE, 103-4

St. Thomas Aquinas, *Summa Theologiae*, I, Q 94, Art 1: He knew God with a more perfect knowledge than we do now. Thus his knowledge was in a way midway between our knowledge in the present state, and the knowledge we shall have in heaven, when we see God through His essence. ST, 903

St. Thomas Aquinas, *Summa Theologiae*, I, Q 94, Art 3: Man named the animals (Gen. 2: 20). But names should be adapted to the nature of things. Therefore Adam knew the natures of all the animals; and in like manner he was possessed of the knowledge of all other things. ST, 906

St. Thomas Aquinas, *Summa Theologiae*, I, Q 94, Art 3: Now no one can instruct others unless he has knowledge; and so the first man was established by God in such a manner as to have knowledge of all those things for which man has a natural aptitude. And such are whatever are virtually contained in the first self-evident principles, that is, whatever truths man is naturally able to know. ST, 907

St. Lawrence of Brindisi, *Explanatio in Genesim*, Ch. 2: Adam, beyond all personal experience, had information of natural things and contemplative knowledge. CF, 125

St. Lawrence of Brindisi, *Explanatio in Genesim*, Ch. 2: It is most probably believed that this imposition of names on all animals was done by Adam himself in the Hebrew language, and that at this time a very holy and complete language was invented and put to use by Adam and continued in use throughout every generation up to the multiplication of languages. CF, 126

Man's Knowledge

St. Thomas Aquinas, *Summa Theologiae*, I, Q 94, Art 3: But those things which cannot be known by merely human effort, and which are not necessary for the direction of human life, were not known by the first man; such as the thoughts of men, future contingent events, and some individual facts, as for instance the number of pebbles in a stream; and the like. ST, 907

St. Thomas Aquinas, *Summa Theologiae*, I, Q 94, Art 3: Moreover, in order to direct his own life and that of others, man needs to know not only those things which can be naturally known, but also things surpassing natural knowledge, because the life of man is directed to a supernatural end; just as it is necessary for us to know the truths of faith in order to direct our own lives. ST, 907

St. Thomas Aquinas, *Summa Theologiae*, I, Q 94, Art 3: Therefore the first man was endowed with such a knowledge of these supernatural truths as was necessary for the direction of human life in that state. ST, 907

St. Thomas Aquinas, *Summa Theologiae*, I, Q 94, Art 3 ad 1: The first man had knowledge of all things by divinely infused species. ST, 907

St. Thomas Aquinas, *Summa Theologiae*, I, Q 94, Art 1: Hence Augustine says that "perhaps God used to speak to the first human beings as He speaks to the angels, by shedding on their mind a ray of the unchangeable truth, yet without bestowing on them the experience of which the angels are capable in the participation of the divine essence." ST, 903

St. Augustine, *De Genesi ad litteram*, Book XI, Ch. 33: Or perhaps it took place with the aid of a creature, either in an ecstasy of the spirit with corporeal images, or in the bodily senses with some object made present to be seen or heard, just as God is accustomed to be seen or heard in a cloud through the ministry of angels. LMG, Vol. 2, 166

St. Thomas Aquinas, *Summa Theologiae*, I, Q 94, Art 3 ad 3: Adam would have advanced in natural knowledge, not in the number of things known, but in the manner of knowing; because what he knew speculatively he would subsequently have known by experience. ST, 907

Genesis 2:20: *but for Adam there was not found a helper like himself.*

St. Ambrose, *Paradise*, Ch. 11:49: Examine, now, the reason why God had by this time created out of the earth "all the beasts of the field and all the birds of the air" and brought them to Adam to see what he would call them. FCAm, 328

St. Ambrose, *Paradise*, Ch. 11:49: In this way he would be able to see that nature in every aspect is constituted of two sexes: male and female. Following these observations, he would become aware that association with a woman was a necessity of his lot. FCAm, 328

St. Ephrem, *Commentary on Genesis*, Part 2:11: Moses called Eve helper because even though Adam had helpers among the beasts and animals he still required one like him of his own kind. FCE, 104

St. Ambrose, *Paradise*, Ch. 10:48: We understand that to mean a helper in the generation of the human family—a really good helper. FCAm, 327

The Formation of the First Woman

Genesis 2:21: *Then the Lord God cast a deep sleep upon Adam: and when he was fast asleep, he took one of his ribs, and filled up flesh for it.*

St. Ephrem, *Commentary on Genesis*, Part 2:12: It is likely that Adam saw in his dream what was done to him as if he were awake. FCE, 105

St. Thomas Aquinas, *Summa Theologiae*, I, Q 92, Art 1: It was necessary for woman to be made, as the Scripture says, as "a helper" to man; not indeed in other works, as some say, since man can be more efficiently helped by another man in other works; but as a helper in the work of generation.[72] ST, 879

St. Lawrence of Brindisi, *Explanatio in Genesim*, Ch. 2: Neither a man nor a woman *per se* is sufficient for the procreation of offspring and the begetting of children. The union of both is required . . .Therefore, God proposed that a 'help like' the man had to be made, *i.e.*, a being of the same nature and form; 'like', not the same thing.[73] CF, 123

St. Thomas Aquinas, *Summa Theologiae*, I, Q 92, Art 2: There is a sacramental reason for this. For by this is signified that the Church takes her origin from Christ. Therefore the Apostle says (Ephes. 5: 32): "This is a great sacrament; but I speak in Christ and in the Church". ST, 882

---

[72] 1Tim. 2:13: "For Adam was first formed; then Eve."

[73] Ecclus. 17:5: "He created of him a helpmate like to himself."

St. Ambrose, *Paradise*, Ch. 11:50: What does the phrase 'deep sleep' signify? Does it not mean that when we contemplate a conjugal union we seem to be turning our eyes gradually in the direction of God's kingdom? FCAm, 328

Genesis 2:22: *And the Lord God built the rib which he took from Adam into a woman: and brought her to Adam.*

St. Augustine, *City of God*, Book XII, Ch. 23: He made also a wife for him, to aid him in the work of generating his kind, and her He formed of a bone taken out of the man's side, working in a divine manner. SA, Vol. 2, 242

St. Augustine, *City of God*, Book XII, Ch. 23: For we are not to conceive of this work in a carnal fashion, as if God wrought as we commonly see artisans, who use their hands and material furnished to them that by their artistic skill they may fashion some material object. God's hand is God's power; and He, working invisibly, effects visible results. SA, Vol. 2, 242

St. Lawrence of Brindisi, *Explanatio in Genesim*, Ch. 1: I hold that the Hebrew word *çela* (translated literally as 'side') primarily and chiefly means 'rib.' CF, 91

St. Thomas Aquinas, *Summa Theologiae*, I, Q 92, Art 2 ad 3: Woman, however, was not produced from man by natural generation, but by the divine power alone. Hence Eve is not called the daughter of Adam. ST, 882

St. Thomas Aquinas, *Summa Theologiae*, I, Q 92, Art 4: Now the matter whence man is naturally begotten is the human semen of man or woman. Therefore an individual of the human species cannot be generated naturally from any other matter. Now God alone, the author of nature, can bring an effect into being outside the ordinary course of nature. Therefore God alone could produce either a man from the slime of the earth, or a woman from the rib of man. ST, 884

St. Augustine, *City of God*, Book XII, Ch. 23: But this seems fabulous rather than true to men, who measure by customary and everyday works the power and wisdom of God, whereby He understands and produces without seeds even seeds themselves; and because they cannot understand the things which at the beginning were created, they are skeptical regarding them as if the very things which they do know about human propagation, conceptions and births, would seem less incredible if told to those who had no experience of them; though these very things, too, are attributed by many rather to physical and natural causes than to the work of the divine mind. SA, Vol. 2, 242

St. Ephrem, *Commentary on Genesis*, Part 2:12: After Adam's rib had been taken out in the twinkling of an eye, God closed up the flesh in its place in the blink of an eyelash. FCE, 105

St. Lawrence of Brindisi, *Explanatio in Genesim*, Ch. 2: Alternatively, from the sole substance of the rib, with nothing added from without, the rib, after being multiplied and increased of itself by the command of God as His all powerful ability, took on larger dimensions, and from it the body of the woman could be shaped by means of that miracle in which later on in Scripture five-thousand men could be fed from five loaves of bread multiplied by the heavenly power of Jesus Christ. CF, 129

St. Thomas Aquinas, *Summa Theologiae*, I, Q 92, Art 3 ad 1: Hence Augustine says that "Christ filled five thousand men with five loaves, in the same way as from a few seeds He produces the harvest of corn"—that is, by transformation of the nourishment. Nevertheless, we say that the crowds were fed with five loaves, or that woman was made from the rib, because an addition was made to the already existing matter of the loaves and of the rib. ST, 883

St. Ambrose, *Paradise*, Ch. 11:50: The word 'built' is well chosen in speaking of the creation of a woman because a household, comprising of man and wife, seems to point toward a state of full perfection. One who is without a wife is regarded as being without a home. As man is considered to be skilful in public duties, so woman is esteemed to be more adaptable to domestic ministrations. FCAm, 328-29

St. Ambrose, *Paradise*, Ch. 10:48: Not without significance, too, is the fact that woman was made out of the rib of Adam. She was not made of the same earth with which he was formed, in order that we might realize that the physical nature of both man and woman is identical and that there was one source for the propagation of the human race. FCAm, 327

St. Ambrose, *Paradise*, Ch. 10:48: For that reason, neither was man created together with a woman, nor were two men and two women created at the beginning, but first a man and after that a woman. God willed it that human nature be established as one. FCAm, 327

St. Thomas Aquinas, *Summa Theologiae*, I, Q 92, Art 3: It was right for the woman to be made from a rib of man. First, to signify the social union of man and woman, for the woman should neither *use authority over man*, and so she was not made from his head; nor was it right for her to be subject to man's contempt as his slave, and so she was not made from his feet. ST, 882-83

St. Thomas Aquinas, *Summa Theologiae*, I, Q 92, Art 3: Secondly, for the sacramental signification; for from the side of Christ sleeping on the Cross the Sacraments flowed—namely, blood and water—on which the Church was established. ST, 883

St. Augustine, *Contra Faustum*, Book XII, 8: As a wife was made for Adam from his side while he slept, the Church becomes the property of her dying Saviour, by the sacrament of the blood which flowed from His side after His death. MH, 209

St. Augustine, *De Genesi ad litteram*, Book IX, Ch. 16: The Lord would have been able to create His flesh from a rib or from any other member of the Virgin; but He who could have demonstrated that He had done again in the case of His own body what had been done before, deemed it more salutary to show that in the body of His Mother there was no cause for shame, where all was chaste. LMG, Vol. 2, 91-92

St. Augustine, *De Genesi ad litteram*, Book IX, Ch. 16: Unbelievers consider both of these events beyond belief. But for believers, why should the account of the Conception of Christ be accepted in the literal sense and the account of the creation of Eve be accepted only in a figurative sense? Are we to say that without any sexual embrace a man could have been made from a woman but not a woman from a man? Did the womb of the Virgin have the power to produce a Man, whereas the side of the man had no power to produce a woman, although in the former case the Lord would be born of His handmaid, and in the latter a handmaid had been born of a servant? LMG, Vol. 2, 91

St. Thomas Aquinas, *Summa Theologiae*, I, Q 92, Art 4 ad 2: As Augustine says, we do not know whether the angels were employed by God in the formation of man; but it is certain that, as the body of man was not formed by the angels from the slime of the earth, so neither was the body of woman formed by them from the man's rib. ST, 884

Genesis 2:23: *And Adam said: This now is bone of my bones, and flesh of my flesh; she shall be called woman, because she was taken out of man.*

St. Ephrem, *Commentary on Genesis*, Part 2:12-13: After the extracted rib had been fashioned with all sorts of beautiful things to adorn it, God then brought her to Adam, who was both one and two . . . Adam said this either as a prophecy or because he had seen it and knew it from the vision of his dream. FCE, 105

St. Lawrence of Brindisi, *Explanatio in Genesim*, Ch. 2: "This now is bone", namely, in this time only it happens that a help like the man was built from the man alone rather than being born. CF, 130-31

St. Lawrence of Brindisi, *Explanatio in Genesim*, Ch. 2: Adam knew supernaturally that the woman was formed from him. Whereupon he spoke prophetically. CF, 131

Genesis 2:24: *Wherefore a man shall leave father and mother, and shall cleave to his wife: and they shall be two in one flesh.*

St. Thomas Aquinas, *Summa Theologiae*, I, Q 92, Art 2: This was most necessary in the human species, in which the male and female live together for life. ST, 881

St. Thomas Aquinas, *Summa Theologiae*, I, Q 92, Art 2: As the Philosopher says, the human male and female are united, not only for generation, as with other animals, but also for the purpose of domestic life, in which each has his or her particular duty, and in which man is the head of the woman. ST, 881

St. Lawrence of Brindisi, *Explanatio in Genesim*, Ch. 2: Also, if his parents suffer any needs or inconveniences, the man is more obligated to his wife than his parents. If he cannot assist both, he must provide for his wife. CF, 131

St. Augustine, *Contra Faustum*, Book XII, 8: And when he says, "A man shall leave his father and mother, and shall cleave to his wife, and they two shall be one flesh. This is a great mystery; but I speak concerning Christ and the Church" [Eph. 5:31–32]. This points most obviously to the way in which Christ left His Father; for "though He was in the form of God, and thought it not robbery to be equal to God, He emptied Himself, and took upon Him the form of a servant" [Phil. 2:6–7]. And so, too, He left His mother, the synagogue of the

Jews which cleaved to the carnality of the Old Testament, and was united to the Church His holy bride, that in the peace of the New Testament they two might be one flesh. For though, with the Father, He was God, by whom we were made, He became in the flesh partaker of our nature, that we might become the body of which He is the head. MH, 209

St. Lawrence of Brindisi, *Explanatio in Genesim*, Ch. 2: Whence the Hebrew words "they will *be*" is the command and injunction of the divine Will so that when by the Will of God they legitimately come together joined by God in the sacrament of matrimony, they are inseparable as one flesh and each has a right to that flesh. CF, 132

St. Lawrence of Brindisi, *Explanatio in Genesim*, Ch. 2: Therefore, it is manifestly clear that in this verse God does not approve of polygamy but rather prohibits it, and that divorce ought always to be illicit, as the Lord said: "What God has joined together, let no man put asunder" [Mt. 19:6]. Nevertheless Moses, because of the depravity and hardness of the Jews, sometimes permitted these things. CF, 132

St. Augustine, *De Genesi ad litteram,* Book IX, Ch. 15: But to form or build a rib into a woman, this could not have been done except by God, on whom every substance depends.[74] LMG, Vol. 2, 88

St. Ambrose, *Paradise*, Ch. 10:47: Yet woman, we are told, "will be saved by childbearing," [1Tim. 2:14] in the course of which she generated Christ. FCAm, 327

St. Irenaeus, *Adversus Haereses*, Book III, Ch. 22:4: And even as she, having indeed a husband, Adam, but being nevertheless as yet a virgin (for in paradise "they were both naked, and were not ashamed" [Gen. 2:25],

---

[74] Ezec. 37:6: "And I will lay sinews upon you, and will cause flesh to grow over you, and will cover you with skin: and I will give you spirit and you shall live, and you shall know that I am the Lord."

inasmuch as they, having been created a short time previously, had no understanding of the procreation of children: for it was necessary that they should first come to adult age, and then multiply from that time onward), having become disobedient, was made the cause of death, both to herself and to the entire human race. WI, Vol. 1, 361

St. Irenaeus, *Adversus Haereses*, Book III, Ch. 22:4: And on this account does the law term a woman betrothed to a man, the wife of him who had betrothed her, although she was yet a virgin; thus indicating the back-reference from Mary to Eve, because what is joined together could not otherwise be put asunder than by inversion of the process by which the bonds of union had arisen. WI, Vol. 1, 361

Genesis 1:28: *And God blessed them, saying: Increase and multiply, and fill the earth, and subdue it, and rule over the fishes of the sea, and the fowls of the air, and all living creatures that move upon the earth.*

St. Thomas Aquinas, *Summa Theologiae*, I, Q 98, Art 1: It is written (*Gen.* 1:28): "Increase and multiply, and fill the earth". But this increase could not come about save by generation, since the original number of mankind was only two. Therefore there would have been generation in the state of innocence. ST, 929

St. Lawrence of Brindisi, *Explanatio in Genesim*, Ch. 1: Nevertheless, I explain this verse as follows. "And God blessed them saying: Increase and multiply". Indeed, this blessing consists first and foremost in the receipt of the power to propagate, so that the human species be multiplied in the number of the persons lest the chief and noblest of species die out. CF, 93

St. Ephrem, *Commentary on Genesis*, Part 1:30: They were blessed on this earth, as if this dwelling place had been prepared for them before they sinned. Although they had not yet sinned, God knew that they were about to sin. FCE, 95

St. Lawrence of Brindisi, *Explanatio in Genesim*, Ch. 1: In that passage, one must note that marriage was made a sacrament because it was blessed by God in order that we consequently understand that grace was given by God to procreate offspring, so that those who came henceforth might come forth sanctified. CF, 93

St. Ephrem, *Commentary on Genesis*, Part 1:30-31: But how was Adam to rule over the fish of the sea unless he were to be in proximity to the sea? And how was he to rule over the birds that fly throughout every region unless his descendants were to dwell in every region? And how was Adam to rule over every beast of the earth unless his offspring were to inhabit the entire earth?... God truly manifested his foreknowledge in His blessing and manifested His grace in the place where he set Adam to dwell . . . And lest it be said that God did not know Adam would sin, He blessed him on this earth. FCE, 95

St. Lawrence of Brindisi, *Explanatio in Genesim*, Ch. 1: If it is a commandment, which I do not refuse to believe, it is a commandment for the time at the beginning, when the earth was empty. CF, 94

St. Thomas Aquinas, *Summa Theologiae*, I, Q 96, Art 1: Therefore in the state of innocence, before man had disobeyed, nothing disobeyed him that was naturally subject to him. Now all animals are naturally subject to man. ST, 918

St. Ephrem, *Commentary on Genesis*, Part 1:31: God did not bless Adam in paradise, because that place and all that is in it is blessed. But God blessed him on the earth first so that by that blessing with which His grace blessed beforehand, the curse of the earth, which was about to be cursed by His justice, might be diminished. FCE, 95

Genesis 1:29-30: *And God said: Behold I have given you every herb bearing seed upon the earth, and all trees that have in themselves seed of their own kind, to be your meat: And to all beasts of the earth, and to* *every fowl of the air, and to all that move upon the earth, and wherein there is life, that they may have to feed upon. And it was so done.*

St. Thomas Aquinas, *Summa Theologiae*, I, Q 97, Art 3: In the state of innocence man had an animal life requiring food, but after the resurrection he will have a spiritual life needing no food. ST, 926

St. Lawrence of Brindisi, *Explanatio in Genesim*, Ch. 1: They ate every kind of herb all at once. And when the sons of Noe rested from the flood, God made meat lawful for them, as it is written, "Every creature that moves and lives shall be food for you; as I have given you the green plants, I give you everything" [Gen. 9:3]. CF, 94-95

St. Ephrem, *Commentary on Genesis*, Part 1:31: On that same day, [God] set [Adam] in the garden to dwell, clothed with glory and made him ruler over all the trees of paradise.[75] FCE, 96

St. Ephrem, *Commentary on Genesis*, Part 2:4: Even though the beasts, the cattle, and the birds were equal [to Adam] in their ability to procreate and in that they had life, God still gave honor to Adam in many ways: first, in that it was said, "God formed him with His own hands and breathed life into him"; God then set him as ruler over paradise and over all that is outside paradise; God clothed Adam in glory; and God gave him reason and thought so that he might perceive the majesty [of God]. FCE, 99

Genesis 1:31: *And God saw all the things that he had made, and they were very good.*

---

[75] Ps. 8:5-9: "What is man, that thou art mindful of him? or the son of man, that thou visitest him? Thou hast made him a little less than the angels, thou hast crowned him with glory and honour: And hast set him over the works of thy hands. Thou hast subjected all things under his feet, all sheep and oxen: moreover, the beasts also of the fields. The birds of the air, and the fishes of the sea, that pass through the paths of the sea."

St. Lawrence of Brindisi, *Explanatio in Genesim*, Ch. 1: I explain this verse as follows: "And God saw all that he had made was very good", or as the Hebrew original has, "good exceedingly". In this verse God commends all the works rather than each work *per se*. For each work is *per se* good by its nature, but all things together, insofar as they constitute the universe itself, are, as it were, one and very good, *i.e.* the best because of the admirable order of the universe. FC, 96

St. Bede, *In principium Genesis*, Book I: But one may rightly ask why this statement, "And God saw that it was good," was not added separately here concerning the creation of humans, instead of reserving their creation for universal praise along with the others? OG, 132

St. Augustine, *De Genesi ad litteram*, Book III, Ch. 24: Perhaps the explanation is that God, knowing man was going to sin and not remain in the perfection of the image of God, wished to say of him, not in particular but along with the rest, that he was good, thus hinting what would be. LMG, Vol. 1, 101

St. Augustine, *De Genesi ad litteram*, Book III, Ch. 24: Man, therefore, before the fall, was good even considered separately from the rest, but instead of declaring so, scripture said something else foreshadowing the future. No false statement was made concerning man. For he who is good individually is certainly better when taken in conjunction with all, he is also good individually. Scripture limited itself to saying what was true at the time and yet intimated God's foreknowledge. LMG, Vol. 1, 102

St. Anthony of Padua, *Sermon on the Third Sunday after Easter*, 9: Note that God sees us in three ways. First, by conferring grace. Hence, He said to Nathaniel: "When thou wast under the fig tree, I saw you" [Jn. 1:48]. Those exiled from paradise had clothing of fig-leaves, which make the flesh itch. A man is 'under the fig tree' if he chooses to live in the shade of idle talk and the itching of the lustful flesh. God 'sees' him when He confers grace on him. Secondly, he 'sees' when he conserves the grace he has given. So Genesis says: "The Lord saw all things that he had made; and they were very good". [Gen. 1:31]. All things God makes in us, when He infuses grace, are good. But when He 'sees' us by keeping it in us, then they are very good, that is, perfect. Thirdly, He will see us when He takes us to Himself. So He says, "I will see you again, and your hearts shall rejoice" [Jn. 16:22]. SSA, 319

Genesis 2:25: *And they were both naked: to wit, Adam and his wife: and were not ashamed.*

St. Ephrem, *Commentary on Genesis*, Part 2:14: [Moses] would neither have said, "They were naked and were not ashamed", nor, "Adam and his wife", if they had not been young adults . . . It was because of the glory with which they were clothed that "they were not ashamed". It was when this glory was stripped from them after they had transgressed the commandment that they were ashamed because they were naked. FCE, 106

St. Ambrose, *Paradise*, Ch. 13:63: They were naked, it is true, before this time, but they were not devoid of the garments of virtue. They were naked because of the purity of their character and because nature knows nothing of the cincture of deceit.[76] FCAm, 343

St. Thomas Aquinas, *Summa Theologiae*, I, Q 95, Art 1: Hence Augustine says that, 'as soon as they disobeyed the divine command, and forfeited divine grace, they were ashamed of their nakedness, for they felt the impulse of disobedience in the flesh, as though it were a punishment corresponding to their own disobedience". Hence if the loss of grace dissolved the obedience of the flesh to the soul, we may gather that the inferior powers were subjected to the soul through grace existing therein. ST, 911

---

[76] Lk. 15:22: "And the father said to his servants: Bring forth quickly the first robe and put it on him: and put a ring on his hand and shoes on his feet."

St. Augustine, *City of God*, Book XIII, Ch. 13: For, as soon as our first parents had transgressed the commandment, divine grace forsook them, and they were confounded at their own wickedness; and therefore they took fig-leaves (which were possibly the first that came to hand in their troubled state of mind), and covered their shame; for though their members remained the same, they had shame now where they had none before. SA, 251

St. Lawrence of Brindisi, *Explanatio in Genesim*, Ch. 2: This absence of shame resulted not on account of their simplicity but from the condition of the state of innocence and because of the gift of original justice, which God gave to the first parents. CF, 134

St. Lawrence of Brindisi, *Explanatio in Genesim*, Ch. 2: In these members especially there appear the disorder and slackening of that bridle, by which the flesh is checked and restrained from behaving extravagantly against the spirit. CF, 134

St. Lawrence of Brindisi, *Explanatio in Genesim*, Ch. 2: They were most splendidly clothed in the beauty of justice; had they preserved it forever, they would never have needed clothing to cover their private parts since those parts did not cause shame at that time. CF, 135

Original Justice

St. Lawrence of Brindisi, *Explanatio in Genesim*, Ch. 2: Accordingly, our discourse has reached the point at which it seemed worthwhile to explain some things about the gift of original justice, which wise King Solomon call "straightness", saying in Eccles. 7:30, "God," from the beginning, "made mankind straight", i.e. endowed with original justice. CF, 135

St. Augustine, *On Rebuke and Grace*, Ch. 11:29: What then? Did not Adam have the grace of God? Yes, truly, he had it largely, but of a different kind. He was placed in the midst of benefits which he had received from the goodness of his creator; for he had not procured those benefits by his own deservings; in which benefits he suffered absolutely no evil. SA, Vol. 5, 483

St. John Damascene, *De Fide Orthodoxa*, Book 2, Ch. 12: He moreover made him sinless and endowed with freedom of will. By being sinless, I do not mean being incapable of sinning, for only the Divinity is incapable of sinning, but having the tendency to sin not in his nature but, rather, in his power of choice—that is to say, having the power to persevere and progress in good with the help of divine grace, as well as having the power to turn from virtue and fall into vice, God permitting because of the freedom of the will. For that which is done by force is not an act of virtue. FCD, 235-36

St. Thomas Aquinas, *Summa Theologiae*, I, Q 95, Art 1: For this rectitude consisted in his reason being subject to God, the lower powers to reason, and the body to the soul. Now the first subjection was the cause of both the second and the third, since while reason was subject to God, the lower powers remained subject to reason, as Augustine says. ST, 911

St. Augustine, *City of God*, Book XIII, Ch. 13: And because it had willfully deserted its superior Lord, it no longer held its own inferior servant; neither could it hold the flesh subject, as it would always have been able to do had it remained itself subject to God. SA, Vol. 2, 251

St. Thomas Aquinas, *Summa Theologiae*, I, Q 94, Art 1: And man was made right by God in this sense, that in him the lower powers were subjected to the higher, and the higher nature was made so as not to be impeded by the lower.[77] ST, 903

[77] Ecclus. 49:19: "Seth and Sem obtained glory among men: and above every soul Adam in the beginning."

St. Thomas Aquinas, *Summa Theologiae,* I, Q 95, Art 1: Man and angel alike ordained to grace. But the angels were created in grace, for Augustine says: "God at the same time fashioned their nature and endowed them with grace". Therefore man also was created in grace. ST, 911

St. Bonaventure, *Breviloquium,* Part II, Ch. 10:5: For this reason, God fashioned for the rational soul a body so obedient that it was free from all stirring to rebellion, any propensity to lust, every bodily weakness, and all corruption of death. The body was so conformed to the soul that, just as the soul was innocent but capable of falling into sin, so the body was without pain and yet able to fall under punishment. Brev, 92

St. Lawrence of Brindisi, *Explanatio in Genesim,* Ch. 3: The first man was adorned with these gifts and received them from God on behalf of all his posterity so that everyone naturally descended from him would obtain these gifts as though by a kind of inheritance. CF, 163

St. Augustine, *City of God,* Book XIV, Ch. 26: In paradise, then, man lived as he desired so long as he desired what God commanded. He lived in the enjoyment of God, and was good by God's goodness; he lived without any want, and had it in his power so to live eternally. SA, Vol. 2, 281

St. Bonaventure, *Breviloquium,* Part II, Ch. 11:6: Thus before the fall, human nature was endowed with perfect natural faculties and was further adorned with divine grace. It is clear, therefore, that if human beings did fall, it was owing to their own fault, for having refused to obey. Brev, 96

St. Augustine, *City of God,* Book XIV, Ch. 26: He had food that he might not hunger, drink that he might not thirst, the tree of life that old age might not waste him. There was in his body no corruption, nor seed of corruption, which could produce in him any unpleasant sensation. He feared no inward disease, no outward accident.

Soundest health blessed his body, absolute tranquillity his soul. As in paradise there was no excessive heat or cold, so its inhabitants were exempt from the vicissitudes of fear and desire. SA, Vol. 2, 281

Chapter Three
The Temptation and Fall

The Divine Command

Genesis 2:16: *And he commanded him, saying: Of every tree of paradise thou shalt eat:*

St. Athanasius, *De Incarnatione Verbi Dei,* Ch. 1:3: And knowing again that free choice of human beings could turn either way, he secured beforehand, by a law and a set place, the grace given. OTI, 52

St. Jerome, *Dialogue against the Pelagians,* Book 3, Ch. 6: For Adam did not sin because God knew that this would be the case; but God knew in advance, as God, that he would do this of his own will. FCJ, 356

St. Athanasius, *De Incarnatione Verbi Dei,* Ch. 1:3: For bringing them into His own paradise, He gave them a law, so that if they guarded the grace and remained good, they might have the life of paradise—without sorrow, pain, or care—besides having the promise of incorruptibility in heaven. OTI, 52

St. Theophilus of Antioch, *To Autolycus,* Book 2, Ch. 27: Neither, then, immortal nor yet mortal did He make him, but, as we have said above, capable of both; so that if he should incline to the things of immortality, keeping the commandment of God, he should receive as reward from Him immortality, and should become God; but if, on the other hand, he should turn to the things of death, disobeying God, he should himself be the cause of death to himself. For God made man free, and with power over himself. ANF, Vol. 2, 105

St. John Damascene, *De Fide Orthodoxa*, Book 2, Ch. 11: Now, this is indeed what is fittingly called the tree of life, for the sweetness of divine contemplation communicates a life uninterrupted by death to them that partake of it. It is just this that God meant by "every tree" when He said: "Of every tree of paradise thou shalt eat." For this is the all, in whom and by whom the universe endures. FCD, 232

St. John Damascene, *De Fide Orthodoxa*, Book 2, Ch. 11: Moreover, it is possible to take "every tree" as meaning the knowledge of the divine power which comes from the things that have been created, as the divine Apostle says: "For the invisible things of him from the creation of the world are clearly seen, being understood by the things that are made" [Rom. 1:20]. FCD, 233

St. John Damascene, *De Fide Orthodoxa*, Book 2, Ch. 11: "Of every tree of paradise thou shalt eat," meaning, I think: By means of all created things be thou drawn up to Me, their creator, and from them reap the one fruit which is Myself, who am the true life; let all things be fruitful life to thee and make participation in Me be the substance of thy own existence; for this thou shalt be immortal. FCD, 233

St. Irenaeus, *The Demonstration of the Apostolic Preaching*, 15: But, lest man should conceive thoughts too high, and be exalted and uplifted, as though he had no lord, because of the authority and freedom granted to him, and so should transgress against his maker God, overpassing his measure, and entertain selfish imaginings of pride in opposition to God; a law was given to him by God, in order that he might perceive that he had as lord the Lord of all. And He set him certain limitations, so that, if he should keep the commandment of

God, he should ever remain such as he was, that is to say, immortal; but, if he should not keep it, he should become mortal and be dissolved to earth from whence his formation had been taken. IP, 83

St. Irenaeus, *Adversus Haereses*, Book V, Ch. 20:2: For the Church has been planted as a garden (*paradisus*) in this world; therefore says the Spirit of God, "You may freely eat from every tree of the garden," [Gen. 2:16] that is, eat from every scripture of the Lord; but you shall not eat with an uplifted mind, nor touch any heretical discord. For these men do profess that they have themselves the knowledge of good and evil; and they set their own impious minds above the God who made them. WI, Vol. 2, 109

Genesis 2:17: *But of the tree of knowledge of good and evil, thou shalt not eat. For in what day soever thou shalt eat of it, thou shalt die the death.*

St. Athanasius, *De Incarnatione Verbi Dei*, Ch. 1:3: But if they were to transgress and turning away become wicked, they would know themselves enduring the corruption of death according to nature, and no longer live in paradise, but thereafter dying outside of it, would remain in death and in corruption. OTI, 52

St. Irenaeus, *Adversus Haereses*, Book V, Ch. 7:1: We must therefore conclude that it is in reference to the flesh that death is mentioned; which [flesh], after the soul's departure, becomes breathless and inanimate, and is decomposed gradually into the earth from which it was taken. This, then, is what is mortal. WI, Vol. 2, 71

St. Athanasius, *De Incarnatione Verbi Dei*, Ch. 1:3: This also the divine scripture foretells, speaking in the person of God, "You may eat from all the trees in paradise; from the tree of knowledge of good and evil you shall not eat. On the day you eat of it, you shall die by death" (Gen 2:16–18). This "you shall die by death," what else might it be except not merely to die, but to remain in the corruption of death? OTI, 52

St. Ephrem, *Commentary on Genesis*, Part 2:8: This commandment was an easy one, for God gave to Adam all of paradise and withheld from him only one tree. FCE, 102

St. Anthony of Padua, *Sermon on the Fifth Sunday after Easter*, 13: God gave the first man (established in so excellent a state) just one short command: Do not eat of the tree of the knowledge of good and evil; and he did not keep even so small a thing! SSA, 383

St. Ephrem, *Commentary on Genesis*, Part 2:17: God, in His justice, withheld one tree from that one to whom He, in His goodness, had given everything in paradise, on earth, in the air, and in the seas. FCE, 108-9

St. Ephrem, *Commentary on Genesis*, Part 2:8: [God] withheld from Adam a single tree, and set death around it, so that if Adam would not keep the law out of love for the One who had set down the law, then at least the fear of death that was set around the tree would frighten him away from overstepping the law. FCE, 102

St. Ephrem, *Commentary on Genesis*, Part 2:19: It was hardly a commandment at all, because it was so small, and it had been given to them for only that short time before the tempter departed from them. FCE, 111

St. Lawrence of Brindisi, *Explanatio in Genesim*, Ch. 3: He established a pact with the first man so that by his obedience to some divine command proceeding from the will of God and by his subjection to recognize divine power and the commanding sovereignty, the man would preserve those gifts for himself and for us. CF, 163

St. Bonaventure, *Breviloquium*, Part II, Ch. 11:1: They were given a double command, namely, one of nature and the other of discipline: The command of nature was, "Increase and multiply"; the command of discipline, "Of the tree of the knowledge of good and evil you shall not eat." Brev, 93

St. Lawrence of Brindisi, *Explanatio in Genesim*, Ch. 2: It was called the "tree of knowledge of good and evil", not by its nature, but from the occurrence of what happened afterwards. CF, 116

St. Ambrose, *Paradise*, Ch. 8:40: Man, on the other hand, had a mental conception of evil, inasmuch as he was enjoined to abstain from evil. FCAm, 318

St. Lawrence of Brindisi, *Explanatio in Genesim*, Ch. 3: God, in giving His command, did not use the words that the prophet Moses used in narrating the history. Rather, God designated the tree with another term. The proof is that the woman, replying to the serpent's question, did not say, "But the fruit of the tree of the knowledge of good and evil", but instead she said, "But the fruit of the tree in the middle of the garden, God commanded us not to eat". CF, 156

St. Lawrence of Brindisi, *Explanatio in Genesim*, Ch. 2: We read in Genesis 1:28 that the man was given by God dominion over the fishes of the sea and the birds of the air, all the wild animals, and the whole earth. At this point, in order that man might know that he is subject to divine authority and that he also everlastingly has as his sovereign the being whom he had as his maker, the man receives this command from God. CF, 121

St. Bonaventure, *Breviloquium*, Part II, Ch. 11:5: Now there is no better way of meriting than through pure obedience. Obedience is pure when a command obliges simply because it was commanded, and for no other reason. Such was the case with the command of discipline. Brev, 95

St. Ambrose, *Paradise*, Ch. 6:32: It was not a question of technical knowledge, but of fidelity. He certainly was aware that God was in a position of preeminence and, as such, heed should be paid to His command. Although he did not understand the precise significance of the commands, he was conscious of the fact that deference should be paid to the person of the commander. FCAm, 310

St. Ambrose, *Paradise*, Ch. 8:38: Another problem. Did God know that Adam would violate His commands? Or was He unaware of it? If He did not know, we are faced with a limitation of His divine power. If He knew, yet gave a command which He was aware would be ignored, it is not God's providence to give an unnecessary order. FCAm, 315

St. Augustine, *Contra Faustum*, Book XXII, 21: Neither was God ignorant of the future, but the author of the precept as well as the punisher of disobedience. MH, 415

St. Ambrose, *Paradise*, Ch. 8:39: No injury was done to Adam in that he received a command, or to Judas because he was chosen. God did not lay it down as a necessary consequence that one should disobey and the other betray Him. Both could have abstained from sin if they had guarded what they had received. FCAm, 316

St. Ambrose, *Paradise*, Ch. 8:39: The fault is, therefore, not in the one issuing the command; the sin is rather in the one who disobeys. FCAm, 316

St. Ambrose, *Paradise*, Ch. 2:9: There was, therefore, in paradise a tree of knowledge of good and evil which appeared to the eye to be beautiful and to the taste to be edible. It was not actually good to eat, for its fruit appeared to have a harmful effect on man. What is injurious to individuals may nevertheless have a beneficial effect on men as a whole. The devil, for example, did harm to Judas, but he bestowed the wreath of victory on all the other Apostles, inasmuch as they were able to face and overcome the force of his temptation. FCAm, 292

St. Lawrence of Brindisi, *Explanatio in Genesim*, Ch. 2: One must think that this tree was forbidden in any way to the man and that, by nature, it was evil and harmful. CF, 121

St. Lawrence of Brindisi, *Explanatio in Genesim*, Ch. 3: The command prohibited something that was not evil of its own nature; it was evil because it was prohibited. CF, 153

St. Lawrence of Brindisi, *Explanatio in Genesim*, Ch. 2: The command was not spoken to the woman who was formed afterwards, but only to the man.[78] CF, 122

St. Ambrose, *Paradise*, Ch. 9:43: Again, let us see why the Lord God said to Adam: "Ye shall die the death." What is the difference between saying "ye shall die" and "ye shall die the death"? FCAm, 321

St. Ambrose, *Paradise*, Ch. 9:44: On the other hand, what does "to die the death" mean if not the disintegration of the body at the time of death, when the flesh is devoid of its customary function of carrying on life and the soul is unable to partake in life eternal?[79] FCAm, 322

St. Thomas Aquinas, *Summa Theologiae*, I, Q 97, Art 1: Therefore man was immortal before sin. ST, 924

St. Thomas Aquinas, *Summa Theologiae*, I, Q 97, Art 1: *God made man immortal as long as he did not sin; so that he might achieve for himself life or death.* For man's body was indissoluble not by reason of any intrinsic vigor of immortality, but by reason of a supernatural force given by God to the soul, whereby it was enabled to preserve the body from all corruption so long as it remained itself subject to God. ST, 924

---

[78] Ecclus. 15:14-16: "God made man from the beginning, and left him in the hand of his own counsel. He added his commandments and precepts. If thou wilt keep the commandments and perform acceptable fidelity forever, they shall preserve thee."

[79] Rom. 5:12: "By sin death came into the world."

St. Lawrence of Brindisi, *Explanatio in Genesim*, Ch. 2: By the gift of immortality he would have always lived happily and joyously, never subject to any misery or disaster, full of every felicity. CF, 139

St. Thomas Aquinas, *Summa Theologiae*, I, Q 97, Art 2 ad 4: In the state of innocence, man's body could be preserved from suffering injury from a hard body, partly by the use of his reason, whereby he could avoid what was harmful; and partly also by divine providence, which so preserved him, that nothing of a harmful nature could come upon him unawares. ST, 925

St. Bonaventure, *Breviloquium*, Part II, Ch. 11:6: Since man was able to fall because of his imperfect nature, formed from nothing and not confirmed by glory, the most kind God conferred on him a four-fold assistance: namely, two of nature and two of grace. He instilled a two-fold rectitude in his nature: evidently, one for judging rightly, which is rectitude of conscience; the other for willing rightly, which is rectitude of synderesis, calling out against evil and inciting to good. Above this He added also a two-fold perfection of grace. One was a grace freely given which was a knowledge enlightening the intellect for knowing himself, his God, and this world that was made for him. The other was a grace making him holy, which was charity, enabling his affection to love God above all things and his neighbor as himself.[80] SB, 269

---

[80] My translation: *Et quoniam homo, ratione naturae defectivae ex nihilo formatae, nec per gloriam confirmatae, poterat cadere; benignissimus Deus quadruplex contulit ei adjutorium, scilicet duplex naturae, et duplex gratiae. Duplicem enim indidit rectitudinem ipsi naturae; videlicet unam ad recte juidcandum, et haec est rectitudo conscientiae; aliam ad recte volendum, et haec est rectitudo synderesis, cujus est remurmurare contra malum, et stimulare ad bonum. Duplicem etiam superaddit perfectionem gratiae: unam gratiae gratis datae, quae fuit scientia illuminans intellectum ad cognoscendum seipsum, et Deum suum, et mundum istum, qui factus fuerat propter ipsum; aliam gratiae gratum facientis, quae fuit charitas habilitans affectum ad diligendum Deum super omnia, et proximum sicut seipsum.*

St. Athanasius, *De Incarnatione Verbi Dei,* Ch. 1:5: But human beings, turning away from things eternal and by the counsel of the devil turning us towards things of corruption, were themselves the cause of corruption in death, being, as we already said, corruptible by nature but escaping their natural state by the grace of participation in the Word, had they remained good. OTI, 54

St. Irenaeus, *Adversus Haereses*, Book V, Ch. 23:2: Now he died on the same day in which he ate. For God said, "In that day on which you shall eat of it, you shall die the death." The Lord, therefore, recapitulating in Himself this day, underwent His sufferings upon the day preceding the Sabbath, that is, the sixth day of the creation, on which day man was created; thus granting him a second creation by means of His passion, which is that [creation] out of death. WI, Vol. 2, 118

The Temptation by the Devil

Genesis 3:1: *Now the serpent was more subtle than any of the beasts of the earth which the Lord God had made.*

St. Lawrence of Brindisi, *Explanatio in Genesim*, Ch. 3: In the opinion of all exegetes, even Jewish exegetes, in this verse, one must understand by the word 'serpent' not only the animal or Satan alone but rather Satan speaking in the animal known as the serpent. CF, 143

St. John Damascene, *De Fide Orthodoxa*, Book 2, Ch. 4: If God give them permission, they have strength and change and transform themselves into whatever apparent form they may desire. FCD, 209

St. Lawrence of Brindisi, *Explanatio in Genesim*, Ch. 3: However, in this passage, the Hebrew for 'serpent' is *nachash,* a word that not only means serpent but also 'sorcerer,' a foreboding deceiver, a tempter, and a diviner of secret things. Perhaps for this reason, Moses used this term to show perfectly in one word both the tempter Satan and the animal serpent in which he deceitfully exercised his treacheries. CF, 149

St. Ambrose, *Paradise*, Ch. 2:9: Hence it follows that the serpent in paradise was certainly not brought into being without the will of God. In the figure of the serpent we see the devil. That the devil existed even in paradise we are informed by the prophet Ezechiel, who in discussing the Prince of Tyre says: "Thou wast in the pleasures of the paradise of God" [Ezec. 28:13]. We maintain that the Prince of Tyre stands for the devil. FCAm, 291

St. Ambrose, *Paradise*, Ch. 2:9: The Lord makes the wickedness of him who stands in opposition to us contribute something to our salvation. The wickedness of the devil has caused the virtue and patience of one holy man to shine in a clearer light. The justice of Job was so disciplined and exercised by the wickedness of his opponent that eventually he gained the crown of victory over his adversary, the devil. No one is crowned "unless he has competed according to the rules" [2Tim. 2:5]. FCAm, 291-92

St. Bonaventure, *Breviloquium*, Part III, Ch. 2:3: Now the devil, who previously was wise and just, but rendered cunning and jealous after falling through his sin of pride, had the will to tempt, because he envied humankind; in his craftiness, he knew how to do so, and with all the might God permitted him to have. Brev, 102-3

St. Lawrence of Brindisi, *Explanatio in Genesim*, Ch. 3: The serpent, however, is said to be 'cunning', in the Hebrew *arum*, from the verb *arom*, which means "to ingeniously take counsel about something with shrewdness, take wicked counsel, to act astutely and conduct affairs wickedly." Above all, the word means 'nudity,' by which we are given to understand how this ancient serpent and most deceitful tempter, already naked and stripped of all his heavenly gifts, filled with envy, armed with all shrewdness, cunning, and foul thoughts, accosted man in order to cast him from happiness and rob him of every heavenly good. CF, 149

St. Ambrose, *Paradise*, Ch. 12:54: The cause of envy was the happiness of man placed in paradise, because the devil could not brook the favors received by man. His envy was aroused because man, though formed in slime, was chosen to be an inhabitant of paradise. The devil began to reflect that man was an inferior creature, yet had hopes of an eternal life, whereas he, a creature of superior nature, had fallen and had become part of this mundane existence. FCAm, 332-33

St. Ambrose, *Paradise*, Ch. 12:54: This is the substance of his insidious reflection: "Will this inferior acquire what I was unable to keep? Will he leave the earth and attain heaven, whereas I have fallen to earth thrust down from heaven? I have many ways and means by which to deceive man. He was made of slime, earth is his mother, and he is involved in things corruptible." FCAm, 333

St. Basil, *Quod Deus non est auctor malorum*, 8-9: Therefore, he was not created our enemy, but he became our enemy because of envy. For when he saw himself cast from the angels, then he could not bear to see man, who was earthy, elevated to the dignity of the angels by his progress. FG, 110

St. Ambrose, *Paradise*, Ch. 12:54: This, therefore, is my first approach, namely, to deceive him while he is desirous of improving his condition. In this way an attempt will be made to arouse his ambition. The next approach is by way of the flesh, promising fulfillment of all his desires. FCAm, 333

St. Basil, *Quod Deus non est auctor malorum*, 8-9: Therefore, garments were not given to him [Adam] immediately, because the rewards of virtue were stored up for man, but the *ambushes* of the devil did not allow these to be obtained. So the devil is our adversary on account of the trial that was induced on us of old through his *ambushes*. FG, 110

St. Lawrence of Brindisi, *Explanatio in Genesim*, Ch. 3: When he wished to deceive, he could not unless he was permitted to be able to act through that animal. CF, 150

St. Ephrem, *Commentary on Genesis*, Part 2:18: Rather, a serpent was allowed to come to them which, albeit cunning, was utterly despicable and hideous. FCE, 109

St. Bonaventure, *Breviloquium*, Part III, Ch. 2:3: And it was through divine dispensation that in this temptation he assumed the form of a serpent, not only that he might entice Eve by his cunning, but so that through that symbol all Adam's children might learn just how sly the devil is whenever he tries to ensnare us. Brev, 103

St. Ephrem, *Commentary on Genesis*, Part 2:18: For this purpose, however, Satan was not permitted to send any of the angels, nor any of the seraphim nor any of the cherubim. Nor was Satan himself permitted to come to Adam in the garden, neither in human appearance nor in divine vision, as he came to our Lord on the mountain. FCE, 109

St. Ephrem, *Commentary on Genesis*, Part 2:16: As for the serpent's speech, either Adam understood the serpent's own mode of communication, or Satan spoke through it, or the serpent posed the question in his mind and speech was given to it, or Satan sought from God that speech be given to the serpent for a short time. FCE, 107-8

St. Ephrem, *Hymns on Paradise*, 15:14: The serpent served as a garment for the evil one to put on: on seeing the innocent ones he became full of guile, he prepared a trap for the hearing of the young couple. EHP, 187

St. Bonaventure, *Breviloquium*, Part III, Ch. 2:5: The devil was likewise very cunning in the manner in which he proceeded with his temptation, for he went about it by probing, instigating, and enticing: testing the woman by his question, urging her on by his assurance, and alluring her with his promise.[81] Brev, 103

[81] Apoc. 12:9: "And that great dragon was cast out, that old serpent, who is called the devil and Satan, who seduceth the whole world; and he was cast unto the earth, and his angels were thrown down with him."

St. Fulgence, *Sermo* 2:6-7: Then the evil angel approached Eve that, through her, man, whom God had made, might be separated from God. FG, 206

St. Ambrose, *Paradise*, Ch. 12:54: Accordingly, he contrived not to attack Adam first. Rather, he aimed to circumvent Adam by means of the woman. He did not accost the man who had in his presence received the heavenly command. He accosted her who had learned of it from her husband and who had not received from God the command which was to be observed. FCAm, 333

St. Ambrose, *Paradise*, Ch. 12:54: There is no statement that God spoke to the woman. We know that he spoke to Adam. Hence we must conclude that the command was communicated through Adam to the woman. FCAm, 333

St. Fulgence, *Sermo* 2:6-7: The devil came to Eve, that he might wickedly deprive us of life. FG, 206

St. Irenaeus, *Adversus Haereses*, Book V, Ch. 23:1: He had indeed been already accustomed to lie against God, for the purpose of leading men astray. For at the beginning, when God had given to man a variety of things for food, while He commanded him not to eat of one tree only, as the scripture tells us that God said to Adam: "From every tree which is in the garden you shall eat food; but from the tree of knowledge of good and evil, from this you shall not eat: for in the day that you shall eat of it, you shall die by death" [Gen. 2:16-17]; he then, lying against the Lord, tempted man, as the scripture says that the serpent said to the woman: "Has God indeed said this, You shall not eat from every tree of the garden?" [Gen. 3:1] WI, Vol. 2, 116-17

St. Ephrem, *Commentary on Genesis*, Part 2:19: That one who was in the serpent then spoke to the woman, through the serpent, saying . . . FCE, 110-11

Genesis 3:1: *And he said to the woman: Why hath God commanded you, that you should not eat of every tree of paradise?*

St. Lawrence of Brindisi, *Explanatio in Genesim*, Ch. 3: Truly, in no way is it suitable that these were his first words. Indeed, the idiom *ki*, "is it so that", indicates that something had been said beforehand. CF, 152

St. Fulgence, *Sermo* 123, *In natalitate Domini*, 7:1: The devil, by speaking through the serpent to Eve, brought death into the world through the ears of Eve. FG, 206

St. Ephrem, *Commentary on Genesis*, Part 2:16: The words of the tempter would not have caused those two to be tempted to sin if their avarice had not been so helpful to the tempter. Even if the tempter had not come, the tree itself, by its beauty, would have caused them a great struggle due to their avarice. Their avarice then was the reason that they followed the counsel of the serpent. FCE, 108

St. Bonaventure, *Breviloquium*, Part III, Ch. 2:5: Accordingly, the devil enticed the woman by means of a threefold desirable object: namely, by knowledge, which is desirable to the mind; by the excellence as like God, which is desirable to the irascible; by the attractiveness of the tree, which is desirable to the concupiscible.[82] SB, 272

St. Lawrence of Brindisi, *Explanatio in Genesim*, Ch. 3: However, since he is a liar and the father of lies, as he was about to approach, he begins his task with a lie. CF, 151

---

[82] My translation: *respectu quarum diabolus allexit mulierem per triplex appetibile, scilicet per scientiam, quae est appetibilis rationali; per excellentiam ad modum Dei, quae est appetibilis irascibili; per suavitatem ligni, quae est appetibilis concupscibili.* Ps. 118:85: "The wicked have told me fables: but not as thy law." Cf. 1Jn. 2:16: "For all that is in the world, is the concupiscence of the flesh, and the concupiscence of the eyes, and the pride of life, which is not of the Father, but is of the world."

St. Ambrose, *Paradise*, Ch. 12:55: The serpent inserted a falsehood in questioning the woman thus: "Did God say, you shall not eat of any tree?" Whereas God had actually said: "From every tree of the garden you may eat, but from one tree you must not eat," meaning, by that, the tree of the knowledge of good and evil which was not to be tasted. FCAm, 335

St. Lawrence of Brindisi, *Explanatio in Genesim*, Ch. 3: The cunning and crafty serpent slyly weakened the force of the commandment. He did not say "Has God really commanded" but instead "Has He really said". The serpent quotes Him as 'saying', not 'commanding'. He is rather silent about God's glorious and fearful name, the Tetragrammaton, for he did not say "The Lord God", but only said "God", partly in order not to introduce into her mind the thought of fear owed at the pronunciation of the Most Holy Name, partly also in order not to appear to disclose to her what he had he sought. CF, 153

Genesis 3:2: *And the woman answered him, saying: Of the fruit of the trees that are in paradise we do eat:*

St. Ambrose, *Paradise*, Ch. 6:32: She knew, therefore, that the command must be obeyed. Hence she said: We shall eat of every fruit which the Lord ordered, but God has given an order that we should not eat of the tree in the middle of the Garden, lest we die. Wherefore, she who knew that the command should be obeyed was surely aware that it was wrong not to comply with the command and that she would be justly condemned for her refusal to obey. FCAm, 311

St. Lawrence of Brindisi, *Explanatio in Genesim*, Ch. 3: Thus the woman, inquiring about the reason for the command and not knowing how to discover one that she could render to the serpent (since the command was of the type for which no reason of usefulness might be evident except the simple pleasure of giving a command) began to think that the command was neither right nor reasonable. She also began to be annoyed at a command the motive of which she did not discover and the utility of which she did not see, as the liberty of her mind also rebelled. CF, 151

St. Gregory of Nyssa, *On the Making of Man,* Ch. 20:4: It is because he saw this that the serpent points out the evil fruit of sin, not showing the evil manifestly in its own nature (for man would not have been deceived by manifest evil), but giving to what the woman beheld the glamour of a certain beauty, and conjuring into its taste the spell of a sensual pleasure, he appeared to her to speak convincingly: "and the woman saw," it says, "that the tree was good for food, and that it was pleasant to the eyes to behold, and fair to see; and she took of the fruit thereof and did eat," and that eating became the mother of death to men. NPNF, Vol. V, 410

Genesis 3:3: *But of the fruit of the tree which is in the midst of paradise, God hath commanded us that we should not eat; and that we should not touch it, lest perhaps we die.*

St. Lawrence of Brindisi, *Explanatio in Genesim,* Ch. 3: Wherefore, having nearly forgotten divine power and dominion, answering the serpent, whom she should have spurned instead, she does not recognize God rightly as her Lord and master with a right to command her of anything He wished. "God ", she says, not "the Lord God"; and she does not say "God's command", which He had imposed on her, but His *utterance.* In accordance with the serpent's persuasion, she believed. As the original Hebrew reads, "God has said", not "has commanded". CF, 154

St. Lawrence of Brindisi, *Explanatio in Genesim,* Ch. 3: Then showing that she was out of spirits, without right or reason, she represented God's command as if it were a very hard burden, for she says: "We shall not touch it", something that God certainly did not command. God forbade tasting it, not touching it. However, the woman, because of her displeasure with the commandment, added another prohibition. Indeed, anyone talking about a commandment imposed on him, which he does not like at all and from which he rather recoils, always seeks to exaggerate it in order to show that it was not imposed fairly or rightly. CF, 154

St. Ambrose, *Paradise*, Ch. 12:56: What is, therefore, at first sight objectionable in the addition made by the woman: "Neither shall you touch anything of it"? God did not say this, but, rather: "You must not eat." Still, we have here something which leads to error. FCAm, 336

St. Ambrose, *Paradise*, Ch. 12:56: There are two possibilities to the addition she made: Either it is superfluous, or, because of this personal contribution, she has made God's command only partly intelligible. FCAm, 336

St. Ambrose, *Paradise*, Ch. 12:56: And many believe that this was Adam's fault—not the woman's. They reason that Adam in his desire to make her more cautious had said to the woman that God had give an additional instruction: "Neither shall you touch it." We know that it was not Eve, but Adam, who received the command from God, because the woman had not yet been created. FCAm, 336

St. Ambrose, *Paradise*, Ch. 12:56: Scripture does not reveal the exact words that Adam used when he disclosed to her the nature and content of the command. At all events, we understand the substance of the command was given to the woman by the man. FCAm, 336

St. Lawrence of Brindisi, *Explanatio in Genesim*, Ch. 3: She, now deceived, also had doubts about His punishment for the transgression. CF, 155

St. Ambrose, *Paradise*, Ch. 12:59: In this incident, as she was on the point of sinning, the woman's faith may appear to have been weak. FCAm, 340

St. Ephrem, *Commentary on Genesis*, Part 2:20: The serpent then realized that God had forewarned them about even looking at it lest they become entrapped by its beauty. With this in mind, the serpent said, enticing Eve to look upon it. FCE, 111

Genesis 3:4: *And the serpent said to the woman: No, you shall not die the death.*

St. Ambrose, *Paradise*, Ch. 13:61: Let us learn, therefore, that the temptations of the devil are full of guile. Of the things that he promised, scarcely one of them seems to be true. He contrived falsehoods, as we can see if we read elsewhere: "And the serpent said to the woman, you shall not die." Here we have one falsehood, for man, who followed the promises of the serpent, is subject to death. FCAm, 342

St. Lawrence of Brindisi, *Explanatio in Genesim*, Ch. 3: He then calls God—who is the highest and chief truth and the author and source of every truth—a liar. God most certainly threatened man with death if he ate of the forbidden tree. CF, 155

St. Irenaeus, *Adversus Haereses*, Book V, Ch. 23:1: When he had [thus] learned from the woman the command of God, having brought his cunning into play, he finally deceived her by a falsehood, saying, "You shall not die by death; for God knew that in the day you shall eat of it your eyes shall be opened, and you shall be as gods, knowing good and evil" [Gen. 3:4]. WI, Vol. 2, 117

St. Irenaeus, *Adversus Haereses*, Book V, Ch. 23:1: In the first place, then, in the garden of God he disputed about God, as if God was not there, for he was ignorant of the greatness of God; and then, in the next place, after he had learned from the woman that God had said that they should die if they tasted the aforesaid tree, opening his mouth, he uttered the third falsehood, "You shall not die by death." But that God was true, and the serpent a liar, was proved by the result, death having passed upon them who had eaten. For along with the fruit they did also fall under the power of death, because they ate in disobedience; and disobedience to God entails death. Wherefore, as they became forfeit to death, from that [moment] they were handed over to it. WI, Vol. 2, 117

Genesis 3:5: *For God doth know that in what day soever you shall eat thereof, your eyes shall be opened: and you shall be as gods, knowing good and evil.*

St. Lawrence of Brindisi, *Explanatio in Genesim*, Ch. 3: He even charged the highest and infinitely good God with malice and envy, saying, *God knows . . .*[83] CF, 156

St. Lawrence of Brindisi, *Explanatio in Genesim*, Ch. 3: He used the ambiguous word *elohim,* which can be applied to God Himself or to the angels. CF, 157

St. Ambrose, *Paradise*, Ch. 13:61: Hence you may note that the serpent is the author of idolatry, for his cunning seems to be responsible for man's error in introducing many gods. FCAm, 342

St. Lawrence of Brindisi, *Explanatio in Genesim*, Ch. 3: The woman, deceived by the lying words of the tempter, believed the serpent that in the tree there was some power for understanding. CF, 156

St. Ephrem, *Commentary on Genesis*, Part 2:20: But Eve failed to discern the import of the words of the serpent, who as tempter, had said the opposite of what God had said . . . But she neglected these things that she ought to have said to the serpent and, just as the serpent desired, she directed her eyes away from the serpent

[83] Isa. 14:14: "I will ascend above the height of the clouds, I will be like the most High."

who was before her and began to look upon the tree to which she had been commanded not to draw near. FCE, 111-12

Genesis 3:6: *And the woman saw that the tree was good to eat, and fair to the eyes, and delightful to behold: and she took of the fruit thereof, and did eat . . . .*

St. Lawrence of Brindisi, *Explanatio in Genesim,* Ch. 3: Certainly from the pleasantness of the fruit and the lovely appearance of the tree, she persuaded herself that what the serpent had said to her was true. CF, 160

St. Bonaventure, *Breviloquium,* Part III, Ch. 3:1: The woman, yielding to the temptation of the devil, wished to possess knowledge and God-like eminence and to taste the sweetness of the forbidden tree, and in the end broke the divine command. Brev, 104

St. Ephrem, *Commentary on Genesis,* Part 2:17: Indeed, she was overcome by the beauty of the tree and by the desire for its fruit. She was not overcome by the counsel that came into her ear; rather, she succumbed to the avarice that came from within herself. FCE, 108

St. Ephrem, *Commentary on Genesis,* Part 2:18: If [Eve] had been victorious in that momentary battle, in that brief contest, the serpent and that one in the serpent would have received the punishment that they received, while she, together with her husband, would have eaten of the tree of life and would have lived forever. FCE, 110

St. Ephrem, *Commentary on Genesis,* Part 2:20: She then went after that which her eyes desired and, being enticed by the divinity that the serpent had promised her, she stole away from her husband and ate. Afterwards she gave some to her husband and he ate with her. Because she believed the serpent, she ate first, thinking that she would be clothed with divinity in the presence of that one from whom she, as woman, had been separated. She hastened to eat before her husband that she might become head over her head, that she might become the one to give command to that one by whom she was to be commanded and that she might be older in divinity than that one who was older than she in humanity. FCE, 112-13

St. Bonaventure, *Breviloquium*, Part III, Ch. 3:1: Not content with this, she offered the fruit of the forbidden tree to the man, involving him as well. And he, not willing to strain his pleasures, did not reprove her, but consented to her bad advice. Tasting the fruit that was offered him, he also became a transgressor of the divine command. Brev, 104-5

Genesis 3:6: . . . *and gave to her husband who did eat* . . .

St. Ambrose, *Paradise*, Ch. 6:33: On realizing this, she should not have invited her husband to share in her sin. By enticing him and by giving him what she herself had tasted she did not nullify her sin; rather, she repeated it. FCAm, 311

St. Ambrose, *Paradise*, Ch. 6:33: Yet this woman, knowing that she could not remain in paradise after the Fall, seems to have had a fear that she alone would be ejected from the garden. FCAm, 311

St. Ephrem, *Commentary on Genesis*, Part 2:21: She then brought the fruit to her husband and made him eat after much entreaty, even if it is not written that she had to persuade him. FCE, 113

St. Gregory the Wonderworker, *Sermo de Nativitate Christi*, 23: Eve, deceived by flattery, brought forth words that were fatal; and Mary, receiving the messenger, brought forth the Incarnate and life-giving Word. On account of the words of Eve, Adam was cast from paradise. FG, 109

St. Ephrem, *Hymns on the Blessed Virgin Mary*, 1:13: Eve and the serpent dug a ditch and threw Adam headlong into it. FG, 145

St. Ambrose, *Paradise*, Ch. 6:34: She ought not, therefore, have made her husband a partaker of the evil of which she was conscious; neither should she have caused her own husband to violate the divine command. She sinned, therefore, with forethought, and knowingly made her husband a participant in her own wrongdoing. FCAm, 312

St. Bonaventure, *Breviloquium*, Part III, Ch. 3:3: By placing too great a value on his association with the woman and the comfort of their relationship, he shrank from reproving the woman or restraining his own pleasures. Since he did not rebuke her when he should have, the woman's sin was imputed to him. Because he was unwilling to curb his own pleasures by driving the woman away, he began to love himself too much, and thus fell away from the divine friendship into his own greed and disobedience. Brev, 105-6

St. Ephrem, *Commentary on Genesis*, Part 2:21: Thus, Adam was to be tested immediately by the seductive pleas of Eve, who having been tested by the counsel of the serpent, had drawn near and eaten, but not become naked. FCE, 113

St. Ephrem, *Commentary on Genesis*, Part 2:22: The enemy, jealous of Adam and Eve both for the things that belonged to them and also for the things that they were soon to receive, set traps, and in a momentary battle took from [Adam and Eve] those things they ought not to have lost even in great battle. FCE, 114

St. Bonaventure, *Breviloquium*, Part III, Ch. 3:4: The woman believed that by eating she would be exalted; Adam, relying on his own importance and God's love, thought he be punished lightly, for he had never yet experienced the rigor of divine severity. Brev, 106

St. Ephrem, *Commentary on Genesis*, Part 2:26: For who would have believed, if it had not actually happened, that Adam would listen to Eve, or that Eve would be persuaded by a reptile? FCE, 117

St. Cyprian, *The Good of Patience*, Ch. 19: Adam, in violation of the heavenly command, was incapable of resisting the desire of the deadly food and fell into the death of sin; he did not preserve, under the guardianship of patience, the grace received from God. FCCy, 281

The Fall from the State of Innocence

Genesis 3:7: *And the eyes of them both were opened: and when they perceived themselves to be naked, they sewed together fig leaves, and made themselves aprons.*

St. Ambrose, *Paradise*, Ch. 6:33: That is, the eyes of their mind were opened and they realized the shame of being naked. FCAm, 311

St. Augustine, *City of God*, Book XIV, Ch. 17: "They knew," therefore, "that they were naked"—naked of that grace which prevented them from being ashamed of bodily nakedness while the law of sin offered no resistance to their mind. SA, Vol. 2, 276

St. Lawrence of Brindisi, *Explanatio in Genesim*, Ch. 2: She did not lose the gift of original justice until the time when the man, tasting the forbidden tree after he also violated the divine command. CF, 136

St. Augustine, *City of God*, Book XIII, Ch. 13: Then began the flesh to lust against the Spirit, in which strife we are born, deriving from the first transgression a seed of death, and bearing in our members, and in our vitiated nature, the contest or even victory of the flesh. SA, Vol. 2, 251

St. Lawrence of Brindisi, *Explanatio in Genesim*, Ch. 3: After the gift was lost, the flesh began to rebel against the spirit and desire things in opposition to it as the law of the members began to fight against the law of the mind. CF, 162

St. Lawrence of Brindisi, *Explanatio in Genesim*, Ch. 3: They began to experience a violent bewilderment and shame that they never felt before . . . Now that they had learned of it through their sin, in order to cover their private parts "they sewed together", perhaps with some bulrushes or something similar, "fig-leaves". CF, 162

St. Ephrem, *Commentary on Genesis*, Part 2:14: The two of them then hastened to cover themselves with leaves—not their entire bodies, but only their shameful members. FCE, 106

St. Augustine, *City of God*, Book XIV, Ch. 17: Consequently all nations, being propagated from that one stock, have so strong an instinct to cover the shameful parts that some barbarians do not uncover them even in the bath, but wash with their drawers on. SA, Vol. 2, 276

St. Anthony of Padua, *Sermon on the Third Sunday after Easter*, 4: Pharaoh means 'dispersing' or 'uncovering', and he stands for the devil who disperses the fabric of virtue and strips the mantle of grace from wretched man, leaving him naked. SSA, 310

St. Bonaventure, *Breviloquium*, Part III, Ch. 4:3: Therefore, through the just judgment of God their own lower natures became disobedient to them, especially those parts designed for the union of the sexes, which are the organs that serve the generative power. And so, because this rebellion of their flesh did not arise from nature, but from their own offense, they blushed for shame and clothed themselves. Brev, 108

St. Bonaventure, *Breviloquium*, Part III, Ch. 4:1: Immediately after their offense, the man and the woman felt their punishment in the rebellion and shame of their own flesh. Brev, 107

St. Augustine, *City of God*, Book XIV, Ch. 17: "The eyes of them both were opened," not to see, for already they saw, but to discern between the good they had lost and the evil into which they had fallen. SA, Vol. 2, 276

St. Bonaventure, *Breviloquium*, Part III, Ch. 5:2: The human race is corrupted by original sin in the following way . . . because they are deprived of the righteousness of original justice. Because of its absence, our souls incur a four-fold penalty: weakness, ignorance, malice, and concupiscence; these are inflicted as a result of original sin. These spiritual punishments are matched in the body by all kind of pain, imperfection, labor, sickness, and affliction. To these are finally added the penalty of death and the return to dust, and the penalty of the deprivation of the vision of God and the loss of heavenly glory. These affect not only adults, but also even unbaptized children. Although these little ones are punished along with the others, they suffer only the "gentlest punishment," since they are deprived of the beatific vision but without enduring suffering in their senses. Brev, 109-10

St. Ephrem, *Commentary on Genesis*, Part 2:23: If the serpent had been rejected along with sin, Adam and Eve would have eaten of the tree of life and the tree of knowledge would not have been withheld from them; from the one they would have gained infallible knowledge and from the other they would have received immortal life. FCE, 114

St. Ambrose, *Paradise*, Ch. 13:64: Scripture relates that the saints are those who find rest beneath the vine and the fig. FCAm, 344

St. Ambrose, *Paradise*, Ch. 13:64: I have information from Adam himself, in fact, about the significance of the leaves. He proceeded to make a covering for himself out of the leaves of the fig tree after he had sinned, whereas he should have had its fruit instead. The just man chooses the fruit; the sinner, the leaves. FCAm, 344

St. Ambrose, *Paradise*, Ch. 13:67: Adam girded himself in that place where it would have been better that he had girded himself with the fruit of chastity. FCAm, 345

St. Lawrence of Brindisi, *Explanatio in Genesim*, Ch. 3: Certain authorities would say that the sin was committed by Adam at around midday, at which time Christ also suffered on the cross to take it away. CF, 167

St. Ephrem, *Commentary on Genesis*, Part 2:23: God tarried in coming down to them for the sole reason that they might admonish each other and so plead for mercy when the judge came to them . . . the judge delayed His coming to them so that He might give them an occasion to prepare their entreaty. FCE, 115

Genesis 3:8: *And when they heard the voice of the Lord God walking in paradise at the afternoon air . . .*

St. Lawrence of Brindisi, *Explanatio in Genesim*, Ch. 3: Both God's speaking and His walking must be understood not according to the shape of the deity, for it is entirely believable that it was made in some created likeness representing God and in it God spoke through an angel to the man, just as we read that he appeared and spoke to Abraham, Moses, and many others. CF, 166-67

St. Ephrem, *Commentary on Genesis*, Part 2:24: Now the sound of feet that went before God, who would soon reveal Himself in the punishment upon the house of Adam, prefigured the voice of John, who was to come before the Son, holding a winnowing fork in his hands in order to clean out his granaries, burning the straw in fire and purifying the wheat to bring into His granaries.[84] FCE, 115-16

---

[84] Jn. 1:21: "They said therefore unto him: Who art thou, that we may give an answer to them that sent us? What sayest thou of thyself? He said: I am

St. Ambrose, *Paradise*, Ch. 14:68: What does 'walking' mean in reference to God, who is everywhere? In my opinion God may be said to walk wherever throughout scripture the presence of God is implied, when we hear that He sees all things and the "eyes of the Lord are upon the just" [Ps. 33:16]. We read, too, that Jesus knew their thoughts and we read: "Why do you harbor evil thoughts in your hearts?" [Lk. 6:8] When we reflect, therefore, on these statements, we have a knowledge of God in the act of walking. FCAm, 346

St. Irenaeus, *The Demonstration of the Apostolic Preaching*, 12: And so fair and good was this paradise, that the Word of God continually resorted thither, and walked and talked with the man, figuring beforehand the things that should be in the future, (namely) that He should dwell with him and talk with him, and should be with men, teaching them righteousness. IP, 82

St. Irenaeus, *Adversus Haereses*, Book V, Ch. 17:1: Now the commandment was given to man by the Word. For Adam, it is said, "heard the voice of the Lord God" [Gen. 3:8]. Rightly then does His Word say to man, "Your sins are forgiven you" [Mt. 9:2; Lk. 5:20]. He, the same against whom we had sinned in the beginning, grants forgiveness of sins in the end. WI, Vol. 2, 101

Genesis 3:8: . . . *Adam and his wife hid themselves from the face of the Lord God, amidst the trees of paradise.*

St. Lawrence of Brindisi, *Explanatio in Genesim*, Ch. 3: Since a wounded conscience makes a man fearful, as Adam sensed the approach of God, whom he knew he had gravely offended, and he hid himself from Him.[85] CF, 167

---

the voice of one crying out in the wilderness, make straight the way of the Lord, as said the prophet Isaias."

[85] Jn. 8:59: "They took up stones therefore to cast at him. But Jesus hid himself and went out of the temple."

St. Lawrence of Brindisi, *Explanatio in Genesim*, Ch. 3: I should most probably believe that, with a gentle and peaceful breeze, He appeared to man in the shape in which he would later come, most merciful and clement, to redeem and save mankind.[86] CF, 167

St. Lawrence of Brindisi, *Explanatio in Genesim*, Ch. 3: Outwardly hearing God's voice, by which He censured them, showed them before their eyes the punishments due, and summoned them to saving penance so that they might obtain, by entreaty, mercy from Him. CF, 167-8

St. Ephrem, *Commentary on Genesis*, Part 2:24: It was not only by the patience He exhibited that God wished to help them; He also wished to benefit them by the sound of His feet. God endowed His silent footsteps with sound so that Adam and Eve might be prepared, at that sound, to make supplication before Him who made the sound. But since they did not come before Him in supplication, neither because of His delay nor because of the sound that was sent before Him, God then made a sound with His lips, just as He made a sound for His footsteps and said . . . . FCE, 115

Genesis 3:9: *And the Lord God called Adam, and said to him: Where art thou?*

St. Lawrence of Brindisi, *Explanatio in Genesim*, Ch. 3: God asks not out of ignorance rather he asked so that Adam would consider where he was, in what state or into what condition he had thrown himself, to what wretched fate he had given himself headlong with all his family and his descendants and thus he might be summoned to penance,

---

[86] 1Kings 19:12-13: "And after the earthquake, a fire: but the Lord is not in the fire. And after the fire, a whistling of a gentle air. And when Elias heard it, he covered his face with his mantle, and coming forth, stood in the entering in of the cave, and behold a voice unto him, saying: What dost thou here, Elias?"

acknowledge his sin, and humbly confess, and so from his answer He would rebuke him for his sin. CF, 168

St. Lawrence of Brindisi, *Explanatio in Genesim*, Ch. 3: God seems to me to summon man with these words so that he should present himself and give an account of his deed.[87] CF, 169

St. Ephrem, *Commentary on Genesis*, Part 2:23: If Adam and Eve had sought to repent after they had transgressed the commandment, even though they would not have regained that which they had possessed before their transgression of the commandment, they would have escaped the curses that were decreed on the earth and upon them. FCE, 114-15

St. Ambrose, *Paradise*, Ch. 14:70: When He says, therefore, where are you? it is not a question of a locality to one who knows what is hidden. God did not have His eyes closed, so that a man in hiding was able to escape His notice . . . What, then, does He mean by "Adam, where are you?" Does He not mean "in what circumstances are you?"; not, "in what place?" It is, therefore, not a question, but a reproof. From what condition of goodness, beatitude, and grace, He means to say, have you fallen into this state of misery? You have forsaken eternal life. You have entombed yourself in the ways of sin and death. Where is that noble confidence and trust of yours? That fear that you show is evidence of your wrongdoing and that hiding place of yours betrays your dereliction. "Where are you?" does not mean "in what place" but "in what condition." FCAm, 348

[87] Ecclus. 23:28: "And he knoweth not that the eyes of the Lord are far brighter than the sun, beholding round about all the ways of men, and the bottom of the deep, and looking into the hearts of men, into the most hidden parts." Heb. 4:13: "Neither is there any creature invisible in his sight: but all things are naked and open to his eyes." Job 26:6: "Hell is naked before him, and there is no covering for destruction."

St. Ephrem, *Commentary on Genesis,* Part 2:26: "Where are you, Adam?" In the divinity that the serpent promised you? Or in subjection to the death that I decreed for you? Would that you had considered the fruits! FCE, 116

St. Irenaeus, *Adversus Haereses,* Book V, Ch. 15:4: Wherefore also the scripture, pointing out what should come to pass, says, that when Adam had hid himself because of his disobedience, the Lord came to him at eventide, called him forth, and said, "Where art thou?" [Gen. 3:9]. That means that in the last times the very same Word of God came to call man, reminding him of his doings, living in which he had been hidden from the Lord. For just as at that time God spake to Adam at eventide, searching him out; so in the last times, by means of the same voice, searching out his posterity, He has visited them. WI, Vol. 2, 98

St. Ephrem, *Commentary on Genesis,* Part 2:24: But Adam, instead of confessing his folly and asking for mercy before the judgment came upon him, said . . . FCE, 115

Genesis 3:10: *And he said: I heard thy voice in paradise; and I was afraid, because I was naked, and I hid myself.*

St. Lawrence of Brindisi, *Explanatio in Genesim,* Ch. 3: He did not correctly understand the sense of the Lord's words . . . he thinks he was questioned about his place and answers that he was hiding in the midst of the trees. CF, 169

St. Ephrem, *Commentary on Genesis,* Part 2:25: Speak to God now, before he asks you about the coming of the serpent and about the transgression that you and Eve committed. Perhaps then, the confession of your lips will absolve you from the sin of eating the fruit that your fingers plucked. But Adam and Eve refused to confess that thing which they had done and they related to Him who knows all only what had been done to them. FCE, 116

St. Ephrem, *Commentary on Genesis*, Part 2:27: Because Adam forgot what was required of him and said instead that which was not required—for, instead of confessing what he had done, which would have helped him, he related what had been done to him, which did not help him at all. FCE, 117

Genesis 3:11: *And he said to him: And who hath told thee that thou wast naked, but that thou hast eaten of the tree whereof I commanded thee that thou shouldst not eat?*

St. Ephrem, *Commentary on Genesis*, Part 2:27: Did you see that you were naked with the sight bestowed on you by that tree, from which you were promised that glorious divine sight? FCE, 117

St. Lawrence of Brindisi, *Explanatio in Genesim*, Ch. 3: God as yet seems to ask that he confess his sin in order to be worthy to receive forgiveness. CF, 169

St. Lawrence of Brindisi, *Explanatio in Genesim*, Ch. 3: The Hebrew reading seems to take this sense: that by His words God wished to elicit a humble confession of the crime from Adam. He did not charge him with a crime as a fact, even if He knew it well as a fact. Rather, He questions him whether it is a fact. CF, 169-70

St. Ephrem, *Commentary on Genesis*, Part 2:27: Adam again failed to confess his folly and blamed the woman who was like him, saying . . . FCE, 117

Genesis 3:12: *And Adam said: The woman, whom thou gavest me to be my companion, gave me of the tree, and I did eat.*

St. Lawrence of Brindisi, *Explanatio in Genesim*, Ch. 3: Adam understands what the Lord is asking of him. Nevertheless, he does not openly confess is sin, but he offers a defense for himself, excuses himself, and, as it were, twists his error around. CF, 170

St. Ephrem, *Commentary on Genesis*, Part 2:27: I neither drew near to the tree myself nor did I dare to stretch out my hand towards the fruit. It is for this reason the Apostle said, "Adam did not sin but Eve transgressed the commandment" [1Tim. 2:14]. If God gave you the woman, O Adam, He gave her to you to help you, not to cause you harm, and as one to be commanded, not one to give command. FCE, 118

St. Ephrem, *Commentary on Genesis*, Part 2:28: Since Adam did not wish to confess his folly, God came down to question Eve. FCE, 118

Genesis 3:13: *And the Lord God said to the woman: Why hast thou done this? And she answered: The serpent deceived me, and I did eat.*

St. Ephrem, *Commentary on Genesis*, Part 2:28: Eve, too, instead of making supplication with her tears and bearing the fault herself so that mercy might take hold of both her and her husband responded, not by saying, "The serpent counseled or seduced me," but simply said, "The serpent deceived me and I ate." FCE, 118

St. Lawrence of Brindisi, *Explanatio in Genesim*, Ch. 3: Just as the man threw the blame on the woman, so, too, the woman, finding no way out, confesses the deed but transfers the fault to the serpent. CF, 172

St. Ephrem, *Commentary on Genesis*, Part 2:29: When the two of them had been questioned and were both found wanting in remorse or true contrition, God went down to the serpent, not to make inquiry but to render punishment. FCE, 118

Genesis 3:14: *And the Lord God said to the serpent: Because thou hast done this thing, thou art cursed among all cattle, and beasts of the earth: upon thy breast shalt thou go, and earth shalt thou eat all the days of thy life.*

St. Irenaeus, *Adversus Haereses*, Book III, Ch. 23:3: But the curse in all its fullness fell upon the serpent, which had beguiled them. "And God," it is declared, said to the serpent: "Because you have done this, cursed are you above all cattle, and above all the beasts of the earth" [Gen. 3:14] And this same thing does the Lord also say in the Gospel, to those who are found upon the left hand: "Depart from me, you cursed, into everlasting fire, which my Father has prepared for the devil and his angels"; indicating that eternal fire was not originally prepared for man, [Mt. 25:41] but for him who beguiled man, and caused him to offend—for him, I say, who is chief of the apostasy, and for those angels who became apostates along with him; which [fire], indeed, they too shall justly feel, who, like him, persevere in works of wickedness, without repentance, and without retracing their steps. WI, Vol. 1, 364-65

St. Lawrence of Brindisi, *Explanatio in Genesim*, Ch. 3: Therefore when we read in this passage that God considered punishment for the serpent, we should understand that the penalty was considered against both . . . those things that seem in this verse to be inflicted by God literally on the serpent as an animal, were not directed principally against the animal but against the serpent as devil, even if they seem to have been aimed at the animal. CF, 174

St. Lawrence of Brindisi, *Explanatio in Genesim*, Ch. 3: He turns to the serpent, and imposes punishment, as it is no longer worth hearing the reply. The serpent did not come to judgment as a defendant who could offer a defense, for he was already unpardonably resolute in sin and already condemned, judged as the eternal enemy, against whom no other thing is proposed except that he be punished according to his merits. CF, 174

St. Ephrem, *Commentary on Genesis*, Part 2:29: For where there is opportunity for repentance, it would be right to inquire, but to one who is a stranger to repentance judgment is fitting. It is so that you might know that the serpent is not capable of repentance.[88] FCE, 118

St. Lawrence of Brindisi, *Explanatio in Genesim*, Ch. 3: However, speech of this sort signifies an expression of the divine will through outward effects. If you will, take the Hebrew original: "Cursed are you before all livestock and every beast of the field". The serpent as animal, from which we must take figurative representation for a demon, is clearly viewed before all cattle and beasts of the field as a creature of this kind; cursed, *i.e.* execrable and detestable, the abhorrent and poisonous betrayer of man. Although the serpent must be cursed by its own nature, nevertheless it is surely fitting to think that He created this curse and malediction for it after the devil used its tongue to work so great a misdeed. CF, 174-5

St. Lawrence of Brindisi, *Explanatio in Genesim*, Ch. 3: It is absolutely not evident or well established whether the serpent had the same natural appearance before it received the curse as it does now. CF, 177

St. Lawrence of Brindisi, *Explanatio in Genesim*, Ch. 3: It was punished in the same way in which the Lord in Leviticus 20:15 ordered the destruction of an animal along with the man who committed sin with it.[89] CF, 177

St. Lawrence of Brindisi, *Explanatio in Genesim*, Ch. 3: The physical transformation of the serpent's nature came about from God, Who visited it with such a punishment that will last for all time, so that by its appearance it may be an example to all in the future lest that infectious counsel be further heard and lest an opportunity be granted to the grievous snares of the serpent . . .

---

88 Jn. 16:11: "because the prince of this world is already judged."

89 Cf. Deut. 13:14-16, 1Kings 15:2-3

Furthermore, the change in appearance occurred so that, seeing the serpent (which the devil used as an instrument) underwent so great an indignation, we may perceive with our intellect the punishments that were inflicted by God. CF, 178

St. Ephrem, *Commentary on Genesis*, Part 2:30: The entire reason God began with this impious creature was so that, when Justice appeased its anger on this creature, Adam and Eve should grow afraid and repent so that there might be a possibility for Grace to preserve them from the curses of Justice. FCE, 119

St. Lawrence of Brindisi, *Explanatio in Genesim*, Ch. 3: By that is meant the devil's heart in which he fosters the wickedest thoughts with all craftiness and cunning and in turn feeds his foulest desires for enticements to which he wanted to draw everyone to be changed for himself as if into the food that is turned into the substance of the one eating. Therefore, scripture adds: "And earth shalt thou eat all the days of thy life", i.e. men of earth who desire, love, and pursue earthy, rather than heavenly, things. CF, 178

St. Anthony of Padua, *Sermon on the Third Sunday after Easter*, 4: Of the earth of avarice, the Lord said to the serpent in Genesis: "Earth shalt thou eat all the days of thy life" [Gen. 3:14]. SSA, 310

St. Lawrence of Brindisi, *Explanatio in Genesim*, Ch. 3: You yourself shall creep over these men on your breast or belly through evil thoughts and by exciting filthy concupiscence by the illicit movements of the sensible appetite. CF, 178

St. Ambrose, *Paradise*, Ch. 15:74: Only those who live for the pleasures of the stomach can be said to walk on their bellies, "whose god is their belly and their glory is their shame," [Phil. 3:19] who eat of what is earthy, and who, weighed down with food, are bent over towards what is of earth. FCAm, 352

St. Ambrose, *Paradise,* Ch. 15:74: The serpent is well called the symbol of pleasure in that, intent on food, he seems to feed on the earth: "On your breast and on your belly shall you crawl, dust shall you eat all the days of your life." FCAm, 352

St. Lawrence of Brindisi, *Explanatio in Genesim,* Ch. 3: He could only tempt man by proposing delightful objects to the senses. Whence as he first undertook to tempt them, he appeared in a sensible form. However, after he overcame them, by the law of war and the rights of the warrior, he made them subject to his power . . . He had the power of undertaking to lure man not only by external temptations but also by internal ones so that he proposes to the internal senses lewd images and wicked thoughts, inserts perverse feelings, excites carnal concupiscence with forbidden movements, and kindles the fire of impure desire. CF, 179

St. Lawrence of Brindisi, *Explanatio in Genesim,* Ch. 3: Thus depraved and wicked men who despise the commands of God are 'earth', since they allow the devil to creep over them and they yield to him, because they consent to his temptations and perform whatever evil thing he will have proposed. Not so are the just, who keep the commands of God. CF, 179-80

St. Ambrose, *Paradise,* Ch. 15:74: God did not condemn the serpent in order to cause injury to man. He pointed out what was to happen in the future. Furthermore, we have demonstrated above how that temptation can be of great service to mankind. FCAm, 352

St. Lawrence of Brindisi, *Explanatio in Genesim,* Ch. 3: Yet Scripture says, "All the days of thy life", because he is said to live for all the time in which he is permitted to live under the cloudy atmosphere and, as it says in 1 Peter 5:8, to go about seeking "someone to devour". That time is until the end of the world, before the last judgment, when he will be shut within the eternal prison as though in a tomb, and he will not be allowed to travel or eat further. Wherefore he is rightly said to end his life. CF, 180

St. Theophilus of Antioch, *To Autolycus*, Book 2:28: Since this Eve was deceived of old by the Serpent, and became the author of sin, the evil-working demon who is also called Satan, who then spoke to her through the serpent, and who works even until now in those men that are influenced by him, calls on her as Eve. Now the devil is also called the dragon from his having revolted against God, for he was at first an angel (Apoc. 12:3 ff.). FG, 95

The Promise of a Future Redeemer

St. Leo the Great, *Sermo* 22, *De nativitate Domini*, 2, 1: The omnipotent and merciful God, as soon as the diabolical wickedness killed us by the poison of its envy, at the very beginnings of the world, signified beforehand the remedies of His mercy prepared for renewing mortal man. FG, 201

St. Leo the Great, *Sermo* 22, *De nativitate Domini*, 2, 1: For He announced to the serpent that there would be the Seed of The Woman who would crush by His own power the haughtiness of the guilty head [the devil's], namely, He signified Christ, who would come in the flesh as God and Man, and who, born of the Virgin, would by His incorrupt birth condemn the violator of the human race. FG, 201

St. Ephrem, *Commentary on Genesis*, Part 2:29: Then [God] made known the enmity that was put between the serpent and the woman and between its seed and her seed when He said . . . FCE, 119

Genesis 3:15: *I will put enmities between thee and the woman, and thy seed and her seed: she shall crush thy head, and thou shalt lie in wait for her heel.*

St. John Chrysostom, *Homilies of Genesis*, Homily 17:7: For I will grant to him so much strength that he will continuously tread upon your head, but you I will make lie under his feet. See my friend, how much care of the *human race* He manifests by the punishment given to the beast. That is said of the *visible serpent.* FG, 123

St. Justin Martyr, *Dialogue with Trypho:* Could not God have cut off the serpent in the beginning, so that he would not exist, rather than have said, "I will put enmity between him and the woman and between his seed and her seed" (Gen. 3:15)? FG, 94

St. John Chrysostom, *Homilies of Genesis,* Homily 17:7: Still it is permissible for one who wishes afterwards to consider and know the sequence of the words that it must be taken *much more* of the intellectual Serpent. For him, too, God humiliated and made subject under our feet and have us the power to tread on his head.[90] FG, 123

St. John Chrysostom, *Homilies of Genesis,* Homily 17:7: Then lest we think he meant sentient beasts, he added: "And upon every power of the enemy" [Lk. 10:19]. FG, 123

St. Irenaeus, *Adversus Haereses,* Book IV, Ch. 40:3: And He turned the enmity by which [the devil] had designed to make [man] the enemy of God, against the author of it, by removing His own anger from man, turning it in another direction, and sending it instead upon the serpent. As also the scripture tells us that God said to the serpent, "And I will place enmity between you and the woman, and between your seed and her seed. He shall bruise your head, and you shall bruise his heel" [Gen. 3:15]. And the Lord summed up in Himself this enmity, when He was made man from a woman, and trod upon his [the serpent's] head, as I have pointed out in the preceding book. WI, Vol. 2, 50

---

90 Lk. 10:19: "Behold, I have given you power to tread upon serpents and scorpions."

St. Isidore of Seville, *Quaestiones in Genesim*, c. 5:5-6: Certain ones have, however, understood "I will put enmities between thee and the woman," of the Virgin, of whom the Lord was born, because at that time (Gen. 3:15) the Lord was promised to be born of her in order to defeat the enemy. FG, 208

St. John Chrysostom, *Homilies of Genesis*, Homily 17:7: Nor will I be content that you shall crawl on the earth; no, I will establish the woman as your implacable enemy; and not only her, but also her Seed I will make the everlasting enemy of your seed. FG, 123

St. Maximilian Kolbe, *Roman Conferences*, II: Mary is the glorious Woman, star of light and salvation, promised by God to our first parents after their sin; of Mary, God was speaking when to put down his pride God said to the serpent: "There will come a Woman who will crush your head and in vain will you try to attack her heel." RC, 7

St. Irenaeus, *Adversus Haereses*, Book V, Ch. 19:1: And thus, as the human race fell into bondage to death by means of a virgin, so is it rescued by a virgin; virginal disobedience having been balanced in the opposite scale by virginal obedience. For in the same way the sin of the first created man (*protoplasti*) receives amendment by the correction of the First-begotten, and the coming of the serpent is conquered by the harmlessness of the dove, those bonds being unloosed by which we had been fast bound to death. WI, Vol. 2, 107

St. Lawrence of Brindisi, *Explanatio in Genesim*, Ch. 3: I now establish another conflict in which another woman must be overcome by you, if you wish safely to have power over your plunder and to attack more widely this assumed tyranny with your deceptions . . . Therefore, in the second battle I choose her as a champion to fight so that she may fight with you. CF, 181

St. Irenaeus, *Adversus Haereses*, Book III, Ch. 23:7: For this end did He put enmity between the serpent and the woman and her seed, they keeping it up mutually: He, the sole of whose foot should be bitten, having power also to tread upon the enemy's head; but the other biting, killing, and impeding the steps of man, until the seed did come appointed to tread down his head—which was born of Mary, of whom the prophet speaks: "You shall tread upon the asp and the basilisk; you shall trample down the lion and the dragon;"—indicating that sin, which was set up and spread out against man, and which rendered him subject to death, should be deprived of its power, along with death, which rules [over men]; and that the lion, that is, antichrist, rampant against mankind in the latter days, should be trampled down by Him; and that He should bind "the dragon, that old serpent" [Apoc. 20:2] and subject him to the power of man, who had been conquered [Lk. 10:19] so that all his might should be trodden down. WI, Vol. 1, 367

St. Irenaeus, *Adversus Haereses*, Book V, Ch. 21:1: He has, therefore, in His work of recapitulation, summed up all things, both waging war against our enemy, and crushing him who had at the beginning led us away captives in Adam, and trampled upon his head, as you can perceive in Genesis that God said to the serpent, "And I will put enmity between you and the woman, and between your seed and her seed; He shall be on the watch for (*observabit*) your head, and you on the watch for His heel" [Gen. 3:15]. For from that time, He who should be born of a woman, [namely] from the Virgin, after the likeness of Adam, was preached as keeping watch for the head of the serpent. This is the seed of which the apostle says in the Epistle to the Galatians, "that the law of works was established until the seed should come to whom the promise was made" [Gal. 3:19]. This fact is exhibited in a still clearer light in the same Epistle, where he thus speaks: "But when the fullness of time had come, God sent forth His Son, made of a woman" [Gal. 4:4]. For indeed the enemy would not have been fairly vanquished, unless it had been a man [born] of a woman who conquered him. For it was by means of a woman that he got the advantage over man at first, setting himself up as man's opponent. And therefore does the Lord profess Himself to be the Son of man, comprising in Himself that original man out of whom the woman was fashioned (*ex quo ea quæ; secundum mulierem est plasmatio facta est*), in order that, as our species went down to death through a vanquished man, so we may ascend to life again through a victorious one; and as through a man death received the palm [of victory] against us, so again by a man we may receive the palm against death. WI, Vol. 2, 110-11

St. Idelphonse, *De cognitione Baptismi*, cc. 7-8: So he added further, "She shall crush thy head, and thou shalt lie in wait for her heel" (Gen. 3:15). This is understood of Christ who is the *virginal* fruit of Mary's womb. That is, you by the malice of the persecutors who are your seed, in whose hearts you dwell, will trip him up so that He will die; and He in turn rising, will crush your head, which is death, and you yourself who have dominion over death. FG, 210

St. Lawrence of Brindisi, *Explanatio in Genesim*, Ch. 3: Nevertheless, a conflict of this type does not end in her. Just as the first battle did not end in the first woman, but you finished it in the vanquished man, so the second conflict ought to end in the man from the seed of this woman. CF, 181

St. Jerome, *Hebraicae Quaestiones in Libro Geneseos*, 6: It has it better in Hebrew "he shall crush your head, and you shall crush his heel". Because our steps also shall be entangled from a serpent and "the Lord shall swiftly crush satan under our feet".[91] CC, 6

St. Ephrem, *Commentary on Genesis*, Part 2:29: not in his ear, but "*in his heel.*" FCE, 119

St. Epiphanius, *Panarion*, Book 3, 78:18-19: Now, nowhere is to be found a seed of woman. Only, according to a figure, in the case of Eve, the enmity is understood between her own progeny and of both

---

[91] My translation: *Melius habet in hebraeo ipse conteret caput tuum, et tu conteres eius calcaneum. Quia et nostri gressus praependiuntur a colubro et dominus conteret satanan sub pedibus nostris velociter.*

the serpent and the devil and envy existing in the serpent. The whole thing, therefore, cannot be fulfilled in a most perfect manner in her [Eve]. It will, however, truly be fulfilled in the holy Seed, the elect, most singular Seed, which was found [born] of Mary without the marriage relation of a man. FG, 115-6

St. Anastasius of Sinai, *In Hexameron*, Book 7: In the latter days "I will put enmities between thee" and the Church . . . Do you not see the invincible and unbreakable weapons by which He [Christ] crushes and severs the head of the serpent? The cross, I refer to, the body of Jesus...and other things that He uses against the serpent? FG, 139

St. Irenaeus, *Adversus Haereses*, Book V, Ch. 24:4: The Word of God, however, the maker of all things, conquering him by means of human nature, and showing him to be an apostate, has, on the contrary, put him under the power of man. For He says, "Behold, I confer upon you the power of treading upon serpents and scorpions, and upon all the power of the enemy," [Lk. 10:19] in order that, as he obtained dominion over man by apostasy, so again his apostasy might be deprived of power by means of man turning back again to God. WI, Vol. 2, 121

St. Isidore of Seville, *Quaestiones in Genesim*, Ch. 5:5-6: The seed of the devil is the perverse suggestion. The seed of The Woman is the fruit of good work, by which the perverse suggestion is resisted. FG, 208

St. Gregory the Great, *Moralia in Job,* 1, 36-53, Book 2: Of course, to observe the head of the serpent is to completely extirpate the beginnings of his suggestion from the approach of the heart. When he is caught in the beginning he tries to strike the heel, because, though he does not strike the intention with the first suggestion, he tends to deceive in the end. FG, 208

St. Cyril of Jerusalem, *Catecheses*, 16, 10: There is also a good enmity, as it is written: "I will put enmity between thee and her seed." For the friendship with the serpent creates enmity with God. FG, 112-3

St. Anthony of Padua, *Sermon on the Fourth Sunday after Easter*, 3: So the text goes on: "And I will turn thee back by the way by which thou camest". He lost his dominion by the same way in which he usurped the lordship of the world. Just as he deceived a man and a woman with the forbidden tree and a serpent, so by a Man (Jesus Christ) and a woman (the blessed Virgin), by the tree of the cross and by the 'serpent' (the death of Christ according to the flesh, signified by the serpent which Moses lifted up on the wood in the desert), the devil lost his dominion over the human race. And so, when the business of our salvation was accomplished, Christ said: "I go to him that sent me" [Jn. 16:5]. SSA, 339

St. Ephrem, *Commentary on Genesis,* Part 2:30: But when the serpent had been cursed, and Adam and Eve had still made not supplication, God came [to them] with punishment. FCE, 119

The Punishment and Expulsion from Paradise

Genesis 3:16: *To the woman also he said: I will multiply thy sorrows, and thy conceptions: in sorrow shalt thou bring forth children.*

St. Lawrence of Brindisi, *Explanatio in Genesim,* Ch. 3: Our first parents led a happy and almost blessed life in the most pleasant paradise of delights. They sensed nothing troublesome, nothing uncomfortable, no pain, or sorrow, and nothing burdensome. CF, 184

St. Lawrence of Brindisi, *Explanatio in Genesim,* Ch. 3: If sin had not intervened, women would have felt the same joy in giving birth, which they feel after the child is born, owing to the fact that they no longer remember the distress and pain that they suffered during birth.[92] CF, 185

[92] Lk. 2:10-11: "And the angel said to them: Fear not; for, behold, I bring you good tidings of great joy that shall be to all the people: For, this day is born to you a Saviour, who is Christ the Lord, in the city of David."

St. Irenaeus, *Adversus Haereses*, Book III, Ch. 23:3: Similarly also did the woman [receive] toil, and labor, and groans, and the pangs of parturition, and a state of subjection, that is, that she should serve her husband; so that they should neither perish altogether when cursed by God, nor, by remaining unreprimanded, should be led to despise God. WI, Vol. 1, 364

St. Lawrence of Brindisi, *Explanatio in Genesim*, Ch. 3: Furthermore, she did not give birth to the Son in pain but with a supreme and ineffable joy, as is held by the firmest belief of the universal Church. For Jesus Christ the Eternal Word of God the Father, made flesh in the womb of the Virgin, came forth from his mother's womb, the sealed and untouched cloister of virginity, leaving no sign of his passage. Wherefore, Solomon said in the literal Hebrew text of Proverbs 30:19, His passage was *the way of a man in a virgin*, which he confessed he did not understand because of the profundity of the mystery. Accordingly, the Virgin Mary gave birth to a son without feeling pain, remaining a virgin before His birth, during His birth, and after His birth. CF, 189

Genesis 3:16: . . . *and thou shalt be under thy husband's power, and he shall have dominion over thee.*

St. Lawrence of Brindisi, *Explanatio in Genesim,* Ch. 3: The woman was given to the man as a solace and delight, as a companion and "a helper like himself", free from servitude. Now, however, she is set under her *husband's power*, so that the man rules over her and reduces her to his power. CF, 185

St. Ambrose, *Paradise*, Ch. 14:72: She was to serve under her husband's power, first, that she might not be inclined to do wrong, and secondly, that, being in a position subject to the stronger vessel, she might not dishonor her husband, but on the contrary, might be governed by his counsel. FCAm, 350

St. Ephrem, *Commentary on Genesis*, Part 2:30: "You shall turn toward your husband," to be counseled and not to give counsel and "he shall rule over you," because you thought that by eating of the fruit you would then rule over him. FCE, 119-20

St. Ambrose, *Paradise*, Ch. 14:72: I see clearly here the mystery of Christ and His Church. The Church's turning toward Christ in times to come and a religious servitude submissive to the Word of God—these are conditions far better than the liberty of this world. Hence it is written: "Thou shalt fear the Lord thy God and serve him only" [Deut. 6:13]. FCAm, 350

St. Ephrem, *Commentary on Genesis*, Part 2:31: After God had set down His judgment against Eve and still no repentance had risen up in Adam, He then turned to him, too, with punishment, and said, FCE, 120

Genesis 3:17: *And to Adam he said: Because thou hast hearkened to the voice of thy wife, and hast eaten of the tree, whereof I commanded thee, that thou shouldst not eat, cursed is the earth in thy work: with labor and toil shalt thou eat thereof all the days of thy life.*

St. Bonaventure, *Breviloquium*, Part III, Ch. 4:1: As a result of the divine judgment, the man incurred the punishment of labor and hardship, of hunger and need, of death and dissolution to ashes, as scripture says, "Cursed is the earth because of you", etc. But upon the woman felt the punishment twice as harsh, for [in addition], she was afflicted with the penalty of much travail in childbearing and cruel pain at childbirth, and of subjection to her husband in their life together. Brev, 107

St. Lawrence of Brindisi, *Explanatio in Genesim*, Ch. 3: Before God inflicts these curses on him, He gives the reasons for the infliction: "Because", He says, "thou hast hearkened to the voice of thy wife", or according to the Hebrew, "because you obeyed the voice of your wife". CF, 191

St. Lawrence of Brindisi, *Explanatio in Genesim,* Ch. 3: But instead, you should have restrained, rebuked, and corrected her from doing what she was persuading you to do. CF, 192

St. Lawrence of Brindisi, *Explanatio in Genesim,* Ch. 3: He now curses the man, in whom the sin was completely consummated, and He hurls five curses against him, as Rabbi Abrabanel notes about this passage. The first is: "Cursed be the ground on account of you". The second is: "In toil or pain shalt thou eat thereof all the days of thy life". The third is: "thorns and thistles shall it bring forth to thee; and thou shalt eat the herbs of the earth". The fourth is: "In the sweat or hard work of thy face thou shalt eat bread". The fifth is: "til thou return to the earth, out of which thou was taken; for dust thou art, and unto dust thou shalt return". CF, 191

St. Lawrence of Brindisi, *Explanatio in Genesim,* Ch. 3: The earth is cursed on account of man's sin since before it brought forth fruit without the work and cultivation of man because man did not exist at that point. Now the earth does not produce the finest vegetation or sweet fruits without the greatest industry, burdensome hardship, laborious cultivation, and even painful work. CF, 192-93

St. Irenaeus, *Adversus Haereses,* Book III, Ch. 23:3: He pronounced no curse against Adam personally, but against the ground, in reference to his works, as a certain person among the ancients has observed: "God did indeed transfer the curse to the earth, that it might not remain in man." etc. But man received, as the punishment of his transgression, the toilsome task of tilling the earth, and to eat bread in the sweat of his face, and to return to the dust from whence he was taken. WI, Vol. 1, 364

St. Lawrence of Brindisi, *Explanatio in Genesim,* Ch. 3: "With labor and toil thou shalt eat thereof", the Hebrew used here, *içavon,* means 'toil,' 'fatigue,' 'sadness,' and 'pain.' Since this work that he had to undergo work to prepare his sustenance which is not easy, delightful, or pleasing, but rather is burdensome, heavy, and irksome, with fatigue, sadness, and pain. It is not brief or short lived, but enduring and perpetual: "All the days of thy life", He says. CF, 193

St. Ephrem, *Commentary on Genesis,* Part 2:31: Had you kept the commandment, you would have eaten without pain. FCE, 120

Genesis 3:18: *Thorns and thistles shall it bring forth to thee, and thou shalt eat the herbs of the earth.*

St. Ephrem, *Commentary on Genesis,* Part 2:31: Because on account of the trifling enticement on the part of your wife you have rejected the most pleasing fruits of paradise. FCE, 120

St. Lawrence of Brindisi, *Explanatio in Genesim,* Ch. 3: For although in the state of our ancient parents before the Fall, the earth produced thorn, caltrops, briars, wild vines, burrs, thistles, wrinkled shrubs, and all manner of plants that are sharp, hard, and prickly, they nevertheless did not injure or harm men. CF, 194

Genesis 3:19: *In the sweat of thy face shalt thou eat bread till thou return to the earth out of which thou wast taken: for dust thou art, and into dust thou shalt return.*

St. Lawrence of Brindisi, *Explanatio in Genesim,* Ch. 3: By the word bread, we ought to understand not only the specific food, which is the principal meaning of that word, but also all food and sustenance . . . Thus, when he committed sin, he received nothing to eat except at the expense of pain, sadness, toil, and sweat. CF, 195-96

St. Lawrence of Brindisi, *Explanatio in Genesim,* Ch. 3: Thus since, as to flesh, you were joined together out of dust, it is necessary that you be resolved into dust. CF, 199

St. Ephrem, *Commentary on Genesis*, Part 2:31: Because "you are from the dust," and have forgotten yourself, "you shall return to your dust," so that, through your state of humiliation, you shall come to know your true essence.[93] FCE, 120

St. Irenaeus, *Adversus Haereses*, Book V, Ch. 16:1: And since Adam was moulded from this earth to which we belong, the scripture tells us that God said to him, "In the sweat of your face shall you eat your bread, until you turn again to the dust from whence you were taken" [Gen. 3:19]. If then, after death, our bodies return to any other substance, it follows that from it also they have their substance. But if it be into this very [earth], it is manifest that it was also from it that man's frame was created; as also the Lord clearly showed, when from this very substance He formed eyes for the man [to whom He gave sight]. And thus was the hand of God plainly shown forth, by which Adam was fashioned, and we too have been formed. WI, Vol. 2, 98-99

Genesis 3:20: *And Adam called the name of his wife Eve: because she was the mother of all the living.*

St. Lawrence of Brindisi, *Explanatio in Genesim*, Ch. 3: After sin, however, he placed on her another name . . . This verse certainly does not seem totally consistent and clear. She should be called death and the mother of the dying rather than the mother of the living, since now the sentence of death had been brought against the entire human race and, in a certain way, she was the chief cause of the punishable state of death. CF, 202

St. Lawrence of Brindisi, *Explanatio in Genesim*, Ch. 3: "She was the mother of all the living" because after her no one is born or made without a woman. For before her, Adam was formed by God without

---

93 Ecclus. 40:11, 41:13: "All things that are of the earth, shall return to the earth again."

a woman, and the woman was built by God from the man's rib equally without a woman . . . but she was also the parent and forbearer of that unique and most singular man, Jesus Christ, she is most worthily said to be "the mother of all the living". CF, 203

St. Augustine, *Contra Faustum*, Book XII, 8: As a wife was made for Adam from his side while he slept, the Church becomes the property of her dying Saviour, by the sacrament of blood which flowed from His side after His death. The woman made out of her husband's side is called Eve, or Life, and the mother of all living beings; and the Lord says in the Gospel: "Except a man eat my flesh and drink my blood, he has no life in him" [Jn. 6:53]. MH, 209

St. Epiphanius, *Panarion*, Book 3, 78:18-19: This one [Mary] is she whom Eve foreshadowed, who merited to be called "the mother of the living" by a figure (Gen. 3:20). For she [Eve] was called "the mother of the living" when after the transgression she had heard: "Dust thou art and unto dust shalt thou return" (Gen. 3:19). FG, 115

St. Epiphanius, *Panarion*, Book 3, 78:18-19: It was indeed a surprising thing that she should have this great title after such a transgression. And, indeed, according to the things perceived by the senses, every birth of men upon earth springs from that Eve. Truly, however, Life Itself has been born to the world through Mary, so that she might give birth to the living (Christ), and become the mother of the living (Christians). So Mary was called "mother of the living" by a figure. FG, 115

St. Bernard, *Homilia* 2, *Super Missus est,* nn. 3, 4, 8: So change the word of the wicked accusation into the voice of thanksgiving and say, "Lord, the woman you gave me, gave me the fruit of the tree of life and I ate; and it has been made sweet to my mouth, and you have given me life through it . . . O Woman singularly to be venerated, admirable above all women, *reparatrix of your parents,* giver of life to your posterity. FG, 220

Genesis 3:21: *And the Lord God made for Adam and his wife garments of skins, and clothed them.*

St. Lawrence of Brindisi, *Explanatio in Genesim*, Ch. 3: Man, however, needs clothing for both decency's sake and the protection of the body. CF, 206

St. Ephrem, *Commentary on Genesis*, Part 2:33: Because it was said that "the Lord made...and clothed them", it seems most likely that when their hands were placed over their leaves they found themselves clothed in garments of skin.[94] FCE, 121

St. Lawrence of Brindisi, *Explanatio in Genesim*, Ch. 3: However, he dressed him in the skin of dead animals for important and germane reasons . . . so that man should recognize from the kind of clothing he wore what he had done to himself through sin . . . He unquestionably showed that man had been changed, in a certain sense into a kind of herd animal because of sin. CF, 206

St. Augustine, *Contra Faustum*, Book XXII, 17: The typical rite of blood-shedding in sacrifice dates to the earliest ages, pointing forward from the outset of human history to the passion of the mediator.[95] MH, 411

St. Caesarius of Arles, *Sermons*, Sermon 11:5: Original sin could not have easily been forgiven, if a victim had not been offered for it, if that sacred blood of propitiation had not been shed. FCCs, 66

St. Lawrence of Brindisi, *Explanatio in Genesim*, Ch. 3: Second, since the skins were from dead animals, by this act he taught Adam and

---

[94] Gal. 3:27 "For as many of you as have been baptized in Christ, have put on Christ."

[95] Jn. 1:29: "The next day, John saw Jesus coming to him, and he saith: Behold the Lamb of God, behold him who taketh away the sin of the world."

all of us, with him and in him, were mortal and destined for death because of sin. In order that we always might remember that we would die at some time, just as the animals, he made their clothing from skins. CF, 207

St. Lawrence of Brindisi, *Explanatio in Genesim*, Ch. 3: God so clothed them in order that Christ, who was promised them as their redeemer through the seed of the woman, might be represented as the One who was always foreshadowed in the animal sacrifices of the Old Testament. Through His death, men ought to be dressed with divine grace, which they had lost, and with justice, and at the end, they ought to be clothed with glory. CF, 207

St. Ephrem, *Commentary on Genesis*, Part 2:33: Why would beasts have been killed in their presence? Perhaps, it was so that by the animal's flesh Adam and Eve might nourish their own persons, and that with the skins they might cover their nakedness, and also so that by the death of the animals, Adam and Eve might see the death of their own bodies. FCE, 121-22

St. Lawrence of Brindisi, *Explanatio in Genesim*, Ch. 3: God . . . also taught them to sacrifice those animals for a divine offering . . . In these first sacrifices, Christ is chiefly symbolized, prefigured, and immolated for the redemption of the offense of the first man. CF, 207

St. Lawrence of Brindisi, *Explanatio in Genesim*, Ch. 3: I also think that it was the kind of sacrifice we call a "holocaust," such that the entire flesh is burned up by fire and consumed as a divine offering, since at that time the eating of the sacrificed flesh was not permitted to men even up to the time of Noe. CF, 207

Genesis 3:22: *And he said: Behold Adam is become as one of us, knowing good and evil:*

St. Lawrence of Brindisi, *Explanatio in Genesim*, Ch. 3: It alludes ironically to what the serpent had said: "You will be like gods, knowing good and evil". Wherefore, as we said above, the clause "You will be like gods" can refer to God Himself, or to the divine persons, as well as to the angels and every knowing higher intellectual creature. CF, 208

St. Lawrence of Brindisi, *Explanatio in Genesim*, Ch. 3: The irony of the verse was of the bitterest kind, since God had clothed man with the skins of dead animals to show by this act that man by his sin had become like the beasts, then mocking him, He said that man had become one of the gods. "Behold", He says, "Adam", who sought to be compared to the gods by the persuasion of the serpent and thus violated my command. What a glorious god he has become! How wise he is, knowing good and evil! Yes, indeed! He who was god and lord of this world, My authoritative representative, the one standing for Me in the world, has become like cattle. CF, 209

St. Ephrem, *Commentary on Genesis*, Part 2:34: [The point] is rather that [God] was mocking Adam in that Adam had previously been told, "You will become like God knowing good and evil" . . . For the glory with which they had been clothed passed away from them, while pain and disease which had been kept away from them now came to hold sway over them. FCE, 122

Genesis 3:22: . . . *now therefore lest perhaps he put forth his hand and take also of the tree of life, and eat, and live for ever.*

St. Lawrence of Brindisi, *Explanatio in Genesim*, Ch. 3: This passage is distorted and must be understood as the Jerusalem Targum supplies: "Now therefore it is good, or fitting that he be cast out of the paradise of delight, lest perchance he stretch forth his hand . . ." In these words we should see the divine sentence of casting man from paradise mixed together with irony and grave reproach. CF, 209

St. Ephrem, *Commentary on Genesis*, Part 2:35: If Adam had rashly eaten from the one tree he was commanded not to eat, how much faster would he hasten to that one about which he had not been so commanded? FCE, 122

St. Lawrence of Brindisi, *Explanatio in Genesim*, Ch. 3: As a result of the food of that tree, owing to its perfection, life still could be extended rather a long time and could become rather long-lasting. That is what is meant by the word 'forever' in this verse. Whence the text has in Hebrew: 'and live' *leolam,* 'forever' for the words here do not properly mean 'eternity' but mean a long-lasting period of time with an end. CF, 211

St. Thomas Aquinas, *Summa Theologiae,* I, Q 97, Art 4: So the power of the tree of life could not go so far as to give the body the prerogative of living for an infinite time, but only for a definite time. ST, 928

St. Thomas Aquinas, *Summa Theologiae*, I, Q 97, Art 4: Therefore, since the power of the tree of life was finite, man's life was to be preserved for a definite time by partaking of it once; and when that time had elapsed, man was to be either transferred to a spiritual life, or had need to eat once more of the tree of life. ST, 928

St. Thomas Aquinas, *Summa Theologiae*, I, Q 102, Art 1 ad 4: The tree of life is a material tree, and so called because its fruit was endowed with a life-preserving power, as was stated above. Yet it had a spiritual signification; as the rock in the desert was of a material nature, and yet signified Christ (I Cor. 10:4). In like manner, the tree of the knowledge of good and evil was a material tree, so-called in view of future events; because, after eating of it, man was to learn, by experience of the consequent punishment, the difference between the good of obedience and the evil of rebellion. However, as some say, it could spiritually signify free-choice. ST, 945-46

St. Irenaeus, *Adversus Haereses*, Book III, Ch. 23:6: Wherefore also He drove him out of paradise, and removed him far from the tree of life, not because He envied him the tree of life, as some venture to assert, but because He pitied him, [and did not desire] that he should continue a sinner for ever, nor that the sin which surrounded him should be immortal, and evil interminable and irremediable. But He set a bound to his [state of] sin, by interposing death, and thus causing sin to cease, [Rom. 6:7] putting an end to it by the dissolution of the flesh, which should take place in the earth, so that man, ceasing at length to live to sin, and dying to it, might begin to live to God. WI, Vol. 1, 367

Genesis 3:23: *And the Lord God sent him out of the paradise of pleasure, to till the earth from which he was taken.*

St. Ephrem, *Commentary on Genesis*, Part 2:35: So that he who had been harmed by the leisure of the garden might be aided by the toil of the earth. FCE, 123

St. Lawrence of Brindisi, *Explanatio in Genesim*, Ch. 3: Adam did not depart from or leave paradise, but he was cast out . . . From this it is evident that man was formed outside of paradise so that he might know that he was in paradise not by nature but by grace. CF, 211

St. Theophilus of Antioch, *To Autolycus*, Book 2, Ch. 25: So also for the first man, disobedience procured his expulsion from paradise. Not, therefore, as if there were any evil in the tree of knowledge; but from his disobedience did man draw, as from a fountain, labor, pain, grief, and at last a prey to death. ANF, Vol. 2, 104

St. Ephrem, *Hymns for the Feast of the Epiphany*, No. 10:1: Adam sinned and earned all sorrows; likewise the world after his example, all guilt. NPNF, Vol. XIII, 280

St. Justin Martyr, *Dialogue with Trypho*, Ch. 100: For Eve, who was a virgin and undefiled, having conceived with the word of the serpent, brought forth disobedience and death. But the Virgin Mary received faith and joy, when the angel Gabriel announced the good tidings to her that the Spirit of Lord would come upon her, and the power of the Highest would overshadow her: wherefore also the Holy Thing begotten of her is the Son of God; and she replied, "Be it done unto me according to Thy word." ANF, Vol. 1, 249

Genesis 3:24: *And he cast out Adam: and placed before the paradise of pleasure Cherubims, and a flaming sword, turning every way, to keep the way of the tree of life.*

St. Lawrence of Brindisi, *Explanatio in Genesim*, Ch. 3: As long as the place lasted, in no way do I doubt that the Cherubim, the celestial spirits, were placed there, as a guardian of that place. CF, 219-20

St. Lawrence of Brindisi, *Explanatio in Genesim*, Ch. 3: He placed a burning and naked sword there, which seemed to disgorge a flame. So great was its splendor! By its appearance it frightened those approaching and inspired a bristling fear. It is said to "turn every way" because by its terror it closes off every path that leads to the tree of life. CF, 220

St. Lawrence of Brindisi, *Explanatio in Genesim*, Ch. 3: Alternately, by this sword, the menace of the death penalty is understood, which, in the custom of scripture, was inflicted by angelic ministry against those presuming to approach that place. CF, 220

St. Ephrem, *Commentary on Genesis*, Part 2:36: That fence was a living being who itself marched around to guard the way to the tree of life from any one who dared to try to pluck of its fruit, for it would kill with the edge of the sword, any mortal who came to steal immortal life.[96] FCE, 123

---

96 Dan. 13:59: *"for the angel of the Lord waiteth with a sword to cut thee in*

St. Lawrence of Brindisi, *Explanatio in Genesim,* Ch. 3: The word *lama,* which as was said above means 'blade', also meaning lightning and a lamp, because there it was able to shine like a sword. CF, 220

St. Lawrence of Brindisi, *Explanatio in Genesim,* Ch. 3: Sinful men would have used that extended life in the worst way. They would have sinned more often and would have remained in their sins for a longer time. CF, 221

St. Anthony of Padua, *Sermon on the Fourth Sunday after Easter,* 5: So it is well said: "Every perfect gift". In six days He made everything, "he spoke and they were made" [Ps. 148:5]. In the sixth age, the Word was made flesh [Jn. 1:14], and on the sixth day, at the sixth hour, He suffered for us and so brought all things to completion; saying on the Cross: "It is consummated" [Jn. 16:30]. As great as the distance between saying and doing, is the distance between creating and re-creating. Creation was light and easy, it was achieved by a mere word: that is, by God's will alone, for to Him to will is to do. But re-creation was very difficult, by means of His Passion and death. Adam was created easily, and fell very easily. Woe to us wretches! We have been re-created and redeemed by so great a Passion, so much anguish and pain: yet how easily we sin, and how gravely, and make of no effect that great labor of the Lord. SSA, 342

---

two, and to destroy you." Josh. 5:13-14: *"he lifted up his eyes, and saw a man standing over against him, holding a drawn sword, and he went to him, and said: Art thou one of ours, or of our adversaries? And he answered him: No: but I am prince of the host of the Lord, and now I am come."* Cf. 2 Sam. 24:16

Conclusion

The Canticle of the Sun
St. Francis of Assisi

Most High, omnipotent, good Lord,
Praise, glory and honor, and benediction all, are Thine.
To Thee alone do they belong, most High,
And there is no man fit to mention Thee.

Praise be to Thee, my Lord, with all Thy creatures,
Especially to my worshipful brother sun,
The which lights up the day, and through him dost
Thou brightness give;
And beautiful is he and radiant in splendor great;
Of Thee, most High, signification gives.

Praised be my Lord, for sister moon, and for the stars,
In heaven Thou hast formed them clear and precious and fair.

Praised be my Lord for brother wind
And for the air, and the clouds, and fair and every kind of weather,
By the which Thou givest to Thy creatures nourishment.
Praised be my Lord for sister water,
The which is greatly helpful and humble and precious and pure.

Praised be my Lord for brother fire,
By the which Thou lightest up the dark.
And fair is he, and gay, and mighty, and strong.

Praised be my Lord for our sister, mother earth,
The which sustains and keeps us
And brings forth diverse fruits with grass and flowers bright.

Praised be my Lord for those who for Thy love forgive,
And weakness bear, and tribulation.
Blessed those who shall in peace endure,
For by Thee, most High, shall they be crowned.

Praised be my Lord for our sister, the bodily death,
From which no living man can flee.
Woe to them who die in mortal sin;
Blessed those who shall find themselves in Thy most holy will,
For the second death shall do them no ill.

Praise ye and bless ye my Lord, and give Him thanks,
And be subject unto Him with great humility.
WSF, 152-53